THE ASHANTI RING

To the Memory of my Grandfather
Colonel Thomas John de Burgh of Oldtown

THE ASHANTI RING

Sir Garnet Wolseley's Campaigns
1870–1882

by

LEIGH MAXWELL

Leo Cooper
in association with
Secker & Warburg

First published by Leo Cooper in association with
Secker & Warburg Ltd,
54 Poland Street, London WIV 3DF

ISBN: 0–436–27447–7

Photoset in Great Britain by
Rowland Phototypesetting Ltd, Bury St Edmunds, Suffolk
and printed by St Edmundsbury Press
Bury St Edmunds, Suffolk

Contents

List of Illustrations

I am also most grateful to the *Illustrated London News* Picture Library for the use of their illustrations.

List of Maps

Acknowledgements

I am very grateful to my cousin Mrs Maeve Davison for sparing the time to research our Grandfather's career. Once again I would like to express my appreciation of the unfailing courtesy and cooperation shown to me by the staffs of the Ministry of Defence and Royal United Services Institution Libraries; and my sincere thanks to the Central Library in Hove for giving me access to the Wolseley letters.

Introduction

Fixed to the wall, at the far end of the entrance hall between the garden door and the school room, was a display cabinet. In the centre, near the bottom, was an Egyptian mummy's leg wrapped in gold-painted rush cloth. On the left was a bottle of water from the Pool of Siloam, and matching it on the other side was a glass jar containing a snake immersed in thick oil. There was a quantity of bric-a-brac, including an Egyptian army biscuit—less one bite. But in pride of place, strung out across the middle of the cabinet, were a pair of torn, tattered and rust-stained braces!

It was told to me when I was a small boy that they had belonged to my grandfather, Colonel T. J. de Burgh. The story went on to say that he had taken part in the battle of Tel el-Kebir; and that he had just bent down to pick up a souvenir when the bullet meant for his heart slashed across his back, cutting the flesh and ripping his trouser-braces to shreds.

Ever since those early days I have been interested in the Egyptian campaign of 1882. Occasionally something happened to remind me of it. For example, there was a Tel el-Kebir battery in my first field brigade which referred to itself as the Broken Wheel. Sadly, when I was part of Middle East Land Forces who were engaged in some static military bickering with Cairo, I was not able to visit the place that we called TEK, though I saw plenty of the Sweet-Water Canal and Ismailia.

At last I got around to proper research, and the first thing I found was that most of the leading personalities in the war had known each other for some years and had often fought side-by-side. So I harked back, through Amajuba, back again through the Zulu war, back until I reached the Ashanti War of 1873–74, when a selected band of

1

British officers fought a hazardous and victorious campaign. Living under the stresses of battle and great hardship, they came to know each other really well and developed a trust and friendship which was to last throughout their lives. Thereafter they preferred to plan and fight their wars together, and were known as the Ashanti Ring. The Ring became very unpopular, because there were not enough wars to go around and other officers wanted their turns too. Most of them were unlucky, for the leading figure in the Ashanti Ring was one of the best commanders, and the outstanding operational and administrative planner, in the British Army. He won wars, he kept within his financial ceiling and his casualties were minimal. So he got his way.

His name was Garnet Wolseley. I have followed his fortunes and those of his officers through six campaigns—from the Red River expedition where he made his name commanding only one British regular infantry regiment and two battalions of locally raised volunteers; until at Tel el-Kebir General Sir Garnet Wolseley commanded a force of three divisions—two infantry and one cavalry.

I have tried to instil continuity and to personalize my accounts by stressing operations in which officers of the Ring took part. Redvers Buller, William Butler and Hugh McCalmont make their impression on Colonel Wolseley during the gruelling toil of paddle and portage along Canada's lakes and rivers. They are joined amid the tropical rain-forests of the Gold Coast by George Colley, Evelyn Wood, Baker Russell and Sir Archibald Alison. In the Zulu War Wood and Buller suffer defeat, but avoid disaster, withdrawing from Inhlobana, then counter with a decisive victory at Kambula Camp, setting the pattern for the final destruction of the Zulu Army at Ulundi. Colley is terribly beaten by the Boers on Amajuba Mountain and loses his life, while Wood and Buller are despatched too late to do more than conduct peace negotiations. Then the survivors come together again for Tel el-Kebir.

Through ten years of valour and endurance, wounded in battle and fighting near-lethal tropical fevers and disease, colonels have become generals, majors have become brigadiers, captains have become colonels.

I have done what I can to bring out the principles of battle, of planning and of war in a way that is easy to read and understand. At the same time I have included sufficient political and economic background to explain why the wars were fought in the first place.

Although I have emphasized the doings of the Ashanti Ring, each campaign is complete in itself.

I have been asked why I do not expand my theme to show the effect of Wolseley's theories and their practice in peace and war on the British military machine. The answer is that my study is not yet complete; there are still the Sudan campaigns of 1884–5 to be considered. The work is in progress, and when it is done I will be in a better position to make an assessment.

I have included a bibliography showing the sources of my material, but I have not written a long, detailed appendix showing the chapter and verse of every aspect and quotation. This is not that sort of book; it is for the general public, a memorial for brave and dedicated professional soldiers.

The Ashanti War 1873–74

CHAPTER 1

Selection and Planning

[1]

Human sacrifice played an essential part in Ashanti religion; it came naturally to the tribe, it was unquestioned by anyone outside the sacrificial levy. But when King Kofi Karikari's armies raided the British Protectorate of the Gold Coast for victims, the Government in England was compelled eventually to take punitive action.

So it came about that, on the evening of February, 1874, local Major-General Sir Garnet Wolseley rode on the wings of a tropical tempest into Kumasi, mounted on a rather inferior mule. He reviewed his victorious troops, then, when the storm broke in full fury, he retired for the night to get what sleep he could on the floor of a hut. Huddled under his water-proof sheet, he lay amid pools of muddy water from rain pouring in through a broken roof. Beside him lay his Military Secretary, tossing in the throes of intermittent fever.

Dr McKinnon had done rather better for himself. He had appropriated a well-appointed dwelling said to belong to a local official of some standing. Later in the evening, the owner dropped in to pay his respects and to chat. It transpired that he was, indeed, a form of civil servant, and was usually contented with his lot, but recently, owing to the war, he had been terribly over-worked. He was King Kofi Karikari's executioner and in normal times would expect to cut off two or three heads a day. This was all part of the job and he had no complaints on that score. There would, of course, be more victims on holy days, but the total over a year would not be more than about a thousand, unless it was an exceptional year in which several great chiefs died, when there would follow great public ceremonial decapitations. This departure from the norm was, again, acceptable. But during the last few weeks the king's

5

need to propitiate his ancestors and invoke their aid, and the fetish men's requirements in the face of imminent defeat had been quite unbelievable. He had been completely worked off his feet, and had not the remotest idea of how many people he had killed. If anyone was glad that the war was over, it was he!

To find how this distressing situation had arisen, it is necessary to go back to the beginning.

[2]

Five hundred years ago the Gold Coast received its name from the innumerable little flecks of precious metal which sparkled amidst the sands of its rivers. The Portuguese were the first to establish trading posts there, but they soon found more worthwhile territories for exploitation elsewhere and withdrew. Others were less particular and competition became brisk. The Dutch and the British even went to war over it and Admiral de Ruyter sacked all the British forts except the castle at Cape Coast. However, amicable relations were restored and more fortresses were built. Contact was established with the interior and business began to prosper. In the early days there was plenty of ivory, but after a hundred years or so all the elephants had been killed. But sufficient quantities of gold remained to form a basis for the local currency for many years, with enough left over for export.

Slaves were available in abundance, and while the plantations of the West Indies and the Cotton States of North America depended on slave-labour the demand was great—and so were the profits. One source of supply was the great Ashanti warrior empire which held sway over primeval forests a hundred and fifty miles inland. They fought wars and took prisoners. Some of these they sacrificed to their fetishes, but there were always plenty more to be sold into slavery. When the trade was at its peak, the British alone were shipping out nearly forty thousand captive men and women every year.

In 1807 two things happened. First, the slave trade was prohibited in all British dependencies. No slaves might be exported from any British-occupied land, nor could they be delivered there. Next, the Ashanti crossed their sacred river, the Prah, and drove down through the forests to the coast. They attacked the Fanti tribes, a loose federation of two kings and a number of chiefs who had indeed

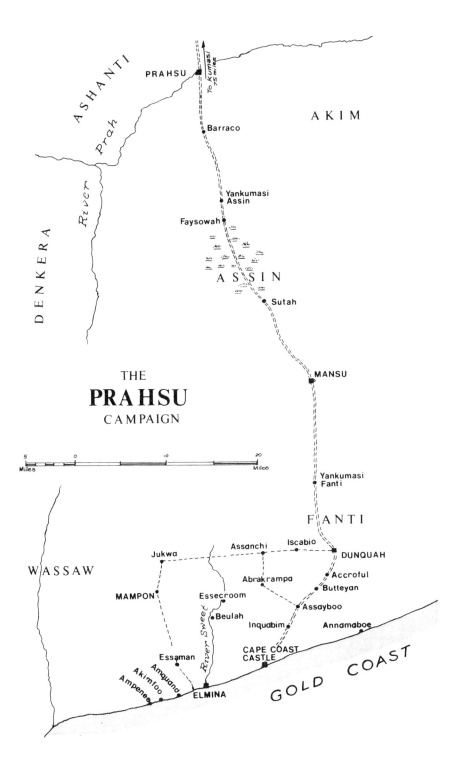

ASHANTI

PRAHSU

River Prah

DENKERA

AKIM

Barraco

Yankumasi
Assin

Faysowah

A S S I N

Sutah

THE
PRAHSU
CAMPAIGN

MANSU

5   0   10   20
Miles   Miles

Yankumasi
Fanti

F A N T I

Jukwa   Assanchi   Iscabio   DUNQUAH

WASSAW   Accroful

                 Abrakrampa   Butteyan

MAMPON   Essecroom   Assayboo

                    Beulah   Inquabim   Annamaboe

                                 CAPE COAST
            Essaman   CASTLE

       Amquana
   Akimfoo   GOLD COAST
Ampenee   ELMINA

River Sweet

To Kumasi 75 miles

given considerable provocation. But the Fanti were unable to back their rude words with military skill and were utterly defeated.

The Ashanti army pursued the flying hordes to the very walls of Annamaboe, one of seven British trading forts, which lay ten miles east of Cape Coast Castle. When they assaulted the fort itself, the Governor-in-Chief at Cape Coast Castle ordered the garrison to hoist the white flag. He then waited on the Ashanti king at his camp outside Annamboe and gave him valuable gifts. He next concluded a treaty acknowledging that all Fanti territory, including the British posts, was part of the Ashanti empire, and agreeing that the British Africa Company would pay annual tribute, cloaked in the guise of a present. In return he obtained a concession that the Company would have jurisdiction over towns near the forts. Thus our first passage of arms with the Ashanti!

There were more invasions and more treaties. In 1821, no longer being allowed to deal in slaves, the Africa Company went out of business and Parliament took over its assets and liabilities. Now, of course, there could be no question of paying tribute. The first Crown Governor, Sir Charles Macarthy, was an ardent abolitionist and repudiated Ashanti authority over the Fanti. The next time the Ashanti invaded Fanti country, he took a few white men with him and went to help stem the advance. Unfortunately, he was deserted by his native allies, was surrounded, ran out of ammunition, and was killed. The Ashanti were most impressed by his effort—no Briton had ever stood up to them before. So they cut off his head and took it home to Kumasi, where the skull was turned into a ceremonial drinking cup. The king used to swear oaths on it on particularly important occasions.

There ensued nearly forty years of peace, during which the British sphere of influence was officially constituted a Protectorate. Then in early January, 1873, King Kofi Karikari of the Ashanti sent an invading army of twelve thousand warriors across the Prah River. The Protectorate tribes were unable to withstand them and dispersed to their homes as a 'heap of scattered fugitives at the mercy of a pitiless and bloody foe, whose delight is to torture, and who will drive them by thousands into slavery, and slaughter all the weak and sick.'

The British Governor, Colonel Harley, had fears for Elmina, a fortified post eight miles west of Cape Coast Castle. His requests for assistance were answered only just in time by HMS *Barracuda*, and a detachment of Royal Marines under Lieutenant-Colonel Festing was landed. Elmina was occupied, while the marines and sailors inflicted a salutory defeat on the Ashanti counter-attacking force. The Ashanti General, Amanquatia, then withdrew to Mampon, where he intended to remain for the rest of the rainy season.

The marines and some of the sailors stayed on shore after the fighting was over and there was not a single case of sickness among them until 20 June. Then the rains began again in real earnest, sheeting down in ceaseless torrents, turning everything into a morass. The results were almost immediate. On the 1st of July a marine died of dysentry. At about the same time smallpox broke out at Cape Coast Castle, and soon the hospital was filled with a hundred and forty patients. Fortunately Doctor Home arrived in station. He had volunteered for service on the Gold Coast for the duration of the emergency, he knew his business and was full of energy. Soon he had organized extra hutted accommodation for the sick, and even got Colonel Harley to give him the drawing-room wing of Government House as an extra ward.

Then he checked up on the condition of the marines. After inspecting the shore-based detachments on 26 July, he found only forty-four out of a strength of a hundred and four to be effective. Soon eighty-seven were in such a dangerous state of health that he insisted they be repatriated to England at once. As the transport *Himalaya* disembarked the second half of the 2nd West India Regiment, so Doctor Home embarked his sick and the ship set sail for Portsmouth. Despite the prompt action, ten marines died on the voyage and fifty-eight of the remainder had to be admitted to hospital on arrival.

None of this was unexpected. The Gold Coast had been known for many years as the white man's grave. Nobody really knew why Europeans were afflicted with fevers from which they often died, sometimes in a few days. It had been deduced, however, from sad experience that sickness was in some way associated with rain and swamps—probably due their poisonous miasma—also with hot, windless coastal areas. People who worked on shore only during the day and returned on board ship at night enjoyed a comparative immunity.

[3]

In the early eighteen-sixties very few Englishmen knew anything much about the Gold Coast, and the majority of these would have liked to abandon the territory altogether. The Government felt much the same; they did not want any more colonies that did not pay their way. On the other hand the Ashanti propensity for slave-trading and human sacrifice had become notorious. Feeling was equally divided between the abolitionists who wanted to extend the British Protectorate to the Ashanti, thereby putting an end to their gruesome practices, and the non-extensionists who were opposed to taking on any more liabilities. Others were stirred by national pride. The Fanti were tax-paying British subjects—how dare this heathen king persecute them!

Mr Gladstone was Prime Minister and was much devoted to a policy of peace on all fronts. So was the Secretary for the Colonies, Lord Kimberley, but he realized that, in view of the proud and intractable attitude of the Ashanti, there could be no hope of lasting settlement until their army had been destroyed. He was shrewd enough to know that the Fanti disaster had offended British national dignity and that further inaction might result in the Government being voted out of office. The Secretary for War, Mr Cardwell, could see Kimberley's point, for he had once been Secretary for the Colonies himself. He was also aware that he would have to proceed very carefully and covertly with his plans before coming out into the open. The British public were incensed by Ashanti behaviour, and by the poor showing of the Protectorate natives, but there was a reluctance to commit British troops. There was a strong feeling that the end could still be achieved by using local levies trained and commanded by some of those British officers capable of inspiring and leading native soldiers, many of whom could always be found in the mid-nineteenth century. Card-well intended to start by paying lip-service to this idea, although he knew it was most unlikely to produce the answer. He would send out a carefully selected and well-briefed commander and staff to make all the necessary gestures, and then produce a cast-iron case for the despatch of British regiments—the only troops capable of thrashing those haughty and skilled warriors, the Ashanti. He would then have no difficulty in persuading Mr Gladstone, who had great confidence in him, of the need to take action.

It was going to be a very intricate operation indeed, one which could lead to political disaster if it were to go wrong. Troops would have to live and fight in a country where the climate was quite appalling for most of the year. They would have to land, penetrate nearly a hundred and fifty miles against warrior opposition into forests where no British force had been ever before, and come out again in such condition that no charges of inefficiency could be laid against the Government. Besides which, it must not cost too much.

There were plenty of generals eager for active service, but Kimberley and Cardwell would require someone in whose loyalty they had complete confidence, and whom they knew to have the ability to carry out a successful campaign within the limitations specified. Fortunately there was an officer who had these qualities, though he was not a general but a colonel.

In order to show why this officer seemed to be so eminently suitable it is worthwhile leaving the Gold Coast for a moment to consider the Canada of 1870.

Fifteen hundred miles west of Toronto among the lakes and forests of the North-West Territory lay a small pioneering settlement along the Red River. There a population of European-Indian half-bred farmers and trappers cultivated the fertile soil or roamed the great woodlands hunting for furs, which they sold to the Hudson Bay Company. They lived under threat of attack by hostile Indian tribes. Winters could be very cold indeed—minus 25 degrees Fahrenheit was nothing to the settlers. In summer the annual invasion of locust swarms could denude the fields of every green leaf and pile insect corpses in heaps three feet deep against the walls of Fort Garry, the primitive defended post of a little town, now the city of Winnipeg.

Recently the Hudson Bay Company had been nationalized. But some of the Red River French-Indian Catholic community did not want to become citizens of the Dominion of Canada, they did not want an English Protestant Governor, they did not even want their province to be called Manitoba. So a few of them banded together, occupied Fort Garry and refused entry to the Governor-elect. They felt safe. It was easy to reach Fort Garry from the south. There was a reasonable road running north from the United States of America; but on that side of the border was living a substantial Irish-American population with no liking for the English and with considerable sympathy for the recalcitrant colonists. From Montreal, however, there was no easy route to the Red River. The journey would mean travelling between one and two thousand miles across lakes, through virgin forests, up fast-flowing rivers with many rapids around which boats would have to be dragged on rollers or canoes carried—portages, as these diversions were called.

All too difficult for easterners and English, thought the Red River rebels.

However, the Dominion Government was not prepared to let them get away with it as there were enormous potential riches in the North-West. They decided to send a military expedition to put down the revolt, despite the physical obstacles. They knew that the climate would impose limitations—the troops would not be able to set out until after the raging torrents of the spring thaw had subsided and they would need to be back in civilization before winter came and made life in the wastes impossible for all but Indians and settlers. Moreover, the approach march would be through a wilderness where no supplies of any kind were to be had, except for occasional fish in the lakes and sometimes blueberries and raspberries.

The Deputy Quartermaster-General of the Armed Forces in Ottawa happened to be an expert military planner, a veteran of many campaigns all over the world, who had made a practice of collecting and collating every type of information pertaining to military projects. He had recently published his *Soldiers' Pocket Book for Field Service*, containing all this data, and his name was Colonel Garnet Wolseley.

He decided that three battalions would be needed. One would be a regular British regiment, the 1st Battalion, 60th King's Royal Rifle Corps, which was stationed in the Dominion. The other two would be formed from local volunteers enlisted specially for the operation. Helped by Mr Irvine, Assistant Controller of Land Transport, he calculated the quantity of supplies that would be required to maintain the expedition and the means of carrying it; also the number of boats needed to embark fighting infantry, artillery, engineers and stores. In minute detail he listed the equipment for every boat down to the last axe, frying-kettle and baling-tin. He obtained skilled Iroquois Indians to man them.

He was also the obvious choice to command the expedition. As well as his expertize as a staff officer, he had commanded Canadian troops in operations against hostile infiltrators (of Irish origin) from the United States. He was popular and respected throughout the Dominion.

There was no trouble in obtaining a staff; everybody wanted to take part. To organize the military side of the line of communication he chose a fellow staff officer, the Military Secretary to the Governor-General, Lieutenant-Colonel J. C. McNeil, VC, who obtained permission to relinquish his duties. A young officer from the Rifle Brigade, Captain G. L. Huyshe, was given the post of staff officer to Wolseley, and Lieutenant W. F. Butler of the 69th Regiment of Foot was appointed Intelligence Officer. Volunteers came from everywhere—a Lancer captain, whose troop had been struck off establishment, arranged leave of absence from his regiment and arrived in Ontario asking to be allowed to join the expedition! Although, strictly, it was against the rules, he had come such a long way that Wolseley stretched a point and let him stay.

The expedition left Toronto on 31 May, 1870. Everybody worked with a will, officers helping to haul boats over portages with their men and taking an oar or a paddle when required. Captain Redvers Buller, commanding a company of the 60th, was a great, strong man and a tremendous driving force. He told his men that he would not overwork them, but that he would be very pleased if they overtook the other boats! This he usually succeeded in doing, sometimes by sheer hard work, at others by using his intelligence to find a more practical route.

There was no alcohol, there was no crime. It rained for forty-five days of the three-month journey but nobody was taken ill. It was exhausting work, but Wolseley kept them at it. One warm morning when nearly all the boat-crews were sitting down and resting, he noted with interest that the little Lancer was still keeping the men of his two boats hard at it, carrying around a portage. They all traversed miles of lakes, rivers and rapids. There were forty-seven portages, and the boats ended their trip at an altitude nearly a thousand feet higher than lake-level at Toronto.

On the way they were met by their Intelligence Officer, Lieutenant Butler, paddling down the Winnipeg River in a canoe. He had seen fit to go to Fort Garry by way of the United States, to see for himself what the threat of a Fenian flank attack was likely to be. He reached the Fort long before the expedition arrived, even had a chat with the rebel leader, Louis Riel, and then slipped away before anybody decided to prevent him.

The rebels fled just before the infantry reached Fort Garry, much to the indignation of the 60th King's Royal Rifle Corps. The leaders could have been pursued and captured, but Wolseley had not been given powers of civil authority and thought it better to let them go. The Fort was occupied and Buller found Riel's breakfast still warm on the table, and ate it. That was on 24 August, and by the 29th, after a Dominion Governor had been installed, the British regular infantry were on their way back home again, arriving safely before winter without the loss of a man. The whole operation had cost only £400,000 of which the Home Government had to pay no more than a quarter.

The Lancer captain, now in water-soaked rags, had never felt fitter in his life, but was quite ready to go home. He had been popular with all the officers, except when he anointed himself with most of their carefully hoarded and treasured bottle of Harvey's Sauce in mistake for anti-mosquito oil. Wolseley had been rather pleased by the conduct of this young gentleman during the expedition, and now paid him the special compliment of selecting him to carry the despatches back to Headquarters in Montreal, a duty which in those days usually brought promotion, or at least a monetary reward, for the courier. The captain, whose name was Hugh McCalmont, was to travel by way of the United States, which would get him back to Headquarters long before anyone else, and he accepted with enthusiasm. He had found an old copy of *The Times* in Fort Garry and in it had read that he had been transferred to the 7th Hussars, an arrangement made in his absence by his father to save him a tour in India! He was not at all sure that he liked the idea, and wanted to get to London to sort things out. So he set off on horseback for Minnesota, passing on his way a bunch of ruffians, one of whom, his guide told him afterwards, had been Riel, and reached St Paul. He was so preoccupied with his own affairs that he had not really appreciated the implication of being despatch-bearer, so he committed his charge to the United States post and headed straight back to England. In his memoirs he excuses himself by pleading that he was a very young officer at the time, with only five years service. He had bought his captaincy (for £5,125) only the previous year.

The Red River Expedition had been an outstanding success. Huyshe wrote it up in a book that was published the following year and then obtained a nomination for the Staff College at Camberley.

Wolseley was in the prime of life, thirty-seven years old. Described by Butler, he was 'somewhat under middle height, of well-knit, well-proportioned figure; handsome, clean-cut features, a broad and lofty forehead over which brown chestnut hair closely curled; exceedingly sharp, penetrating, blue eyes from one of which the bursting of a shell in the trenches of Sevastopol had extinguished sight without in the least lessening the fire that shot through it from what was the best and most brilliant brain in the British Army. He was possessed of a courage equal to his brain power. He could neither be daunted nor subdued. His body had been mauled and smashed many times. In Burma a gingall bullet fired within thirty yards of him had torn his thigh into shreds; in the Crimea a shell had smashed his face and blinded an eye. No one ever realized that he had only half the strength and the sight with which he had started life.'

He now became Colonel Sir Garnet Wolseley and was posted to the War Office in Whitehall.

[4]

On reaching Whitehall Sir Garnet was appointed Assistant Adjutant-General and worked under Cardwell, advising him and helping with his work in bringing the Army into line with the international standards of that time. In due course they gained complete confidence in each other and earned the thorough dislike of the die-hard military clique. The Colonel now was just forty years old, in the best of health, full of initiative and enthusiasm, dedicated to a modern and unorthodox approach to military problems, and his selection to command the Ashanti Expedition was a foregone conclusion.

Wolseley accepted the task, but made several requests. He was very young for his rank and position and had trodden on a lot of toes during his climb up the ladder of promotion. He had been an ardent supporter of Cardwell in his drastic reforms of the military system, for, though fully justified by results, they were anathema to the establishment. Many officers of senior and middle rank would have been only too pleased if he were diverted into a faraway backwater and left there. So, first he asked to be assured that he would not be expected to stay on in the Gold Coast after the campaign was over. In this case his request was granted. He wanted also to pick his own officers. He maintained afterwards that 'he could not have done the work with the very ordinary humdrum men usually told off from a Horse Guards register, and that the claims of seniors should never be allowed to interfere with selection of the best officers in the Army for all the little campaigns we so often have to carry out.' In this, too, his wishes were granted, causing much ill-feeling and many jealous gibes in military circles. He was soon besieged by applications to join his force, but preferred officers who had served with him already, and in whose known capability he had confidence.

In his personal entourage were Colonel McNeil, as Chief of Staff, and Deputy Controller Irvine, both of whom had served him well on the Red River Expedition. The two Deputy Assistant Adjutants and Quartermaster-Generals were to be Buller and Huyshe, who was given special permission to leave the Staff College before completion of his course. His Military Secretary was Captain Brackenbury, taken from his post as Professor of Military History at the Royal Military Academy, Woolwich. As Private Secretary he appointed Lieutenant Maurice, also of the Royal Artillery, currently serving as an Instructor in Tactics and Organization at the Royal Military College, Sandhurst. This young officer had won the Wellington Prize Essay on 'The System of Field Manoeuvres' for which Sir Garnet had himself submitted an entry! There were to be two Aides-de-Camp: Lieutenant The Honorable A. Charteris of the Coldstream Guards, and Captain Hugh McCalmont of the 7th Hussars, who had been forgiven his little lapse. Finally, Major Baker would be Assistant Adjutant-General.

All these officers were to travel with Sir Garnet in the same ship, together with eight others from the commissary, pay and medical departments, and nineteen officers for special employment with native personnel. The number of the latter more than doubled before the campaign was over, and they too were chosen with care. One of them was Brevet Lieutenant-Colonel Wood, who had just happened to drop in at Wolseley's office in Whitehall to find him poring over a map of the Gold Coast. Wood had transferred from the Royal Navy and jokingly offered to navigate Wolseley up the River Prah. 'So you shall, if we go,' said Sir Garnet. That had been in May; Wood got his letter of appointment and the sailing date at the end of August. He also chose a young officer from his regiment, the 90th Light Infantry, into which he had bought a transfer for £2,000 just before the system was abolished. This was Lieutenant Eyre, who had greatly impressed Wood with his self-possession, good manners and determination. So when Eyre asked for a recommendation to be included in the expedition, Evelyn Wood had no hesitation in granting his request.

Butler, unlike Hugh McCalmont, was lacking in this world's goods. So, during twelve years of service he had five or six times been purchased over by officers, most of whom were many years junior to himself. When promotion by purchase was finally abolished, he had at long last been promoted to captain, but only in a half-pay vacancy. Having, therefore, no duties to perform, he made his way back to Canada and, while he was there, read in a newspaper about preparations being made for Sir Garnet to lead an expedition to the Gold Coast. He immediately telegraphed asking to join him, and took ship for England in hopeful expectation. Fortunately, all had been taken care of, and on arrival he received instructions to follow on and meet up with the others at Cape Coast Castle.

[5]

Next, Sir Garnet asked for British troops. But again, not just that—he did *not* want what would normally be allotted to him, the first two battalions on the foreign service roster after those already ear-marked for India. He wanted to pick suitable officers from the twelve best battalions in Britain, and let them choose their non-commissioned officers and men. This special selection was too much for the Whitehall traditionalists and was refused on the grounds that there was no military precedent (the last resort of the hidebound) and that it would weaken the Home Forces. In any case, the Government as a whole was still influenced by the gloomy council of officials who had served on the Gold Coast and by the fate of the Marine shore detachment whose ailing survivors had but recently returned to England. They would not countenance the use of British troops—officially. Some of them did not want to send anyone at all, and Sir Garnet only got away after Lord Kimberley had announced to his colleagues that 'either this expedition comes off, or I cease to be Colonial Minister'. He was quite sure that British soldiers would be required in the end. So Cardwell quietly brought the Royal Welch Fusiliers and the 2nd Battalion of the Rifle Brigade up to war strength and put them on stand-by for embarkation. Whether or not they would ever be despatched would depend on Sir Garnet's report after arrival at Cape Coast Castle and his assessment of the situation.

Now he tried to find out all he could about the projected theatre of operations, but herein he encountered considerable difficulty. There was little or no intelligence, as the Army Department of Intelligence in Whitehall had only just been formed. But he pored over all the old Colonial Office reports, read all the memoirs written by previous officials and interviewed everyone who professed any knowledge of the Gold Coast. The majority were most discouraging about an advance to Kumasi. *They* had never done it; how could anyone else? There were some who thought it quite possible if set about in the right way, but, on the whole, pessimism was rife. One officer asked advice from an 'expert' about the kit that he should take. 'Take a coffin—that's all you will need!' came the reply.

Sir Garnet appreciated that 'it was evident that the most serious enemy to be encountered was the climate, usually considered the worst in all our foreign possessions.' He was convinced that he would never reach Kumasi without the support of British troops. Nor would he get there if they all fell sick, as they surely would without special precautions. 'I did not mind how many I lost in action, for soldiers are made to die there,' wrote Field-Marshal Sir Garnet Wolseley in later years, but he hated to waste them through sickness. Therefore he must complete the operation during the healthiest months of the year, December to March, when there was little or no rain, and a hot dry wind blew down from the Sahara in the north. They must spend as little time on land as possible; the ideal would be for them to march straight up country on the very day they disembarked. The road on which they would march must be completed as far forward as possible before they arrived. This would entail pushing the Ashanti north at least to the River Prah using local forces. Fortified staging posts with fields of fire cleared around them must be constructed to avoid any delay or unnecessary fatigue to the British battalions on their way; their job was to spearhead the attack.

All known and feasible sanitary precautions must be installed at these staging posts. Supplies and ammunition must be dumped forward, the operation must not be delayed by a slow baggage convoy. There would inevitably be sick and wounded, despite all precautions, so arrangements must be made for casualties to be evacuated all the way down the line to Cape Coast Castle, and back to England if necessary. All officers and men must be given a rigorous medical inspection before leaving England; it would be a waste of time and medical effort to bring out men unlikely to stand up to the physical stress of active service.

Ordinary British home and tropical dress would be quite unsuitable for the campaign, so Sir Garnet arranged for a simple grey uniform of serge or homespun to be issued. Officers were to have Norfolk jackets, riding breeches, gaiters and shooting boots; they were to leave their swords behind—too long for close-quarter fighting in thick bush—and instead carry sword-bayonets which could cut and thrust, and revolvers. They would be limited to fifty pounds of kit, packed in such a way that it could be carried on the head of a native, as at that time no four-legged transport was expected to survive on the Gold Coast. The men would wear smock-frocks, trousers and long sailors' boots. They would be armed with the short rifle and sword-bayonet. All ranks would have cork sun-helmets.

Minds were made up, officialdom began to stir and Sir Garnet was appointed Administrator of the Government of the Gold Coast. He was to come directly under the Home Government and correspond direct with them. He was specifically not under the Governor-in-Chief of the West African Settlements in Sierra Leone; in fact this official was forbidden so much as to visit the Gold Coast during Sir Garnet's tour of duty. Still more, he was made Commander of Her Majesty's Land Forces in the whole of the West African Settlements, with the local rank of major-general. One supreme commander for everyone except ships of the Royal Navy.

Cardwell sent him a carefully worded directive on 8 September, telling him to do all the things that he had already decided to do, and stating that 'nothing but a conviction of necessity would induce Her Majesty's Government to engage in any operation involving the possibility of its requiring the service of Europeans at the Gold Coast.'

Lord Kimberley's directive was dated two days later. Briefly, on arrival Sir Garnet was to tell the Ashanti to get out of the Protectorate, make reparations for injuries and losses inflicted on its natives and give security for the maintainance of peace—or else! He was to tell the Protectorate kings and chiefs that Her Majesty's Government would help them against the Ashanti, but 'unless they unite together cordially in their own defence, and show themselves prepared to make every sacrifice in their power to maintain themselves against the invader, they must not look for aid to Her Majesty's Government.' If Sir Garnet should find it necessary to ask for any considerable reinforcement of British troops, Kimberley requested that 'you will enter into full explanations as to the circumstances in which you propose to employ them, and the reasons which may lead you to believe that they can be employed without an unjustifiable exposure, and with a well-grounded anticipation of success.' Sir Garnet had already been told that the whole thing would have to be on the cheap! It must on no account cost more than £800,000. In a separate letter Lord Kimberley made suggestions for a treaty with King Kofi Karikari if he should prove amenable.

It should be mentioned here that another expedition to the Gold Coast was already on its way, led by Captain Glover of the Royal Navy. An expert on West Africa with a great reputation for being able to influence the local tribes, he had volunteered to take out a party of officers. On arrival he would recruit a large native force around a nucleus of Hausas, probably about ten thousand men in all. When ready, he would take them up the River Volta by steamer, then advance west towards Kumasi as a powerful diversion in support of Wolseley's operation. It was made quite clear, however, that he was very definitely under Sir Garnet's orders.

Harley had been told to give Glover everything he wanted, so when he stopped at Cape Coast Castle and requisitioned all the Hausas in the Protectorate, Harley, although reluctant, felt that he was in duty bound to hand them over, with their rifles. He also let his Colonial Secretary and Director of Customs depart with the expedition, but was able to replace him with Captain Owen Lanyon of the 2nd West India Regiment.

CHAPTER 2

The Build-Up at Prahsu

[1]

Sir Garnet and his party took ship at Liverpool on 12 September, 1873. He wrote that morale was high and everybody full of zest for the enterprise. All the relevant papers and books had been brought, so the voyage was spent in daily discussion and planning, interspersed with lectures by Brackenbury and Huyshe. Brackenbury's alleged high morale must have improved considerably since the beginning of the voyage, when he complained that even this collection of high calibre officers was 'dispirited and disgusted long before blue water was reached. Sent to sea in a ship whose berths were being painted twelve hours before they had to be slept in, through whose cabin-floors bilge-water oozed, which was absurdly underhanded for all purposes of attendance, was reeking with foul smells below, and flooded above due to the absence of bulwarks—the passengers on the West African Company's steamship *Ambriz* were as miserable as they could be made'!

They anchored off Sierra Leone on 27 September, where they were given every consideration by the Governor-in-Chief, Mr Berkeley, in no way put out at the Major-General's charter of independence. Then on to Cape Coast Castle where they arrived on 2 October.

Sir Garnet was determined to recruit native levies if he could, though he would rather do so outside the Gold Coast, as they would be less likely to drift back to their villages. He hoped to raise ten thousand, and had already tried for technicians and retired NCOs for use as drill-sergeants in Sierra Leone, and for Kroomen in Las Palmas. He had also sent two British officers to the Gambia to see who they could enlist. He intended to form two regiments of local

21

troops under Brevet Lieutenant-Colonel Evelyn Wood and Brevet Major Baker Russell.

On the day of arrival Evelyn Wood and his officers were landed through the great, rolling surf and sent to Elmina, which they reached in time for afternoon tea. Three officers of the garrison were down with fever, but the remaining three turned out to offer hospitality. Wood was startled to find that there was no tea available —nobody had drunk anything like that for a long time—but instead he and his friends were offered square face (trader's gin). Eyre declined, so one of the hosts gratefully drank his glass as well as his own. As Wood explains, the climate was, admittedly, intensely depressing!

Harley gave the newcomers at Cape Coast Castle an excellent dinner and then left for England. It had been made clear to him that he had done well under great difficulty, but that the current project called for the appointment of a senior military officer.

Next morning Huyshe, who had been put in charge of survey, left for Dunquah to start work in the forward area, leaving Lieutenant Hart to deal with the mapping around Cape Coast Castle and Elmina.

On the 4th Sir Garnet had his meeting with the Protectorate kings and chiefs. Not all were able or inclined to get there at such short notice, but to those who showed up he passed on the message of Her Majesty's Government. There was little enthusiasm, so he gave them some gin and sent them away to think things over. After some delay they reported that their people would much prefer to work as carriers at the proffered wage of a shilling a day than enlist as soldiers at sevenpence half-penny. They seemed to have little authority over their tribes. One chief complained that he had no power to coerce his subjects; in the good old days he would have ordered general mobilization and cut off the head of any man holding back. There would have been a magnificent turn-out. But the British Government had stopped all that sort of thing and what could he do? So Sir Garnet allotted to all chiefs with a large potential following a British special liaison officer as support for their recruiting drive, whom they accepted gratefully. It transpired subsequently that they considered that this gesture effectively relieved them of all responsibility.

The difficulty lay in finding the nine officers required for the task. He found six himself, and Captain Fremantle bent the rules to lend him three naval officers. Fremantle was doing everything he could to help, but he had been forbidden to land any officers or men for offensive operations, nor were they to go up river by boat. A recent expedition up the Prah had proved a costly failure in which the Commodore himself had been so badly wounded that he had to be evacuated to Cape Town. Fremantle had been reminded that 'the loss of one human life from his forces would but inadequately compensate for any amount of injury he might do to the savage natives'.

The same day Sir Garnet sent a message to the War Office requesting twelve more specially employed officers. It went by sea to Madeira, whence it was telegraphed to Lisbon and relayed from there to London. It reached Whitehall on 21 October. This was the only means of communication and depended very much on the movements of civil mail steamers. In fact, things soon got worse when the Madeira-Lisbon cable parted and the British Admiralty had to send a warship to stop the gap.

The General now had time to look around and check his resources. The Hausas had all gone with Glover to Accra and the 2nd West India Regiment was split between five settlements and three outposts. If he collected together the men at Cape Coast Castle, Elmina and the outposts, he could put about four hundred men into the field. Under his powers as Civil Governor, he had told the native armed police that they were to consider themselves as part of the military command, only to be told that, apart from recruits and men employed on civil police duties, there were only ten available to go to war!

As regards the enemy, Lieutenant Gordon had established with reasonable certainty that there were about forty thousand Ashanti around Mampon. Local scouts were inclined to lie up in the scrub not far from their bases until they had eaten up their rations and then return to report what they thought would please their officer most. Gordon had originally done much to offset this by sending a reliable Hausa with each party. On return he would de-brief the Hausa and the scouts separately. There was no likelihood of collusion, as the Hausas and the local people had no common language. But the Hausas had gone with Glover!

Sir Garnet now put Redvers Buller, old colleague and mighty man at poling boats up Canadian rivers, in charge of intelligence; and Buller immediately set about recruiting spies and interpreters. With the help of the latter he interrogated everybody who might be able to produce information—disaffected Elminas, escaped slaves, captured Ashanti tribesmen. It was very difficult to get anything out of anybody, but he was able to confirm that there were indeed about forty thousand Ashanti around Mampon and that they were commanded by Amanquatia. They were suffering from dysentery and Amanquatia was in two minds as to whether or not he should withdraw north of the Prah. In order to be able to do so at short notice, he had started cutting a new path through the forests to join the main road north of Mansu. What was of more immediate interest, he was short of provisions for his army and was being supplied from his friends in Elmina and the fishing villages to the west, channelling both sources through Essaman.

Hearing this, Evelyn Wood summoned the chiefs of the villages involved to a meeting, and told them that if this traffic did not stop he would burn down their villages. But British prestige was very low. Even close to Elmina, British officers on their own were subjected to insults and threats. The chiefs, confident that the white men would never dare come through the bush to their homes, and encouraged by the presence of small Ashanti garrisons, refused to attend—with contumely!

The Essaman chief replied, 'Come and fetch me. White man no dare go bush.' The Amquana headman said, 'I have smallpox today, but I will come tomorrow.' (He never did.) While the Ampenee villagers decapitated and mutilated a loyal native sent with the message, and exposed the body on the beach as an insult and as a fetish charm to keep the enemy away.

They had made an unfortunate choice. Sir Garnet was looking for a short, sharp, successful engagement to raise morale in the Protectorate, and what better operation than to destroy the delinquent villages? Provided, of course, that the forty thousand Ashanti in Mampon did not get to hear of it and reinforce the targets. Surprise was essential if that was to be avoided, yet everything that happened in Cape Coast Castle was supposed to be known to Amanquatia in a matter of hours.

The General realized that he could not conceal troop movements, nor even that some sort of operation was under preparation. So the enemy must be made to think that something quite different was being organized.

The first move was simple. On 10 October a company of Hausa recruits who had escaped the Glover net arrived by sea from Lagos. There were always rumours of impending attacks on Cape Coast or Elmina, and Sir Garnet let it be spread abroad that Evelyn Wood expected to be attacked. He would send the Hausas to reinforce Elmina and he himself would accompany them with some of his personal staff to discuss the matter with the local commander on the ground. They all took ship next day, and the two-hour voyage was usefully employed in issuing the recruits with Snider rifles, weapons they had never seen before, and teaching them how to use them and look after them. The Hausas thoroughly enjoyed it all, even though the ship was rolling heavily. Only Brackenbury found the smell of rifle oil rather disturbing! After disembarking, Sir Garnet had a private talk with Wood and told him what would be required of him, himself returning to Cape Coast Castle in the evening.

The time had come to repay the Senior Naval Officer's official call, so next day he went to visit HMS *Barracuda* in full regalia. He knew that Captain Fremantle had received fresh instructions which gave him very much more freedom of action. Then the General went back on shore to tell everyone that Captain Glover in Accra was in serious trouble, and that a full scale operation would be needed to get him out of danger. He told his true intentions only to those who absolutely had to know, leaving many of his own staff in complete ignorance of what was really going to happen.

While this news was spreading through Cape Coast, and through Elmina to the Ashanti (Wood had told the same story about a Glover relief expedition), Sir Garnet cleared his pending tray. On 13 October, as he had been told to do, he sent his ultimatum to King Kofi Karikari, giving him until 12 November to be clear of the Protectorate. He also signed a long despatch to the Secretary of State for War to bolster his request for British troops—two battalions of infantry with artillery and engineers. This was just going through the motions; the despatch contained hardly anything that he had not known before departure and discussed with Cardwell. It was probably drafted during the voyage out from England. However, he did add some satisfactory 'nil' sick returns to show that the troops up-country were healthy and well. All signed and sealed, the missive then lay in Cape Coast Castle for two weeks until the next mail steamer called by.

At two o'clock on the same day an administrative column of two hundred and fifty carriers loaded with stores and cots (litters manned by four native bearers) set off by road for Elmina. During the previous forty-eight hours, Wood had made no preparations whatsoever, but when this column arrived in the evening he brought them all into the fort and raised the drawbridge for the night, thereby making sure that the carriers would not disperse but would be ready when required in the early dawn. When no one could get out to tell the tale, he began his preparations for battle. Later that night he sent out armed police to cordon the town to prevent news of the arrival of Sir Garnet's task force filtering out to the hinterland.

Back at Cape Coast Castle a naval detachment took over the defences, relieving a hundred and fifty soldiers of the 2nd West India Regiment to embark, ostensibly for Accra. The General and his officers joined Fremantle in *Barracuda* and all set sail at midnight. Landing at Elmina began at three o'clock in the morning to take full advantage of the high tide. Unfortunately, the Gold Coast had made different arrangements, and it turned out to be low water! Sir Garnet and Fremantle went ashore in the Captain's gig, but the troops took very much longer. Redvers Buller, Brackenbury and Mr Winwood Reade (correspondent of *The Times*) were soaked repeatedly by the ocean rollers as their boat bumped its laborious way across the bar, during a trip that took almost two hours. But everybody got ashore in the end, and the main body was able to march at a quarter past five. Evelyn Wood was Force Commander, although the General went too, to show the natives that they now had a fighting man as Governor, not a fortress-domiciled civilian. Fremantle was there as well, to command the equivalent of a platoon of sailors with a rocket-launcher. The rest of the column consisted of Redvers Buller with a party of native axe-men to cut paths through dense jungle; a company of Royal Marine Light Infantry; a detachment of Royal Marine Artillery with a 7-pounder gun; two companies of the 2nd West India Regiment, of which Eyre was allowed to command a detachment; and several hundred native carriers for water, ammunition and cots, in the charge of Chiefs Essevie and Andoo, brave men who comported themselves well throughout this operation and the whole campaign.

The advance guard had been formed from the new Hausa recruits, and had moved off at half-past four in the morning, but they had only gone about a mile and a half when they stopped and hung around waiting for the main body to catch up. This was unfortunate as they were in sight of a village, whence some warning of impending trouble must have gone ahead to Essaman. After the column had closed up, the route of advance lay through eighty yards of knee-deep swamp, and then along a narrow path, in places one foot wide. All around were 'beautiful creepers, purple, red and mauve; many-coloured sweet-peas and bright yellow convolvuli met the eye at every moment'. Thick jungle remained on each side of the way until first contact with the Ashanti was made about a mile from the village.

The leading Hausa fell mortally wounded by a bullet fired from point-blank range, and his fellow-recruits immediately began to fire wildly in all directions. Their excitement was infectious and some of the marines started to do likewise, but were quickly brought under control by an officer.

Resistance faded away and the Hausas, sailors and marines moved slowly forward while Buller and his axe-men cut through the scrub to the left until the ground became more open and Ashanti could be seen on two hills left and right of the track. Again the Hausas began firing in all directions, making it quite a hazardous business to leave the path and go into the bush!

The head of the column now came under heavy fire from the front and right, so Wood deployed for action. Officially Commander of the expedition, he says ruefully of the General: 'Himself and the HQ staff having no definite duties were free to enjoy themselves, which they did by leading the advance with a lively vivacity, which, while exciting admiration, caused some uneasiness to those who reflected on the nature of the void their fall might create.'

The Hausas were collected from the bush and brought back on to the track, where it was easier to keep them in order. Buller had already cut his way through to a point where he could see into the village, and reported seeing armed men and hearing drums beating. Sir Garnet sent Captain Crease and his marines to deal with the hill on the right and to make a frontal attack on the village. He realized that the Captain could not possibly control so many men in the very dense bush, so he sent with him two of his personal staff, Brackenbury and his aide-de-camp, Charteris. The Chief of Staff, Colonel McNeil, led a party on a left hook, while Captain Fremantle brought his gun and rocket launcher into action on a small clear space left of the track, whence they could engage the village with direct fire.

Crease decided to lead his men personally in the attack on the hill, leaving Brackenbury and Charteris to head the frontal assault. Slashing their way through the scrub with their sword-bayonets, they reached the village to find that resistance in that sector had dispersed. The gun had made excellent practice once a vital tool for fusing the shells had been found; so had the rocket-launchers, even though the first one fired was deflected by trees and caused a sensation by making a U-turn and returning to its starting point! At the beginning of the action they were under heavy musket fire from short range and Fremantle was hard hit in the arm.

On the left, McNeil was very severely wounded in the wrist, so Buller took over and cleared his side of Essaman. In the meantime the Ashanti resorted to their traditional tactics of going for the flanks, and in this case attacked the West Indians who were still at the point of first contact. They made an initial local penetration, but Wood and Major Baker took charge and restored the situation. Evelyn Wood then called the West Indians forward along the path cut by Buller through the bush on the left of the road. By half-past eight the enemy had vanished and the column sat down to eat their breakfast in Essaman. There was one alarm when drums suddenly began beating close by, but they were found to be captured drums which some of the soldiery had been unable to resist! Then the village was set on fire, after Crease had rescued a small child left abandoned in one of the huts.

At a quarter to ten the column marched for Amquana, a distance of four miles, which took two and a half hours, despite meeting no resistance on the way. Brackenbury says, 'The march was intensely fatiguing. The thick bush shut out every breath of air, and there were no forest trees to give shade. The path was rugged, and the way seemed never-ending. Then for the first time we learnt the terrible strain of performing staff duties on foot in such a climate; yet no one would give in.' In other theatres of war, staff officers rode horses.

Lieutenant Eyre volunteered to take his detachment of West Indians and act as flanking party, harder work than anyone else had taken on. He struggled on until he dropped from exhaustion, but nothing would induce him to travel in a cot. After a short rest he went on again.

Some of the men were in pretty poor shape when they reached the beach at Amquana, so they were sent back to Elmina as escort for the wounded in their cots. Sir Garnet left all the marines at the fishing village, except for Crease and twenty volunteers, who he led on, together with his staff, twelve sailors with their rocket-launcher, and the two West Indian companies, west along the coast to Akimfoo and Ampenee. On the way they were intercepted by ships' boats with sailor reinforcements who had brought some very welcome supplies of water and biscuit, which were quickly disposed of. Then to Akimfoo, which was deserted—the news had spread! They burned it, and the same again at Ampenee. As they finished, there was some desultory musket fire from the bush, and the newly-landed bluejackets were anxious to engage; but the General had achieved his aim, and it was time to go home. He went on board ship and returned direct to Cape Coast Castle. The West Indians covered the departure of the boats before marching back to Amquana, where they joined up with the marines and all returned together to Elmina, arriving at eight o'clock in the evening.

The greater part of the column had covered twenty-one miles in difficult conditions after having been up all night, but they had stood it well. There were only two admissions to hospital from heat exhaustion, and four others with minor complaints.

The bush had been so thick that very few Ashanti bodies had been found; there had been no point in searching, nor the time to do so. Wood's casualties had been very light: sixteen Hausas had been wounded, one of whom died of his injuries. Colonel McNeil was so badly hit in the wrist that he had to be evacuated to England; Captain Fremantle was severely wounded, but recovered quickly, and a total of four sailors and marines were also wounded. The only casualty among the West Indians was a wound to Captain Forbes. Three carriers had been wounded during the Ashanti raid on the West Indians south of Essaman, causing the whole party to drop their loads and go to ground, but they had had the sense not to run away through bush country full of Ashanti, and returned to their duties after the attack had been repulsed. The reason why the column had escaped so lightly was because the Ashanti gunpowder was of very poor quality, and the slugs fired were harmless over about fifty yards. During the subsequent campaign 'a large proportion were hit by slugs which gave a severe stinging and painful blow without entering the flesh. The only harm was a bad headache or stomach-ache for a few hours.'

This small punitive raid gave a great boost to morale throughout the Protectorate. It also provided Sir Garnet with some strong arguments to support his case for the despatch of British troops from England. One might wonder why the General, who never left anything to chance, should have decided to head his advance with a company of newly-joined recruits, equipped with unfamiliar weapons, with only one British officer to control them, when he could just as easily have used some of the West India Regiment. Whatever his aim may have been, the fact remains that he was now able to write back to Cardwell that 'I have been shown how little reliance can be placed on even the best native troops in this bush-fighting', and 'The Hausas showed undeniable courage and spirit; but their uncontrollable wildness, the way in which they fired volley after volley in the air, or at imaginary foes in the bush, expending all their ammunition, shows how little use they are for the work we have in hand.' He reported also that the dress of the West Indians was utterly unsuited for bush-fighting, thereby stressing his wisdom in arranging for special home-spun uniforms. Moreover, the special circumstances of bush-fighting where officers could control only those men close to them demanded an exceptionally large proportion of officers, at least one for every twenty men.

Hugh McCalmont had not accompanied the expedition. He went down with fever a few days before it was mounted and became so bad that, to his fury, he had to be sent first aboard the *Simoom*, which was acting as a hospital ship, and then back to England. His place as ADC was taken by Lanyon.

[2]

The Essaman operation had only been a side-show. The long-term aim was still to smash the Ashanti war-machine, and that meant capturing Kumasi. The first step was to render the tortuous jungle track from Cape Coast to the Prah River suitable for a rapid advance by British troops. Progress had been made already, in that men could march four abreast as far as Mansu, though they still had to wade through a great many streams and swamps. But Amanquatia and his army, now estimated by Buller to be twenty-five thousand men, were encamped around Mampon, only fifteen miles west of the road at its nearest point, and there was nothing to stop him moving in to kill the pioneers and disperse the road gangs. There was also the possibility that he might be aroused by the Essaman affair sufficiently to try another attack on Elmina, so fortified patrol bases had to be manned to ensure against surprise attacks.

As regards the road, by 22 October Lieutenant 'Hausa' Gordon had brought the defences of Assayboo, Abrakrampa, Accroful, Dunquah and Mansu to a reasonable state of readiness. The difficulty lay in finding garrisons for all the posts. The 2nd West India Regiment was dispersed in detachments all over the Protectorate and there were no other regular troops. It had been established quite clearly before the General's arrival that the local Fanti tribesmen were almost useless; however, it was just possible that they might be better than nothing, so he sent messages to all his special liaison officers, telling them to order the kings and chiefs to report with their men to Dunquah by 20 October. He realized now that the recruiting drive outside the Protectorate was unlikely to raise more than a few hundred men, nowhere near the thousands which he had envisaged while still in England. But there had been limited successes and some men were coming in. For example, Captain Nicol, a volunteer from his post as Adjutant to the Royal Hampshire Militia, had found two tribes, the Opobo and the Bonny, who were always fighting each other. He described to each king separately how inadvisable it would be if his rival provided a contingent, which would receive excellent military training and experience in battle, and he did not. As a result he obtained a company from both, though it was considered tactful to post them to different regiments.

Evelyn Wood's basic organization was to be four companies. He was eventually to have sixteen special service officers, five native officers and over four hundred men. Increments which kept dribbling in were offset by sickness or unsuitability. He had no great opinion of his men during the early days! The 1st Company consisted of Fanti enlisted from the area around Cape Coast Castle, and it would be difficult to imagine a more cowardly, useless lot of men. The 2nd Company, the only one of fighting value, and the one which did nearly all the scouting work, was obtained from the disloyal part of Elmina, the area which sympathized with the Ashanti; it also contained a few freed Hausa slaves, taken and liberated during the early reconnaissance patrols. No 3 Company were Kossoos from the interior east of Sierra Leone. They claimed to be swordsmen, so they were armed with naval cutlasses, but it transpired that their only marked characteristic was intense cruelty. The 4th and last Company contained the Bonny men under Prince Charles of Bonny, a young man who had been educated in Liverpool. They were small, beautifully made and very clever at all basket-work, but with no special aptitude for war.

Baker Russell was to have about the same strength, but divided into six companies—the Hausas who had been on the Essaman expedition, the Opobo Company, Sierra Leones, Mumfords, Winnebahs and Annamaboes. Captain Rait, helped by Lieutenant Eardley-Wilmot, was doing much better than anyone had expected with his Hausa gunners. He had the advantage in that his non-commissioned officers were British, giving him a much higher proportion of English to native personnel than in the two regiments. The extraordinary state of affairs was that all his Hausas had been slaves, captured by Ashanti, and sold in the Coastal Territories. There had been a great many of them in Lagos, where the owners had to put them in chains to stop them enlisting. In Accra Glover had to buy them from their masters at £5 a head! All this was quite in order as slavery was recognized in the Territories, though it is doubtful if the British public was aware of the fact. An English magistrate paid by the Home Government sat as Judicial Assessor in Court with the native chiefs to administer law and order according to local customs, restoring runaway slaves to their rightful owners. Wood managed later to augment his Elmina company with twenty-five slaves liberated from Amanquatia's army.

It was obvious that the British-officered levies would be too few to deal with Amanquatia if he decided to fight, and that there were not sufficient marines and sailors for the task. The General made no change to his original appreciation that two British battalions would be sufficient to force a crossing of the Prah and advance to capture Kumasi. But, if they also had to fight Amanquatia south of the river, they might suffer such heavy casualties as to render them too weak for the final phase of the operation. So now he wrote to Cardwell at the War Office asking for a third battalion to be ear-marked, and for the 1st West India Regiment to be called forward from Jamaica. In the meantime the two regiments of levies must go into action. Their officers had been on shore for three and a half weeks and there was no more time for individual training. Evelyn Wood commented ruefully at a later date that never throughout the whole war had he time to convince the majority of his soldiery that shooting was more accurate if one put the butt of the rifle to the shoulder!

As it happened, Amanquatia had no stomach for offensive action at this time and had for some weeks been considering withdrawing north of the Prah. He was short of provisions, and now that his source of supply from the Elmina coast had been cut off his soldiers would soon be hungry and his slaves starving. He was also disturbed on two counts. First, by Sir Garnet's demonstration that white men and rockets could penetrate into the bush; secondly, by the construction of forts flanking his line of retreat at Abrakrampa and Dunquah. He decided not to wait for permission from King Kofi Karikari but to start pulling out at once, striking the main Cape Coast Castle to Prahsu road at Mansu and marching up it to the north. Wary of the now unpredictable British, he would put out strong flankguards to protect the vulnerable right of his route of withdrawal. He started to move on 22 October. It was three days before Sir Garnet's intelligence staff received indications that this was going on. Buller was doing his best, but everybody preferred to kill Ashanti prisoners rather than bring them in for questioning. He astonished Evelyn Wood by appearing in Elmina carried in a cot and saying, 'Please order me a cup of tea and give me some information as quick as you can. I feel I have got fever coming on and I am not certain how long my head will last.' He received his intelligence, wrote it down, had his tea and departed. Shortly afterwards he became delirious, imagined that the Fanti carriers were Ashanti surrounding him, drew his revolver and fired three shots at them, fortunately missing everybody.

Butler had arrived soon after the Essaman operation and now relieved Buller as Intelligence Officer. On hearing his assessment, Sir Garnet despatched Evelyn Wood from Elmina to find out what was going on. Wood's advance party of marines soon established that there were less than two thousand Ashanti still in Mampon and he would have liked to retain contact and follow up the withdrawal, but his Protectorate tribal allies made it quite clear that they had no intention of becoming involved in anything so risky, so he had to return to base.

At the same time the General and his staff, two hundred and fifty marines and sailors, and Russell's regiment, now a hundred strong, left Cape Coast Castle for Assayboo, staged there and moved on to Abrakrampa on 27 October. There he found Huyshe in charge, very busy completing the defences. The key point was a Wesleyan mission house in the centre of the village, where he had removed the thatch and built a platform for a light naval gun and a rocket-launcher on the roof-trees.

Sir Garnet had ordered Lieutenant-Colonel Festing, Royal Marines, now enrolled in the elite corps of specially employed officers drawing their extra guinea a day, to probe with the whole of his Dunquah garrison towards Iscabio, supported by Russell who had marched up to join him. They succeeded in surprising a camp of three thousand Ashanti a mile short of the village, dispersing them and driving them away into the forest. The West Indians did well, so did Rait's Hausa artillery. Moreover, Russell's Annamaboes fought creditably under their baptism of fire, led by their king who, unfortunately, was seriously wounded. Of the Protectorate tribal allies, some had to be thrashed into action by their officers, others sat miserably in huddles and refused to move, despite being belaboured by blows from sticks and umbrellas; some simply disappeared.

The General took his column to Assanchi, whence a few shots were fired at his Abra scouts, causing considerable confusion. Here it was that Butler managed with certain difficulty to obtain a live Ashanti prisoner, who had been caught asleep among the plantains. He describes the incident: 'I came upon six or eight men struggling in the dense brushwood, some on the ground and some on their legs. In the centre of the mass there was a short, stout savage with his hair twisted into spiral spikes which stood straight out from his head. He was fighting for his life; and so strong was he that he was able in his twistings to move the three or four Abras who had him down. A couple of other Abras were striking him on the back of his head with the butts of their long Dane guns; but they were unable to stop his writhings. At the edge of the group stood a tall Hausa soldier with a long knife in his hand, ready for an opening which should enable him to draw it across the throat of the Ashanti. . . . He leaned forward to get a better draw for his knife across the man's neck; but as he did so I caught him full on the ear with my fist, and over he went, knife and all into the bushes. At the same instant the Ashanti rose, and seeing a white man close to him he threw himself forward, caught hold of my hand and was safe.' Under interrogation he declared that there was nobody else in Assanchi, so the General returned to Abrakrampa. Brackenbury described the day as one of the worst of the whole campaign—a drenching thunder-storm, a track often knee-deep in water and so overhung with branches and creepers that it was impossible to carry a cot along the path. Charteris was completely exhausted at the end of the day after a ten-mile march with no water fit to drink; there had been difficulty in getting the man-drawn water carts as far even as Assayboo.

Festing wanted to go out again to harry the Ashanti flank, but his Protectorate kings and chiefs would not move; they were discouraged by losing the King of Annamaboe, the bravest of them all in battle. So Sir Garnet went back to Cape Coast Castle where he wrote to Whitehall to say, 'My position is somewhat humiliating; the enemy's main column of retreat is within easy march of my Headquarters, and I have no force capable of attacking it.' The Protectorate tribesmen would not even pursue a retreating foe; scarcely could they be persuaded to reconnoitre any direction in which an Ashanti might be found. Wood, however, managed to get his locals as far as Beulah by invoking the services of the Chief Magistrate at Cape Coast Castle, known and trusted by the chiefs, who consented to advance under his leadership. Eyre got his tribesmen as far as the Sweet River opposite Essecroom by holding a pistol to the head of their leader. But he could not make them cross, though he set an example by swimming over himself.

However, a few days rest did wonders, and both the Dunquah and Abrakrampa garrisons sent out columns in 3 November. Festing, from Dunquah, tried the Iscabio track again and made contact with a large enemy camp, but this time the Ashanti would not be driven out, and instead came forward to attack. Eardley-Wilmot went up front with his Hausas and rockets to support the West India company, which was bearing the brunt of the assault, and was wounded. He insisted on carrying on until an hour later, when he was shot through the head and died instantly, the first of the original *Ambriz* party to be killed in action. Festing was wounded when he went out to bring in his subaltern's body. The eighty men of the 2nd West India Regiment stood firm for two hours until the enemy began to leave the field, hastened on their way by a lucky rocket which landed among a group of Ashanti chiefs and captains, killing or wounding six of them. Then Festing took his column back to Dunquah. Nine British officers had been in action, of whom one had been killed and five wounded. The Protectorate men had bolted back to Dunquah and safety at the start of the fray.

The Abrakrampa patrol was led by Hausa Gordon and his men, supported by Russell's Winnebah company commanded by the Adjutant, Lord Gifford, who thought that he would like a day in the field. Contact was made, but the Winnebahs suddenly panicked and made off, knocking over Gifford and Mr Winwood Reade in their rush. So Gordon, too, took his men back to camp.

Abrakrampa was furthermost west of all the road-protection defended posts, and there was always the possibility that Amanquatia might attack it on his way home. But nothing happened and the General decided to call back the Naval Brigade of an officer and sixty men. At four o'clock in the afternoon of 5 November they were actually on parade and ready to march when Russell, now Garrison Commander, was, as Sir Garnet put it, 'so fortunate' as to be attacked by a large force of Ashanti on his western perimeter. Russell and Huyshe had cleared a lot of ground in this sector and had established sentry posts in the surrounding belt of scrub. These were soon driven in, to the shouts and cheers of the Ashanti, some of whom now ventured into the open to perform a war dance. When there were about two hundred within sixty yards the West India Regiment gave them a volley, then charged with the bayonet, whereupon the enemy promptly ran back under cover. Russell then managed to make his men hold their fire, hoping to lure the enemy into the open again, but the Ashanti had no intention of being caught twice. The enemy fusillade continued with great volleys of booming musketry, but the defenders were in trenches and had little to bother about. The gunners on the Wesleyan mission roof fired thirty rounds of gun-ammunition and twenty-eight rockets which kept the enemy in the scrub, although they themselves had the only serious casualty of the action, a sailor struck in the eye. Nearly everybody was hit, including Mr Boyle, special correspondent to the *Daily Telegraph*, but it was all long range fire, far too great a distance for Ashanti powder. The results were mostly 'such slight touches by slugs as the officers took no notice of'!

Then the Assaybbo road was cut and the Ashanti launched a furious assault across the cleared ground on the left and left rear of the defences, which was again repelled by disciplined volleys. Attacks continued until midnight, when the fighting faded to a desultory exchange of shots dying away by four in the morning. The battle began again half an hour before midday, but with very much less enthusiasm on the part of the Ashanti, few of whom ventured out of the scrub.

Despite the Assayboo road being closed, Russell had been able to keep in touch with Accroful, whence he was sent a fresh supply of rockets during the night.

By this time Cape Coast Castle could be reached by telegraph, through the initiative of Lieutenant Jekyll. Two hundred miles of cable had been sent from England, but on board the slowest ship. Jekyll, however, had managed to bring with him two instruments and twenty miles of line in his private baggage, which was quite a feat considering that he had an allowance of only fifty pounds weight. He had erected his poles and fixed his cable as far as Accroful before the official consignment arrived. There had been delays, as he had other duties to perform as well as working on the telegraph; he was short-handed and had no skilled labour, everybody had to be taught and then supervised. The line had to be at the side of the road, so quantities of boughs and creepers had to be cut, and kept cut back, lest they foul the wire. The weather also played its part; in December's storms a month later, the wire became so charged with electricity that the instruments could not be touched, and on one occasion a set was struck and melted by lightning. But he had refused to accept defeat and communications had been established. Russell was able to telegraph a message through Butteyan to tell the General what was happening. At first the news was treated with some scepticism at Headquarters; they thought it was 'too good to be true', some officers offering odds of fifty to one against Abrakrampa being attacked. But when it became evident that an attack really had been made, and was still in progress, Sir Garnet took immediate steps to reinforce his outpost. He marched north with all available sailors and marines from the five warships in the roads, twenty-two officers and three hundred men, also Rait with fifty 9-pounder rockets and their launchers. But although life on shipboard may have protected the men from illness, it had left them in no condition for a long march. The heat was terrific, there was very little shade, and a tenth of the force fell out along the road suffering from heat-stroke. So exhausted were the remainder after the ten miles to Assayboo that the General rested them for some hours and managed to find some warm chocolate which cheered them up considerably. Then, with the hundred and forty sailors and marines who were able to go on, and led by fifty marines from the Assayboo garrison, Sir Garnet marched on through Butteyan to Abrakrampa, which he reached at sunset on the second day of the battle.

Wood had orders to advance through Essecroom from Beulah to Abrakrampa and take the enemy in rear. Relying on local guides who had no intention of doing anything so stupid, he was led by a wide detour around the danger area and finished up at Assayboo, whence he was sent on to Butteyan.

The General's column entered Abrakrampa to the accompaniment of a light exchange of small-arms fire. They put out the necessary piquets and settled down for the night. The Headquarter staff officers, who had all marched on foot from Cape Coast Castle, took over responsibility for the outlying piquets so as to let officers of the garrison get some well-deserved rest. They found the Hausas always alert at their posts, but the tribal men were almost invariably asleep and nearly impossible to wake.

Evelyn Wood and his men arrived from Butteyan next morning, 7 November. Their first task was to help persuade the Cape Coast tribes to reconnoitre south-west of the village, where everything had become very quiet. It was not a great success. The Kossoos drove the tribesmen on with the flat of their swords and the occasional prod, which got them a few yards into the bush, when they all without exception lay down. One British officer broke his best umbrella encouraging a chief into action! The majority of chiefs and kings were not popular. They would not work, dared not fight and were unable to control their men. They were described as useless mouths.

Amanquatia had been in command himself and during the night he had held a great council. Many slaves had been sacrificed, but the omens were all inauspicious. Much to his annoyance, the Ashanti General was compelled by his fetish men to withdraw. Disgusted, he then got so drunk that next day he was unable to walk and had to be carried. Luckily for him he was taken away before his rearguard was surprised by a fighting patrol of Gordon and his Hausas, and Captain Bromhead and his Abra tribesmen. Their appearance was so unexpected that the Ashanti abandoned everything and took to their heels. They left quantities of property, ceremonial stools, drums and slaves—more Hausa recruits for Evelyn Wood. Things had moved so quickly that an Ashanti chief who was busy cutting his concubine's throat had to leave the job half done to ensure his own escape; the lady recovered in due course and married one of the companies of the West India Regiment.

That was the end of the reconnaissance in force. The Abras started to loot the camp, and it proved too much for the Hausas to just stand by and watch them, so they joined in. When Gordon had only six men left of his entire company, he turned around and took them back to Abrakrampa.

Next day they collected enough men to try again, taking with them the Cape Coast Fanti tribesmen. After a while they met some minor resistance, but all was going well until suddenly the Fanti lost their heads and began a wild, random fusillade. The panic spread, until even the Hausas joined in, some of them firing off nearly all their ammunition. Captain Bromhead decided it would be better to withdraw to camp before anything worse happened, and set off back with the Abras, to be followed by the Hausas and then the Fanti. This did not suit the Fanti at all: they thought they were being abandoned to the mercies of the Ashanti! They made a frantic rush for safety along the narrow bush track. They hit Gordon and his Hausas while they were crossing a deep stream, knocking him and several of his men into the water as they charged by, one unfortunate Hausa never being seen again. The Ashanti had realized what was going on and harried them from behind, which made things worse. Bromhead halted some Abras to stop the rout and even opened fire on the Fantis, who nonetheless overran everyone in their path and trampled them down. They did not stop at Abrakrampa, but made straight for their homes in the south.

The Ashanti were in full retreat, marching four to five miles a day through the thick bush west of the road, moving in three columns. Sir Garnet wanted Amanquatia out of the Protectorate as soon as possible, so he ordered that nothing was to be done to prevent him reaching the Prah road north of Mansu. After that, Evelyn Wood was to follow him and harass his tail.

Amanquatia was in Sutah on 24 November. Wood, with a regiment now two hundred strong, was there two days later. On the 27th he moved out and captured a prisoner who said that Amanquatia and several of his more important chiefs were at Faysowah, ten miles up the road. The man also said that they were celebrating an Adai day, a very holy sacrificing of slaves, and that nothing would make them move. Wood pressed on regardless of this warning, through jungle where the light was so dim that he could not see to read his English letters—the mail had just arrived— until he came to a clearing. He drove some enemy outposts right through the village of Faysowah, then came up against some of the main army who began to threaten him by encirclement with greatly superior numbers. He thought it better to pull back, and all was going well until the Cape Coast company, coming up to form a lay-back through which the remainder could safely withdraw, sud- denly ran off without having even been in contact with the enemy. This fright spread to the Kossoos and the Hausas; only the Elminas stood firm. They and some British officers, including Eyre, who was now Adjutant, formed sufficient of a rearguard for the regiment to be extricated, leaving a broken officer's hammock and somebody's suitcase to be borne proudly away as spoils of war and later presented to King Kofi Karikari in Kumasi as symbols of a great victory over the British. Far from being a victory, this clash started Amanquatia moving at once, marching by torchlight through the night, scarcely stopping until he reached the Prah River. Behind him, the path was strewn with his dead and his dying; the great Ashanti army was in a miserable condition. Be that as it may, the British tribute to Amanquatia was that no army of a civilized nation need have been ashamed of a retreat conducted with such skill and such success.

It took Amanquatia three days to recross the Prah by canoe. Another phase of the campaign had been completed, and everybody was suffering from overstrain. Brackenbury said that, until it had been felt, no one could possibly realize the exhausting, depressing, enervating nature of the climate, which rendered every exertion a burden and sapped the powers of mind and body. The advance to Kumasi from the Prah was to be a pleasant picnic compared with the arduous toil south of the river. Yet a large army of a great warlike nation had seen fit to withdraw in the face of 'a little band of officers, who had been looked upon almost as lunatics when they volunteered for such a task, who had been sent out in a filthy steamer and not even been allowed to take soldier-servants, that the experiment should be made on the bodies of officers only, whether white men could stand a campaign in the West African bush.' Brackenbury had rather strong feelings on this subject.

They had withstood the environmental hazards of the country —just! On most mornings a sad little cortege had wound its way from Cape Coast Castle through the noisome streets of thatched hovels to the sloping beach. The fever-stricken, dysentery-wracked invalids, some still able to walk without help, others carried in cots, were being taken to the dubious amenities on board *Simoom*, the improvised hospital ship. Escorting them were a medical officer and some orderlies, while a few patients had friends to see them off and wish them luck.

The long, shallow coffin-like cots were slung by rope to wooden bars front and rear, carried on the heads of two pairs of native porters. In these cots lay the sick, fully dressed, blankets up to their waists, heads protected by cork helmets or swathed in cloth. Quietly they lay, gazing up at the canopy a foot or so above their heads. Out in the roads was anchored the small British fleet of warships and transports; while, hauled half out of the water, the surf-boats were waiting.

The Medical Officer checked off names, the walking sick were helped into the boats to seat themselves on the forward thwarts. Then a cot with its patient was carefully lifted in amidships and laid flat. Sometimes behind the cot would be secured a wooden box containing the sufferer's effects. Meanwhile, little native boys who had come to see the show lost interest and began to fight and squabble among themselves.

When all was ready, the Cape Coast paddlers chose their time, rushed the boat forward on the crest of an incoming roller, leaped aboard five to a side and paddled vigorously through the surf, surmounting three more great heaving waves until they reached the easier swell of the open bay.

The General went sick and had to be evacuated from Abra-krampa to the coast on 8 November, and had such a high fever on arrival there that he had to be embarked on board the *Simoom*. Nursed devotedly by his secretary, Lieutenant Maurice, he was able to return to Government House on the 20th of the month. Eyre, whose irrepressible energy always led him to overtax his strength, had been evacuated suffering from fever from Faysowah, and he too spent some time on the *Simoom*. So did Charteris; he had never been fit since the Abrakrampa—Assanchi reconnaissance, when he had exhausted himself carrying messages. He had contracted dysentery, and now fever. From among the sixty-odd officers who had disembarked on the Coast between 2 and 16 October, half had been ill with dysentery or malaria, though the majority recovered within ten days or so. Seven had had to be evacuated to England already, and one had died. Not only the British suffered; the King of Abra died of smallpox, which mercifully never attacked the British contingents throughout the whole war.

The General was confident that British regiments were on their way, and there was a great deal of preparation to be completed before their arrival. They must be able to disembark and start marching for Prahsu that day, reaching their destination with no delay, healthy and ready to fight. His first need, therefore, was for a road from Cape Coast to the Prah, twelve feet wide and cleared of roots, with bridges and culverts for the rivers and streams, causeways across the swamps. In this way the regiments would march in fours to the operational assembly area, arriving dry-shod and in first-class physical condition. Despite labour shortages, Major Home, the Commander of Royal Engineers, had achieved this for him by Christmas, when the road was in excellent order except for a bad swampy patch between Sutah and Faysowah. He had constructed two hundred and thirty-seven bridges.

Now staging camps had to be made ready where the troops could spend the nights on their way north. They would not be marching-fit after the sea voyage, and there was no shade for the first fifteen miles, so the first day would entail only six miles to Inquabim, the next day seven more to Accroful; the next four stages about a dozen miles each by way of Yankumasi Fanti, Mansu, Sutah and Yankumasi Assin; finally nine miles to Barraco and six more to Prahsu. Apart from considerations of distance, sites had been chosen in comparatively dry and healthy areas with a plentiful supply of clean water. Each camp was designed to accommodate four hundred British officers and soldiers in transit and a permanent garrison of fifty. The standard hut was to have wattle walls and to be thatched with palm-leaves to keep off sun and rain. As lying on the bare earth, with its smell of damp and decaying vegetation, was thought to be a potential source of illness, sleeping shelves of split bamboo raised on palm stakes two feet off the ground were to be constructed all around the inside walls. There would be separate huts for senior officers, while their juniors slept four to a hut; a large open-walled mess-shed and the usual ablution and sanitary facilities; a hospital tent and a secure shed with plank walls to protect attractive stores. All around the perimeter the ground would be cleared for at least a hundred yards to deny cover to an attacking enemy, and to give fields of fire.

Mansu, half-way point on the seventy-three-mile route to Prahsu, was to be built on a more elaborate scale with a large central parade-ground; surface drains were dug all over the camp as it seemed always to rain there more than anywhere else.

Major Home had two worries—the insufficiency of labour to get all the work completed in the time required and the behaviour of the natives. They found the finished huts provided excellent privacy for their more intimate personal functions, better even than the main road, which they normally preferred to going off into the bush. Home found one of his huts being used as a slaughter-house for sheep, another as a harem.

The health of British soldiers was paramount. Columns would march out at daybreak to avoid as much as possible of the heat of the day, and proceed at a moderate pace with frequent halts. Before they left they would be given a mug of cocoa, a local product; bread or biscuit, and quinine—the latter under supervision! Daily rations were to be good, a pound and a half of bread or biscuit, a pound and a half of meat, vegetables, tea, sugar and half an ounce of salt. Although the authorities were not fully aware of the dangers of salt deficiency, this small ration was to be a great help in strengthening the men's resistance to the climate.

Bakeries were planned at four camps and a fresh meat supply at six. Marching troops would be given fresh lime-juice with sugar four times a week. Water was to be sterilized as much as was considered necessary to meet the rather dubious standards of the time. At least one well at each camp would be lined and fitted with a special filter, but unfortunately water from native wells and village pools could be used if the local sanitary officer thought it looked clean enough. Sentries were posted over all water-points to ensure that they were not fouled, and every camp would have its sanitary orderlies and scavengers—rubbish collectors and sweepers.

On arrival in camp men would be told off to their accommodation and given a good meal. After dark, fires would be lit either inside the huts or in the doorways 'to dry the air and keep away miasma'. One has to remember that malaria was supposed to come from the noxious odours of swamps, their concomitant swarms of mosquitoes were nothing more dangerous than a nuisance. However, these fires would have kept off mosquitoes and flies of all kinds, so the aim was achieved, albeit unwittingly. Heaps of dried wood were collected and stacked, readily available.

Despite all this there would be a sick list, and battle casualties in times to come. So there was to be a large hospital with a hundred beds at Prahsu, another with sixty at Mansu and a smaller one at Accroful. At Cape Coast Castle there would be sixty-six beds for British soldiers and sailors, and eighteen for officers. Smaller stations would not have hospital accommodation as such, but the best huts could be used as wards after the north-bound columns had all passed through.

Evacuation of sick and wounded was to be by the local brand of hammock with roof and sides, slung on poles and carried by four men, ideally with two reliefs. Thirty-five of these conveyances were to be kept at each staging post, and eighty-five would accompany the Kumasi column from Prahsu. The carrying power of hammocks returning up the line after delivering their patients would not be wasted; they would be used to carry light loads of stores.

Back in England special arrangements were being made to evacuate casualties by sea. Three warships between them could carry four hundred and forty patients, and more could be shipped on mail steamers chartered and specially fitted; hospital orderlies would be in attendance on the invalids. As there might be some sick who would recover quicker in a warmer climate than in England, arrangements were made to accommodate them in Gibraltar if necessary.

Stores, ammunition and supplies would have to be stock-piled at

Mansu and Prahsu, and the only way of getting them there was by native porter. There was a corps of six hundred carriers at Cape Coast Castle when Sir Garnet arrived, but now he needed ten times as many. There were no local pack-animals. The General's dedicated staff, who were quite prepared to give their lives to further the success of the operation, and made a point of ignoring hardship, were greatly angered to find that the local natives, although men of fine physique, did not *like* carrying fifty-pound loads over seventy miles to Prahsu again and again in Brackenbury's 'exhausting climate which rendered every exertion a burden'. Women worked: there is a sketch showing a gang of cheerful ladies setting off from Cape Coast Castle with sixty-six-pound boxes of Australian beef on their heads. Boys worked: Brackenbury's servant was a happy little black imp who would march twenty miles if necessary, and still look after his master properly when they got in to camp. But when boys reached man's estate, that was the end of it all. The man lay back in the shade, while the women of his household brewed his beer and fed him. He was not interested in pay, as compared to a quiet life. He reckoned that he was no longer threatened with slavery and that it was a white man's war. Pressure was now put on chiefs and kings to provide manpower, and they would detail some unwilling men; but they had very little power to coerce their subjects since British rule had removed their right to cut off heads and inflict torture. Gangs would turn up at Cape Coast Castle and report to harassed commissariat officers, who were overworked in a beastly climate and had no time to pander to proper man-management, so the natives all ran away home again.

Women were recruited, particularly from Annamaboe, and they worked well but there were not enough of them who could be spared from ministering to their men-folk. Elmina chiefs who now began to come in and sue for peace were told to back their protestations of goodwill by producing labour, and this produced a thousand men. Huyshe was sent all around the Dunquah-Mansu area to order the kings to provide men and women carriers, with a message from the General that he would take ship and leave them to the mercy of the Ashanti if they would not cooperate. This threat produced no less than five thousand men, quite enough for all requirements, but they soon started to drift away again and the project fell behind schedule.

Fortunately Brevet Lieutenant-Colonel Colley arrived from England in mid-December. He had worked with Sir Garnet at the War Office over the Cardwell reforms, which were to bear the test of time so well. Now he had voluntarily given up his post of Professor of Military Administration at the Staff College to take part in the Gold Coast campaign. The General knew all about his energy and ability, and was also aware that he had some years of experience with natives in South Africa where he had been a Magistrate in Kaffraria—just the man to tackle the transport problem. Sir Garnet could not actually *force* a military officer on to the Commissary, but he had not picked a difficult, hide-bound civilian staff and Commissary O'Connor readily agreed to accept Colley as his Director of Transport.

With three specially employed officers to help him, Colley took over his duties just before Christmas and proceeded systematically to reorganize the system, with the basic aim of giving the carriers decent working conditions and humane treatment. He divided the line of communication into sections and allotted carriers to them; men would not be expected to work outside their own section, which would be commanded by a British officer, who would get to know them and they him. Allocation to sections would be by tribes under their own headmen. Porters would be paid on return from each journey, and what was more they would be paid by their British officer, who would not delegate the task of giving them their money to chiefs or kings. When possible, they would be given one day's rest in five. Complaints were to be investigated properly and minor offences met by fines. Corporal punishment was to be avoided in all except very serious cases, and would rarely exceed twenty-five lashes.

This was to be the system for line-of-communication carriers. When the British regiments disembarked they would be allotted their own regimental carriers who would stay with them throughout the war. Nonetheless, the porters' own British transport officer would stay with them and continue to pay and watch over them.

It was hoped that these measures would reduce desertions to an acceptable drain, but it was not to be. More severe methods became necessary, which will be described in due course. Colley was eventually to employ twenty-two military officers and six controllers.

The War Office had received General Sir Garnet Wolseley's despatches written between 13 and 27 October on the afternoon of 17 November and had taken immediate action. A Cabinet meeting was called, it was agreed that three battalions should be sent and orders were telegraphed the same evening. The regiments already held in readiness, which were the 2nd Battalion, The Rifle Brigade, and the Royal Welch Fusiliers (23rd Regiment of Foot) sailed on the 19th, only two days after the arrival of Sir Garnet's official request. The 42nd Royal Highland (The Black Watch) Regiment were brought up to Sir Garnet's stipulated strength of six hundred and fifty by a draft of a hundred and seventy men from the 79th Highlanders. They were kitted up and equipped, a civil steamship was chartered for them and they sailed on 3 December. There had been a delay in producing the short rifles and sword-bayonets, so that both the 23rd Foot and the 42nd had to sail with standard weapons, but Cardwell was able to send off the right arms to arrive in time to be issued before the regiments disembarked for action. The Rifle Brigade was off Cape Coast Castle on 9 December, the 23rd Foot on the 12th; and the 42nd, who had made the fastest voyage ever, on the 17th of the month.

But nobody was ready for them. The essential preparations had not been completed, and, as the General had promised that they would not be landed a moment before they could march up country, he had to order the ships away to cruise until 31 December. So that they should not waste their time, Commanding Officers were given a training memorandum of lessons learnt during the campaign to date, with some instructions for reorganization.

At that time the infantry company was the lowest unit at which command was exercised, and this was impossible to do in bush warfare when visibility was often limited to only a few yards. The General decreed that all companies were to be split forthwith into four sections and that each section was to be commanded by an officer or an NCO. Section commanders and the men in them were to remain unchanged throughout the war except in extraordinary circumstances, and then only by order of officers commanding battalions. Even fatigue duties were to be arranged on a section basis, except for small guards and suchlike, which could be done by half-sections. In this way every man would fight in the special, individual circumstances of bush warfare with comrades and a leader who he knew well, and who knew him.

Wolseley told them of the Ashanti habit of yelling and howling to demoralize their enemies. He told them of the Ashanti doctrine of encirclement and attacking from the rear; but they were not to worry, and trust *him* to deal with that sort of thing. He explained that a British soldier with his breech-loading rifle was equal to twenty Ashantis, whose rifles were not lethal over fifty yards, and that the enemy had a superstitious fear of white men.

He stressed also that everyone must be kind to the native carriers, or they would desert, and then where would breakfast and ammunition come from? Finally, he told them how important it would be to conserve ammunition, which would have to be carried up to them over many miles of road.

'Fire low, fire slow, charge home!'

He then had time to open his mail, which included a despatch from Lord Kimberley, reminding him that what Her Majesty's Government would really like would be a treaty on their terms. Sir Garnet was not to go any further inland that was necessary to obtain peace. The British contingent was to be re-embarked as soon as this peace was signed, and in any case not later than the end of March, 1874. His Lordship was worried also lest 'if Kumasi should be occupied, the King might take to the bush, and the conquering British General might have no one to treat with!'

Although Sir Garnet had sent the troops away on a cruise, he allowed certain officers to land. Foremost of these was Brigadier-General Sir Archibald Alison, an officer senior to himself under normal conditions and a well-known historian with a number of publications to his credit. He was to command the British brigade of three battalions and must have been a willing volunteer for this much sought-after appointment. His task now would be to organize the British brigade's disembarkation and to despatch it up the road to Prahsu.

Colley had been on the same ship and also Colonel G. R. Greaves, who would replace Colonel McNeil as Chief of Staff.

The ships would be back by the New Year and all seemed to be well along the road, so the Headquarter Staff left Cape Coast Castle for the Prah on Boxing Day. They were sad to hear before they left that Charteris's fever had got much worse aboard the *Simoom* and that he had died at sea. Eyre had recovered and had left to rejoin Wood at Prahsu.

Nearly everybody walked. It was customary in the Gold Coast for officers to be given allowances to maintain their personal hammocks, but now there were neither the hammocks nor the bearers to go around. It had been decided that there would no longer be any such allowance issued and that officers would march on foot except in very exceptional circumstances. On such occasions hammocks would be provided at public expense, subject to sanction by the

Quartermaster-General. Eight very poor-class mules had been obtained from Madeira, but they were scarcely worth their keep. Three or four could be ridden at a pinch and officers have been portrayed on mule-back in several sketches of the campaign. Mr Henry Stanley, who was representing the *New York Herald*—his famous meeting with Dr Livingstone at Ujiji had taken place two years earlier—had a mule!

The road through Inquabim to Accroful passed through low brush and after that entered the great primeval forest. It was all very dreary, an endless passage of dark-green, none of the dappled sunlight and bright colours that Sir Garnet remembered from his campaign in the jungles of Burma. There was no game to shoot for the pot; there did not seem to be any animals. There were supposed to be hyaenas, but if so they kept well away from the fighting areas; bodies were left lying in the bush for days and were never eaten.

The General was still suffering a bit from his old wound, so he travelled all the way in a light American buggy, which gives some indication of the excellent work put in by Home and his road-gangs. He reached Prahsu on 2 January, 1874.

On arrival he inspected the garrison. Evelyn Wood was there with a regiment that was now four hundred and fifty strong. Chief Essevie had joined him in early December with 'twenty-two sons of his own body begotten, between the ages of twenty and twenty-three, he himself being a man of about forty years of age, and the finest of the family'. He brought also about twenty of his relations, and all his men were engaged on the condition, approved by Sir Garnet, that they be discharged on the day upon which Evelyn Wood, from any cause whatsoever, ceased to command the regiment.

Russell was there with five hundred men. Rait and his battery were in camp, fifty gunners to serve three 7-pounder guns, two 4⅖-inch howitzers and six rocket-launchers. The howitzers had been dragged most of the way by oxen—meat on the hoof delivered at Cape Coast Castle, and misemployed as draught-animals.

Prahsu was a nice camp; there was room to breathe. A great swathe of bush had been cleared. The River Prah flowed gently by at a walking pace, more than sixty yards wide, and one could see up and down for five hundred yards in each direction, a very welcome change after the claustrophobic conditions of the jungle trek. Huts were ready for the staff, and more and more were being completed every day. The whole camp had to be ready for two thousand Europeans by 15 January.

The Naval Brigade had landed on 27 December and marched in to camp on 3 January. So well-planned and organized had been the camps and march stages that not one man had fallen out along the seventy-three-mile journey.

Disembarkation of the first British infantry began on New Year's Day and continued at the rate of half a battalion a day (the camps were designed to take only this amount at any one time). They began at the early hour of a quarter to two in the morning, and every man of the first wing of the Rifle Brigade was on shore and marching north two hours later, led by their commander, Major Stephens, on a donkey. They were accompanied by their baggage, which had been landed the day before, carried on the heads of their own native carriers. Everybody covered the six miles to Inquabim without any trouble, except for an unfortunate sergeant-major of the Royal Engineers who threw an apoplectic fit, possibly an occupational hazard, and had to be invalided home.

So in their turn disembarked the 42nd Highlanders, and the Royal Welch Fusiliers, the 23rd Foot. All went well at first, but now that work had really started the carrier desertion rate from all stations along the line reached such proportions in early January that it seemed the operation would either have to be abandoned altogether or that it would have to be carried out with less troops —fewer mouths to feed and fewer weapons to supply with ammunition. Brigadier-General Alison on his own initiative stopped the disembarkation of the second half of the 23rd Foot and the British gunners; hearing which, the General himself ordered the leading half of the regiment to return to base and re-embark. They had already got as far as Accroful with no casualties except for the regimental goat, which had passed away in Inquabim, and were greatly disappointed at being denied a part in the war. But Colonel Mostyn, the Commanding Officer, made a special representation to the General, who saw his point and relented. There was still no question of bringing more than the equivalent to two battalions of British soldiers up to the front, but a hundred men of the 23rd under Colonel Warren were now allowed to continue their march north; while a hundred of the least fit officers and men of the 42nd were sent down the line and re-embarked in their stead. The British gunners received no such concession, which was bad luck. But the General was really rather glad of an excuse to get rid of them. He had asked for them to be sent before he had realized what a first-class job Rait, his officers and NCOs would do in forming a native battery, which had already proved itself. Moreover, he did not want Rait, whom he later described as one of the best officers he had ever served with, to be superseded in command by a more senior officer! In any case Rait had made it standard drill for his Hausa gunners to dismantle and carry their guns for considerable distances when necessary, and British gunners would have been unable to do this in the climatic conditions of the Gold Coast.

The advance was stopped. The Rifle Brigade halted with the leading wing at Barraco, only six miles short of Prahsu, and the rear half one stage behind at Yankumasi Assin; the 42nd Highlanders stayed at Mansu and Yankumasi Fanti. The regimental carriers of both regiments were taken away to be used along the line of communication to stockpile thirty days supply at Prahsu by 15 January. This was of the greatest urgency if the Kumasi operation was to be launched in time, so the 1st West India Regiment at base and the 2nd West India Regiment along the line were all turned into carriers. So was Wood's regiment, just when he was hoping to fit in some musketry training! But Russell's regiment had fifty more men and they had behaved well in a proper battle at Abrakrampa, so the General had chosen them to lead the advance across the Prah and kept them for this purpose only. The 42nd volunteered to act as carriers, and actually did several journeys, but the General forbade this when he heard of it. He wanted them fresh for their real task of fighting.

Whole tribes were deserting in mass and stern measures had to be taken. The General so far had not used force to conscript labour, though he had exercised his powers as Civil Governor and arranged for the Judicial Assizes Court at Beulah to pass the legislation enabling him to do so. Now he decided that he must implement this law and Colley was authorized to take action. Although he had a fever, he mounted an operation to comb the villages for deserters and able-bodied men who had so far avoided service, starting among the Agoonah who had gone absent as a tribe and ill-treated messengers sent to fetch them back. Colley made a ten-mile night march along a bush track, surrounded the offending village in darkness and collected all the serviceable manpower living there. He then burned the village and fined the local chief £20 for not having punished the men who had beaten his messengers. He and his officers repeated this operation for several days and at all hours, until chiefs and men came pouring in; they realized that there was no escape.

There was no more trouble about a sufficiency of labour. Colley had, and kept, about eight thousand carriers. Even though there was a wastage of about a hundred and twenty a week through genuine sickness, there were enough men and women for the task. The whole machinery was set in motion again. The Rifle Brigade were all in Prahsu by 20 January, the Highlanders by the 22nd.

Meanwhile, on 2 January envoys from King Kofi Karikari had arrived at Prahsu. They were met by Buller in his capacity as Intelligence Officer, told that Sir Garnet would give audience only to the King or to a prince of the royal blood, and were confined to a hut under guard. The King seemed to be rather behind the times as both his letters were addressed to Colonel Harley. The first letter, dated late November, was reasonably conciliatory, though it stated that he would not let Mr Dawson, the Governor's representative, or the missionaries go until the ransom had been paid. When the money was received they would be released at once. The second, signed on 26 December, was very different in tone. It appeared that Amanquatia and his captains had got together and agreed, very wisely, not to tell the King the whole story. They had represented the affair at Faysowah as a great victory, producing the broken hammock and Lieutenant Woodgate's box as proof. So Kofi Karikari now demanded that suzerainty over the Denkeras and Assin be restored to him, and that an explanation should be given for the 'attack' on his army at Faysowah. A short time limit was set for Sir Garnet's reply!

The General was in no hurry; he wanted the envoys to see the Naval Brigade, who were due in next day. He wrote his reply at once, however, refusing to cede the Denkera and Assin and pointing out that Amanquatia had attacked both Elmina and Abrakrampa, and had been soundly thrashed on each occasion. The Faysowah affair had been nothing but a minor skirmish involving local troops who had been given orders not to attack. Even so, this minor brush had caused the Ashanti to retreat in utter disorder.

The General repeated the terms which he had sent to the King on arrival at the Gold Coast and reiterated his desire for peace. He insisted on the release of all prisoners, white and native, and said that 'having unjustly forced this war on the Queen of England, thereby entailing immense expense on her, you will pay Her Majesty 50,000 ounces of approved gold.' Hostages for Kofi

Karikari's good behaviour would have to be produced and would be nominated at a later date.

Sir Garnet added that if these terms were not met, white troops already on their way from the coast would invade Ashanti territory on four fronts—from the west through Wassaw into the lands of the King of Becquah; two thrusts in the centre from Prahsu to capture Kumasi and further east aimed at the King of Kokofoo's possessions; fourthly from the Volta River towards Juabin.

All this was quite true. On the left Captain Dalrymple would reach Jukwa on 5 January with orders to raise an army of Wassaws and Denkeras. The General himself was at Prahsu and his troops were moving up. Butler had left on 18 December with arms, ammunition and rocket launchers to recruit two thousand Akim and cross the Prah twenty miles further east on 15 January, while Glover was on his way from the Volta.

Things had not been easy for Glover. He had trouble buying Hausa slaves for his army. Then he had the same problem as everyone else in getting kings and chiefs to join him. He had asked Whitehall to send him a thousand bottles of duty-free gin as presents to these dignitaries, but a frugal government department had decided that three hundred would suffice. He could not even obtain enough small change in silver for paying his men. Next, one of his officers was found to have a predisposition for brandy, which left the expedition short-staffed after his dismissal. However, in the end he brought together all the kings and chiefs to make them take a mighty oath to march with him against the Ashanti. They swore on the red coat, and by the head of Sir Charles Macarthy, a vow held with the same veneration and awe in the West African Settlements as the King's Great Oath in Ashanti. Anybody breaking it would suffer the disgrace of proving himself unmindful of the fact that Sir Charles's sacrifice had been for him and his country. It was even administered on the anniversary of his death in battle.

All the usual evasions and delay ensued, so Glover sent a despatch to the General saying that he could never make the schedule; it was most unlikely that he would be able to cross the Prah before early February. There ensued a smart exchange of messages. Sir Garnet said that he must at all costs cross into Ashanti territory on 15 January, even with only seven hundred men. Glover replied that in that case he could not be held responsible if his force met with disaster. In answer to this Colonel Greaves's despatch on behalf of Sir Garnet was: 'While the Major-General is fully prepared to accept responsibility for the directive issued by him to you, he must count on your using the ordinary precautions of a military commander of troops in the field.' Glover pressed on.

Major Home's bridge over the Prah had not been completed when the Naval Brigade marched in to Prahsu, so the Ashanti envoys remained held in their hut, except when taken out to witness a demonstration of Gatling gun fire-power. This was so impressive that one of the envoys shot himself that night. This was not what Sir Garnet had intended and he wrote to Kofi Karikari apologizing for such a thing happening in his camp, and enclosing proceedings of the Court of Inquiry which he had convened. The king was uninterested, he brushed it aside, commenting testily that it seemed an awful lot of fuss about a man who was, after all, only a common fellow!

The surviving envoys were released on 6 January and escorted by Redvers Buller across the new bridge over the Prah through columns of marching, singing sailors heading north into Ashanti-land, (they crossed back as soon as the envoys were out of sight and ear-shot), through Russell's foremost elements already eight miles up the road, past Lord Gifford's scout-screen at Essiaman further on, and then sent on their way.

There was still plenty to be done preparing for the British infantry. Sailors and marines were put to work clearing scrub and felling trees to make room for a new, large encampment. They worked only in the early mornings and late evenings, avoiding the heat of the day, but the weather conditions at Prahsu were not in fact too bad. The harmattan wind had begun to blow dry and fresh from the northern deserts; it was so dessicating that soon some of the bush could be burned instead of cut, saving a lot of trouble. The temperature only rose to seventy-five degrees Fahrenheit in the shade, while the nights were actually cool. Sickness among the men was negligible—only thirteen out of four hundred and twenty-seven; but the staff, who had been exposed to all the dangers of the environment for very much longer, were in comparatively worse health. Mr Irvine had fever; Maurice was not well; Baker, the Assistant Adjutant-General, had fever and ague; Huyshe gave some cause for worry, he had driven himself harder than anyone else. He had gone straight off to Dunquah on arrival in the Gold Coast; then he had taken over the road from Hausa Gordon. He had fortified and then fought for Abrakrampa. Next he was sent to persuade the kings to produce labour. Recalled from this, he was despatched on reconnaissance north-east of Mansu. In early December he had gone to map tracks through all the old Amanquatia camps from Mampon to Jukwa. Now he had gone surveying new areas and had returned feeling very ill indeed. His condition deteriorated rapidly.

On 12 January another Ashanti embassy passed through Lord Gifford's scouts at the Foomoosu River, bringing with them one of the missionaries, Mr Kuehne. Kofi Karikari was now very much more amenable, blaming everything on his subordinates and asking Sir Garnet to stay where he was to avoid clashes with the Ashanti Army. He asked that Mr Dawson should stay to act as scribe and interpreter for the short time remaining before everything could be settled.

According to Mr Kuehne, Amanquatia had reached Kumasi on 22 December and had paraded his men through the market-place carrying with them the bones of two hundred and eighty Ashanti captains who had died of disease or had been killed in battle. His force was then disbanded and the men dispersed to their homes. There were no Ashanti units closer than the Adansi Hills, over thirty miles north of the Prah, but beyond these hills lay the army of Cobbina Obbin, King of Adansi.

Kuehne said also that Kofi Karikari had already killed all his Assin and Akim prisoners, though there were still some of the Fanti left alive. He did not believe that the King was anything like as rich as everybody supposed, and thought that he would be quite unable to pay a large indemnity. For example, when he had, in accordance with tradition, to give away money on Adai religious occasions, he had to sell slaves in order to be able to find the ready cash.

Sir Garnet replied to the King agreeing that Dawson might stay, but insisted that all prisoners must be released and all other demands met before he would call off the now imminent invasion. He was well pleased with Kuehne's news that Amanquatia had disbanded his army; he was sure that it could not be reassembled again in time to stop his own advance on Kumasi. Though he did not know it at the time, his stratagem of deliberately announcing details of his four-pronged attack had resulted in several kings removing their men from the main Ashanti army to go and defend their own threatened territories.

CHAPTER 3

The Battles for Kumasi

[1]

Buller had been sent to the Prah in early December to raise a company of native scouts from among the men who had been employed on such duties during the advance. They found some of the canoes used by Amanquatia for his crossing and used them to get over the river and reconnoitre to the north. During their sweep they captured a prisoner who confirmed that the Ashanti army had marched away towards Kumasi. The General was so pleased with the way that they had carried out their task that he decided to recruit more of them. They were all picked men. The majority were Assins, who spoke the Ashanti language; some of them knew every village as far as Kumasi; all were hunters skilled in field craft. Also included were a couple of dozen Hausas and Kossoos chosen for their proven courage in battle, and a few West Indians for the same reason. Lord Gifford, adjutant of Russell's regiment and an officer of exceptional bravery and initiative, was put in command of this band.

British troops were still to be preserved as unscathed as possible until the time arose when only they could win the day. Until that time the local levies, now including veterans of three months' service and several frays, were to lead the way. On 5 January, 1874, Gifford's scouts and Russell's regiment were ferried across the Prah. Gifford pushed forward twelve miles to Essiaman, which he found clear of enemy. As soon as he reported this, a company of Russell's regiment came forward to dig in and form a defended post. At the same time the rest of the regiment did the same at Attobiassie, eight miles from the river, clearing fields of fire and erecting huts for the main body. Next day they started helping the engineers clear the road north to Essiaman. This became standard procedure during the rest of the advance to contact; every time that

55

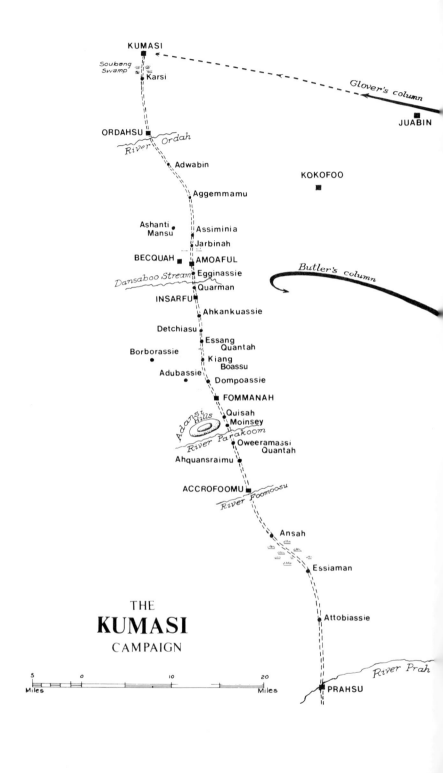

KUMASI

Soubang
Swamp
Karsi

Glover's column

JUABIN

ORDAHSU
River Ordah

Adwabin

KOKOFOO

Aggemmamu

Ashanti
Mansu
Assiminia

Jarbinah

BECQUAH AMOAFUL

Egginassie
Dansaboo Stream
Quarman

INSARFU

Butler's column

Ahkankuassie

Detchiasu

Essang
Quantah

Borborassie
Kiang
Boassu

Adubassie
Dompoassie

FOMMANAH

Quisah
Moinsey

Adansi Hills
River Parakoom
Oweeramassi
Quantah

Ahquansraimu

ACCROFOOMU
River Foomoosu

Ansah

Essiaman

THE
KUMASI
CAMPAIGN

Attobiassie

River Prah

5   0   10   20
Miles   Miles

PRAHSU

Gifford made a bound forward, so the places occupied would be turned into firm bases for the main force. The carriers accompanying Russell brought up a week's supply of food and the regimental reserve of ammunition. Then they were sent back for more supplies to establish forward depots. They were disconcerted to find sentries on the bridge, which had now been completed, and that they were not allowed over on to the south bank. Colley had decided to make things a little less easy for would-be deserters!

So the advance continued with Gifford and his scouts working ahead of Russell and his five hundred men. Over a swamp to Ansah, where a fetish goat-skin stretched across the road failed to deter them; on to the Foomoosu River, thirty to sixty feet wide but fordable. Then to Accrofoomu, which was found to be full of enemy. Gifford collected what he considered to be sufficient men for an attack, but Russell decided that the opposition was too strong and stopped him. The last thing that was needed at this time was any kind of reverse. So there was a day's delay, after which Gifford moved in to find the town deserted except for ten Ashanti scouts who fled on his approach. On they went through Ahquansraimu and Oweeramassie, over the Parakoom River to the foot of Moinsey Hill, which they reached on 16 January, thirty-two miles from their jumping-off point on the Prah. The fetish men had fought an unsuccessful rearguard action with splayed remains of goats and chickens, all to no avail. Next morning Gifford attacked a formidable Ashanti position on Moinsey Hill and manoeuvred so well, and the scouts responded so well to his orders after only two weeks under his command, that they outflanked the enemy. According to the conventions of Ashanti warfare you were supposed to retreat when outflanked, in the same way as you were supposed to admit defeat if you were surrounded, so the Ashanti in this case cleared off without firing a shot. Up came the Royal Engineers and their Sierra Leone labourers to clear ground and form a camp at Moinsey for the equivalent of four battalions. Essiaman and Accrofoomu were already able to take two battalions, garrisons of sixty soldiers and large supply depots.

It remained now to capture and consolidate the crest of the Adansi Hills. Gifford went down the far side of Moinsey Hill to the town of Quisah, unoccupied except for a few Ashanti scouts, with whom he parleyed. Both sides maintained that they were quite ready to fight each other, but the Ashanti said that they must ask their chief first; so Gifford for his part said that he would have to consult his General! Next day, however, when Gifford came forward for battle there was nobody there, so Russell promptly occupied the place.

It was now 19 January. Gifford, Russell's regiment, Wood's regiment, Rait's artillery and most of the 2nd West India Regiment were deployed along the new depots and staging posts north of the Prah. They were now to be called the advance guard and be a separate command under Colonel M'Leod, Commanding Officer of the 42nd Highlanders, called forward from Mansu to take up the appointment. He arrived that day; so did Colley, to report that the transport difficulties were solved. Carrier trouble so far had cost the General a battalion of British troops and five days from his timetable. But now the great good fortune of his advance having been able to penetrate so deeply and so quickly into Ashanti territory, when he had expected to have to fight his way up the road, had put him right back on schedule. Such extensive preparation had been made north of the Prah that Sir Garnet assessed that the British troops could reach Quisah four days after the crossing.

Huyshe died on 19 January. Next day his friends, the General and staff crossed over, followed by the Naval Brigade. Captain Blake, Royal Navy, had to be left behind suffering from severe dysentery, from which he died soon after being evacuated to Cape Coast. Commodore Hewett came up to take his place, catching up next day.

Gifford moved a short distance forward to Fommanah. 'All along the road from Quisah to Fommanah the fetish priests had been at work. A white thread was stretched from tree to tree the whole way, and in Fommanah itself strips of white cotton or linen were nailed to the trees. Before reaching Fommanah, Lord Gifford had found, planted in the middle of the road, a gun roughly carved out of wood, with a number of knives stuck into it; and a dead man was impaled on a stake close by, horribly mutilated, with the severed parts of his body hung around his neck.' Near this horror, at the side of the road, was a deep pit containing the remains of sacrificed victims, thrown in without even a covering of earth.

Fommanah was empty of inhabitants, as was Dompoassie which Gifford reached next day, 24 January. By then all the fighting troops were over the Prah. The 42nd Highlanders had crossed, so had the hundred-strong detachment of the 23rd Royal Welch Fusiliers, also the field hospital and the ammunition reserve. More troops were on their way. Buller estimated that King Karikari was trying frantically to collect his army, and that there would be a battle at Amoaful; so two hundred more of the 23rd were ordered to disembark and start up the road. Information was hard to come by, but the scouts had been offered substantial bounties for Ashanti prisoners brought in alive and able to talk.

Now good news came in from the outposts. Two envoys arrived with another letter from the Ashanti king, and with them were all the remaining white captives—M. Bonnet, a French medical missionary, and Mr and Mrs Ramseyer and their two children. Now at least there was no longer the fear that they might be murdered or sacrificed.

The King was very upset at Sir Garnet's rapid rate of advance, which was not going to give him time to collect his soldiers. He asked the General to stop and discuss things in a sensible manner; and he had hit on a good idea about the gold—Amanquatia could pay the indemnity as a punishment for disobedience in attacking the British.

The General decided now to halt at Fommanah for a few days, seemingly in accordance with Kofi Karikari's request. If the King really meant to make peace, it gave him an opportunity to do so. But Sir Garnet's true reason was that he wanted to stock-pile ten days supplies in Fommanah before moving his British contingent any further forward.

Colley had now been given complete command over the whole line of communication, over all military and civil personnel, over all troops, posts and transport. All normal protocol had been set aside, and he was now in a position where no post commander could thwart his intentions and no civilian officer could plead difficulty or delay by referring to higher authority. Woe betide an officer who commandeered a hammock and kept it for his own use! He had collected thirty days' supplies at the Prah and now more and more carriers were reporting in to Mansu, so he formed them into divisions to work north of the river. He despatched divisions to work from Prahsu to the north, from Accrofoomu, from Fommanah and from Insarfu, even though Gifford and his scouts had not yet got there. Everything was ready by 27 January; then Colley turned his attention to the next priority, that of medical evacuation, getting everything in order before battle casualties added to the steadily increasing stream of sick on their way to Cape Coast.

The British contingent had now lost three officers and two hundred and fifteen men through sickness out of a total of one thousand eight hundred all ranks. The General never for one moment forgot the vulnerability of Europeans to the Gold Coast climate, and he now ordered that all night duties and the harder day-time work should be done by native troops.

He was forthright in his reply to King Kofi Karikari. He said that he was now going to Kumasi anyway and that it was up to the King to decide whether he came as a friend or as an enemy. If it was to be as a friend all the native prisoners must be released and half the gold was to be sent at once. The King's mother and his heir, Prince Mensa, the two most important people in the kingdom, were to be delivered to the British camp as hostages, under a guarantee of good treatment. The General was not to know it at the time, but this last term would be quite impossible for the king to agree to; it would be out of the question, on religious grounds, for him to surrender these two relatives.

The missionaries had confirmed that the Kings of Becquah and Juabin had left Kumasi to defend their own lands. None of the chiefs north of Kumasi had rejoined the King's army, but the King of Mampon was believed to have five thousand men somewhere south of Aggemmamu; and Cobbina Obbin was not far away at Adubassie, only two miles west of Dompoassie; he had met and talked to the missionaries on their way south. The Ramseyer family were sent down to the coast, but M. Bonnet remained with Force Headquarters where he was of great assistance to the intelligence department and a devoted minister to the wounded under the hottest fire.

On 26 January Colonel M'Leod reconnoitred in force to Adubassie where he surprised two hundred Ashanti. Prisoners told him that Cobbina Obbin had been there with a thousand soldiers, but that he had now withdrawn north and would fight near Amoaful. It transpired that he had cut into the road at Essang Quantah just ahead of Evelyn Wood, who was advancing from Dompoassie. Hot on his rear, Wood had by evening occupied Essang Quantah and exploited on towards Detchiasu.

Sir Garnet wrote furiously to Kofi Karikari to say that he would not tolerate the presence of armed men near his force and that he would march immediately on Kumasi unless all the terms were met. 'This is the last time that I shall warn you!'

Gifford was still checking the west and north and confirmed that the Ashanti were indeed retreating. He found Ahkankuassie empty and occupied it, while the engineers toiled to make the road suitable

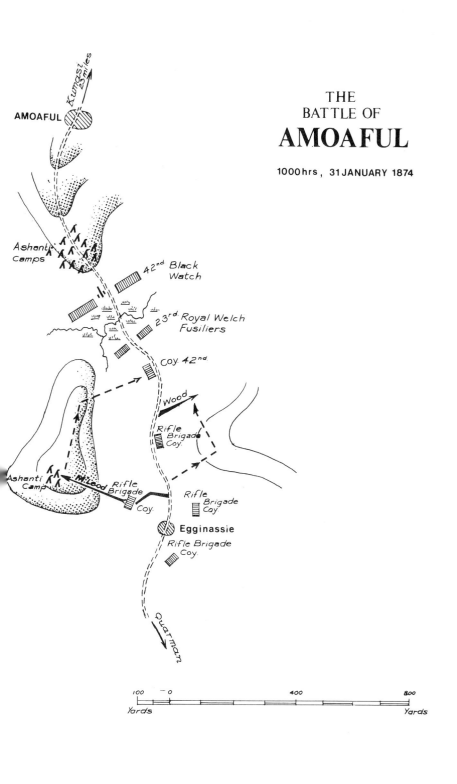

AMOAFUL

Kumasi 25 miles

THE
BATTLE OF
AMOAFUL

1000 hrs, 31 JANUARY 1874

Ashanti Camps

42nd. Black Watch

23rd. Royal Welch Fusiliers

Coy. 42nd.

Wood

Rifle Brigade Coy.

Ashanti Camp

M'Leod

Rifle Brigade Coy.

Rifle Brigade Coy.

Egginassie

Rifle Brigade Coy.

Quarman

100   –0   400   800
Yards   Yards

1. Lord Gifford's skirmish at Egginassie.

for further advance. They got as far as Detchiasu, to find that beyond that point the track became very bad indeed. The General ordered that they were no longer to take part in local skirmishes, a pastime dear to many officers of the Royal Engineers, but to put their whole effort into their proper task of making good the road.

Colonel M'Leod's advance guard was now augmented by the Naval Brigade and the 23rd Royal Welch Fusiliers, whom he took with him on 29 January to reconnoitre Borborassie. Russell's Annamaboe company surprised and stormed the village, but Captain Nicol who had done such good work recruiting Opobos and Bonnys was shot dead leading his men. His place was taken by the General's ADC, Lieutenant the Hon H. Wood, who had been given permission to have an outing that day. After an hour M'Leod withdrew his force to Kiang Boassu, while the Naval Brigade dealt efficiently with an Ashanti attack on the rearguard.

Ten days' supplies were now in Fommanah, so the General continued his advance. On his way he received two more letters from King Kofi trying to gain time, but wrote back saying that he would wait no longer. By the evening of the 30th the advance guard was dug in across the Dansaboo Stream north of Quarman, and the fighting force teeth arms were at Insarfu just behind them.

Early that morning Gifford, with his motley band of scouts, magnificent in their savage finery, had probed forward to Egginassie, a village a mile south of Amoaful. His Opobos led the way, fantastic figures in their caps of monkey skins; behind them specially-picked Kossoos and Bonnys, their head-dresses decorated with long feathers, porcupine quills, hanks of rope, braided sticks of hair standing straight out from their heads at all angles; compared to them the more staidly attired Hausas and uniformed West Indians seemed drab and colourless.

Cautiously they approached Egginassie, a typical Ashanti village of straggling huts lining both sides of the jungle path. In the middle was a great tree, social centre of the community, beneath which the inhabitants would sit and conduct their business. Some form of conference was actually in progress when an Ashanti sentry gave the alarm, and in a trice the tree was deserted except for abandoned string-beds, chairs and overturned earthenware pots. Then at the far end of the village Ashanti warriors began to gather in great numbers, fleetingly discernible through the clouds of gunpowder-smoke from their muskets. Three scouts fell and Gifford withdrew out of range, maintaining contact while he sent back his report of enemy in strength.

This looked like the real thing at last and Redvers Buller went forward to see for himself, while the Royal Engineers were given an escort and began to cut a road through to within a hundred yards of the village. Buller gave his opinion that Amanquatia was in command of the Ashanti opposing force and that he would fight at Amoaful, and again, if necessary, in front of Kumasi.

The General decided to attack next day, 31 January, and issued his instructions for the operation.

[2]

The fighting regiments and units of Major-General Sir Garnet Wolseley's expeditionary force moved out from Insarfu in battle order at daybreak. Lord Gifford and forty of his scouts led the way. Then came the advance guard, based for the first time on a British battalion, the 42nd Highlanders, and commanded by Brigadier-General Sir Archibald Alison, leading his brigade in action. In front marched two companies of the 42nd, with the essential Royal Engineers and their Sierra Leone labourers, under Major Home, right up with his men now that action was certain. Next came the Brigadier-General and the regiment's remaining six companies, followed by Captain Rait and two of his 7-pounder guns.

Gifford passed through Quarman without incident, but as he neared Egginassie, three-quarters of a mile further on, heavy but long-range and therefore ineffectual musket-firing broke out from his front and left. Undeterred by this, the scouts pressed on, brushed aside an ambuscade and took possession of the village in the face of only token resistance. But from the great roar of fire and the clouds of black powder smoke it was clear that there was a great host of Ashanti across and around the road leading out of Egginassie.

Now, after all these weeks, it was time for the British infantry. Alison deployed his two forward companies and passed them through the scouts. Soon they were heavily engaged from left and front. Whenever they could they extended in line to the left of the road, but there were times when the bush was so dense that this was impossible. Worried about his left, under heavy fire from an enemy he could not see, Alison sent two companies up a track leading to the left just outside Egginassie hoping that it would turn right and enable him to outflank the enemy west of the road. If it should diverge in the wrong direction, however, the companies were to turn north and cut themselves a path parallel to the road.

The two leading companies were having a hard time, so he sent forward another company to support them, and two more under Major Baird to take over responsibility for the left of the road, giving the others a chance to push forward. Major McPherson, acting Commanding Officer of the 42nd, was put in charge of the forward companies. It was no longer spent bullets that the Highlanders were meeting; the Ashanti in the bush lay in wait and fired at nearly point-blank range. Lying flat on the ground they were almost invisible until they fired; then, unclothed and without accoutrements, they would crawl away backwards on their hands and knees through the tangled undergrowth almost unmolested by the British who were quite unable to follow them. Baird's companies killed a man within four yards, never spotted until he fired his musket.

Engaged by short-range musketry, British casualties became significant for the first time in the war. Wounded Highlanders began to stream back from the front, others lay along the road awaiting hammocks to take them to the rear. More men were needed and Alison sent his last company to join McPherson. Luckily, the two companies sent off to the left reappeared; the track had turned the wrong way and the bush had been too thick for a path to be cut fast enough to keep up with the advance up the road. Alison made them replenish their ammunition, then kept one and sent the other forward. Except for this one company retained by the Brigadier-General, McPherson now had the whole of his regiment under his orders.

After advancing a few hundred yards beyond Egginassie Alison came to a small rise in the track from where he was at last able to get some idea of what was going on. The road descended into a low swampy area three hundred yards ahead, through which ran a small stream, and all the way it was open to fire from the hilly bush rearing up on the left, occupied, judging by the slugs flying around, by a great number of the enemy. Crossing the stream, the track wended its way up half a mile of rising ground, and on each side was a big Ashanti encampment. The Brigadier-General describes the situation as follows: 'The peculiarities of Ashanti warfare were now strongly developed. We were in the midst of a semi-circle of hostile fire, and we hardly ever caught sight of a man. As company after company of the 42nd descended with their pipes playing into the ravine, they were almost immediately lost sight of in the bush, and their position could only be judged from the sharp crack of their rifles, in contrast to the loud, dull boom of the Ashanti musketry.'

This was exactly what the General had visualized when he had drafted his training instructions to be read on shipboard. Apart from Alison being unable to see his men, the men themselves often could not see more than one or two of their comrades in the scrub. Control at company level would have been quite impossible without the delegation of sectional command (forerunner of the later platoon command) to junior officers and NCOs. Now there was somebody responsible in charge of every small detachment, who knew the men, and in whom they had confidence. Discipline was excellent; there was no wild firing. There was no loss of direction, even though extended two hundred yards into the bush to the left of the road and one hundred to the right, for leaders were told to regard the road as if the Regimental Colour was on it and never lose touch. Nor did any section coming up from the rear to take its turn in the forefront of the battle shoot the section ahead in the back.

The Ashanti were fighting bravely and well. With immensely superior numbers they opposed the central advance, while they kept enveloping with a constant series of well-directed flank attacks. Their fire was lethal at the very short range at which it was now being employed. Baird was wounded, Home was wounded, so were a great number of NCOs and men. 'Our loss in wounded is pretty severe,' wrote Alison in a message asking for more surgeons to be sent forward.

As soon as Alison's advance guard had cleared Egginassie Colonel M'Leod, who had been following close behind with Russell's regiment and half the Naval Brigade, took his force off to the left up the path for three hundred yards, the distance laid down in Sir Garnet's battle drill. Then he set the Royal Engineers under Major Buckle to cutting a path uphill parallel to the road, trying to catch up with the 42nd advance and protect their flank. Urged on by their major, the Sierra Leone labourers made tremendous efforts, but they were under continual heavy fire from both sides. Buckle fell mortally wounded and was taken back to the road where he soon died, but the path-cutters carried on until near the top of the hill where they found an Ashanti encampment across their path. M'Leod mounted an attack, supported by Lieutenant Palmer and his rocket-launchers, and Russell's Hausa and Opobo companies swept forward with a roar of cheering and put the enemy to flight. But all this had taken time and the 42nd were a long way ahead. Besides, M'Leod now had to cut his own path; things had been a little too much in one day for the Sierra Leones who had quietly made themselves scarce. He was also out of touch with the General at Egginassie who realized this and sent a company of the Rifle Brigade a short way up the path to re-establish communication.

Evelyn Wood had been behind M'Leod, with his regiment and the other half of the Naval Brigade, and his task was to advance a few hundred yards beyond the village and then to cut a path off to the right for the stipulated three hundred yards before turning to advance parallel to the road, guarding the right flank. But he was held up by such heavy fire that he had to halt and dig in. Exasperated, he tried to see for himself what was going on, pushing through the bush and parting it with his hands as he went. This was too much for Eyre, who pulled him back by the skirt of his Norfolk jacket, protesting, 'It is really not your place' and thrust in ahead of him. The adjutant found an enormous Ashanti, stark naked, with a huge heavy gun. A couple of volleys cleared that part of the bush, but soon Wood was repelling attacks from both the north and the south.

This was all standard Ashanti practice—let the head of the column in and then attack the flanks. The General knew all about it. He had told the troops not to worry about their rear, he would be responsible for that, so now he sent the 23rd Royal Welch Fusiliers (strength now reduced by sickness to eighty-three all ranks) to keep touch with the rear of the 42nd Highlanders, and a company of the Rifle Brigade two hundred yards beyond the village to keep in contact with *them*. He already had a company up the path to the left and now he had to deploy another into the bush on the right and a fourth to the right rear of the village. He was soon beset on all sides by what he described as a howling mass of many thousand savages. The smoke of bad Ashanti powder hung heavily around them, there was no wind to disperse it. Mr Winwood Reade was in the fighting line, Mr Henry Stanley had a rifle which he put to excellent use; Commodore Hewett, sword in hand, charged in counter-attack to restore a wavering sector of the West India Regiment's line.

It was not yet ten o'clock in the morning. The 42nd Highlanders were over the swamp but McPherson, who had already been hit twice, was wounded so badly in the ankle that he had to hand over command and be helped to the rear. He told Alison that further progress up the hill on the far side was impossible without support. But Home found and cleared a gun platform on the north side of the swamp, so Rait hurried a 7-pounder gun across the morass and came into action. There was no question of not being able to see the enemy now! The Ashanti had shown remarkable passive courage in sustaining Snider fire, but now they had Rait banging away at them over open sights at fifty yards range. Fifteen rounds of rapid fire caused such slaughter among their packed ranks that they flinched; then the Highlanders charged forward, drove them from their position and captured the camp. But the Ashanti were not beaten yet; there was another position along a ridge beyond their camp, and there they resisted again. The 42nd kept up the pressure; Rait went with them, moving his gun sometimes only twenty yards at a time. More shelling, some effective Snider volleys, the Highlanders charged again and the Ashanti warriors gave way. It was their last attempt at serious resistance in the centre that day. There was a brief rather half-hearted try to hold Amoaful village, but a few rounds from Rait's guns, a last assault by the Highlanders and the enemy went flying in all directions in utter disorder.

Alison decided to go no further as his rear was by now quiet, and he could hear heavy firing on his right. Home and his labourers started to prepare Amoaful for defence and Alison sent back to tell Sir Garnet that there would be room in the village for the whole force. It was nearly half-past twelve.

As the 42nd had fought their way forward from the swamp, so the Ashanti had come in behind them to cut the road. Colonel Mostyn and his men of the 23rd, on their way to support Alison, had to fight their way through the swamp, just as the Highlanders had done, and on up to the captured enemy camp beyond. There they halted, now in touch with the rear companies of the 42nd. Their rear was in the air but Captain Somerset's company of the Rifle Brigade came up to establish contact, settling down to hold the road in the swamp area. They too had fought their way forward. Between them and Egginassie was one company of the 42nd, left to keep the road open. So now the whole road from Amoaful to Egginassie was held by British troops—four hours fierce fighting to advance three-quarters of a mile!

M'Leod was cutting his way painfully through very thick bush back to the main road and had strong views when his men were shot at by the company of his own 42nd Highlanders south of the swamp. He eventually slashed his way through to their position.

On the right, Evelyn Wood had been sufficiently badly wounded to have to hand over command to Captain Luxmoore of the Royal Navy. He had been hit over the heart by a nail fired from a musket and had to be helped back to Egginassie. The doctors were worried; they could not find the piece of metal and dared not probe any deeper. The senior medical officer told Sir Garnet that Wood was dying and asked him to come and say goodbye; but the General refused to believe it, saying that he would see him at the head of the road within a week!

Luxmoore's wing of the Naval Brigade was unable to make any progress, so the General decided that the time had come to clear the area. He deployed two companies of the Rifle Brigade north-east of Egginassie and ordered Wood's Bonnys and Kossoos to charge. Shouting war-cries, they drove the Ashanti before them up the Egginassie Hill, over the crest and down the far side. Then they swung north to make contact with Luxmoore's sailors and marines. It was all over by a quarter to two in the afternoon. Gradually, as news of the Ashanti defeat in the centre became known on the enemy flanks, the firing died away. By four o'clock Gifford and his scouts were able to report that the enemy centre and right were in full flight. But the left had not finished yet.

It now remained to bring the ammunition reserve and the baggage up to Amoaful and evacuate the wounded to Insarfu. Colley, who had managed to catch up with Headquarters in time for the battle, had made himself very useful throughout the action as a staff officer. Now he started back to Insarfu to make the necessary administrative arrangements. He had some difficulty in getting there, as Ashanti were still active along the road and were attacking the two Rifle Brigade companies holding Quarman. The hammock-bearers carrying wounded refused to go any further, but Colley himself with an escort of levies forced his way through. He collected the ammunition and baggage, took an escort from the 2nd West India Regiment and headed back. But in the meantime, starting at five in the evening, Quarman had come under heavy attack from north and south. Colley got to within half a mile of the village before the enemy noticed him and then they called off their assault and attacked him instead. This was far too much for the carriers, some of whom threw down their loads and bolted, sweeping a furious Colley back with them to Insarfu. The commander of Quarman sent a company out to help, which fought the Ashanti until dark began to fall at half-past six. Then the enemy drifted away—they did not like night-fighting—and the company withdrew to the village. Colley, in Insarfu, assembled the most reliable porters he could find—they were all individuals now, their characteristics known to the transport officers—and sallied out several times to bring in abandoned loads. What he could not bring in he dumped centrally under guard of a detachment of the 2nd West India Regiment.

The General made his dispositions for the night. All troops north of Egginassie were called in to Amoaful: Egginassie itself was garrisoned by Colonel Warren and a wing of the Rifle Brigade. A company of the Rifle Brigade escorted a convoy of wounded back to Insarfu and arrived safely, although fired at all the way. Colley, quite tireless, went back up the line with this company when it set off again for Quarman. From there he joined a band of police and labourers and was in Amoaful at midnight. He reported to the General and suggested that three companies of the 42nd Highlanders and six companies from the Rifle Brigade should go out in the early morning and picquet the whole road at short intervals all the way from Amoaful to Insarfu, then bring everything up and send all the wounded back under their protection. The General agreed and Colley sat up for the rest of the night writing his instructions. Next day the whole of the ammunition and baggage was brought to Amoaful less what had been thrown away and lost. Some officers were out of luck—Brackenbury never saw his bedding or groundsheet again and Greaves lost all his notes on the campaign.

The 42nd Highlanders had borne the brunt of the action. Only two had been killed, both private soldiers, one of whom had got too far ahead of his detachment and had been shot down and instantly beheaded. But Major Baird and several others died later from wounds received during the battle. A quarter of the regiment, nine officers and one hundred and four men, had been wounded, sixty per cent of the casualties suffered by the whole force. The Ashanti had fought bravely and stubbornly, showing great fortitude; but they had been staggered by seeing the British advance in spite of their comrades falling all around them, and the sight of the white men closing with the bayonet appalled them more than the hottest fire. The Ashanti had closed with the British, their leaders to the fore, and had fought to win. Amanquatia had been killed; the King of Mampon had been severely wounded. In the end the rout of their centre had been complete. Brigadier-General Alison estimated that they must have lost two to three thousand in killed and wounded. Only a hundred and fifty corpses had been left lying on the road;

they always took great care to carry off their dead if it was at all possible to do so. Brackenbury had gone forward from Egginassie on an errand—all the staff officers were continually walking from one end of the battlefield to the other throughout the action, accompanied sometimes by reluctant escorts—and he had noticed the body of a chief propped against a hut. On his way back half an hour later the body had gone! Conditions were so fluid that the Ashanti were continuously running to and fro across the road between the British units, making things hazardous for staff officers carrying messages.

Before the battle the sick list had reached twelve per cent of the fifteen hundred British who had landed a month earlier. Now there were the same amount of wounded to be evacuated to the coast. No question of two relief bearers to each hammock; there were sufficient hammocks, not enough men; it was four carriers to a hammock, and that was that! There is a sketch of hammocks being carried up a steep bank after crossing a stream, the doctors with their sticks raised to keep the bearers moving.

All the natives were extraordinarily callous about the sick and wounded, even their own. There was a good example of this a week or so later when Wood and his regiment were on their way back to the coast. One of the Bonny men had been taken seriously ill, and eight of his comrades had been ordered to carry him, but the moment that Evelyn Wood's back was turned they took him fifty yards into the bush and abandoned him. Wood, returning, happened to hear his cries and had him fetched back by some of Baker Russell's men. Next morning, however, the Bonny men absolutely refused to carry him, Prince Charles maintaining that they always left their sick and wounded to die. So Wood had one Bonny flogged until he personally was nearly sick at the sight, all to no avail. Then he started on the next, who was less stubborn; after twenty-five lashes he turned his head and said, 'I will carry'. Surly and reluctant, eight Bonnys picked up their sick countryman and carried him down to the coast with no further nonsense.

The Brigadier-General wrote: 'It is impossible for me to speak in too high terms of that magnificent regiment the 42nd Highlanders; their steadiness and discipline, the admirable way in which they were kept in hand by their officers, and the enthusiastic gallantry with which each charge was executed exceed all praise.' But without Rait's artillery support 'I do not think that even all the gallantry of the 42nd could have carried the position.'

At daybreak on 1 February, as troops were being deployed to line the road from Insarfu, Buller and Gifford scouted towards Becquah, a mile from Amoaful and the highest feature of the Ashanti defensive complex. The enemy were in occupation of the town, so as soon as the administrative column was safe in Amoaful, Alison went off to capture the position. Gifford's scouts led the way along an ordinary native track with thick bush on both sides. He reported contact at Becquah and was ordered to take it by storm, supported by Gordon's Hausas. The enemy fought hard at first and nearly half of the scouts were wounded, but he and Gordon got a foothold until the Naval Brigade came up; then the Ashanti withdrew, carrying their dead with them. This was a very sticky action for the scouts and Sir Garnet recommended that Lord Gifford be awarded the Victoria Cross for the part he had played.

The town was set on fire and the force withdrew, leaving an ambush of Highlanders hidden behind some houses; so when the enemy returned to harass the rearguard they were surprised and dispersed by several well-directed volleys of rifle-fire. Lieutenant Maurice, the General's Private Secretary, did well in this action, now a very different man from the young academic who had won a Prize Essay. M'Leod had observed his conduct and commended him to the General.

Meanwhile the Rifle Brigade reformed as a regiment and marched up to Amoaful from Egginassie along a road completely clear of living enemy.

[3]

At daybreak on 2 February the whole force marched out of Amoaful with an advance guard under M'Leod of Gifford's scouts, what remained of Russell's regiment after leaving garrisons along the line of communication, one of Rait's guns—the pistol gun of the future—and a company of the Rifle Brigade. They were to fight their way to Aggemmamu, seven miles ahead, and then report.

They encountered about a thousand Ashanti defending a strong position in swampy ground before the first village, Jarbinah, but the enemy morale had been shaken badly at Amoaful. They opened fire while the Opobo company was still well out of range and there was little difficulty in driving them out of their position and back into the village. The Sierra Leone company was passed through to take

Jarbinah with a rush, which they did. Unfortunately the Ashantis' trigger-happiness had proved to be infectious and Russell's regiment of two hundred and eighty-six men had in a very short space of time expended over two thousand rounds of ammunition! So M'Leod got permission from the General to put the Rifle Brigade company in the lead to avoid any more waste. He then moved on through village after village, overcoming slight opposition in every one. Lessons learned the hard way in this campaign sunk in quickly! He left a picquet in every village, and across any path leading in to the main track, to prevent the Ashanti from re-occupying ground vacated by his onward-marching troops. He was in possession of Aggemmamu by a quarter to one and the main body came up and joined him soon afterwards.

The General decided to stay the night and bring up all the baggage, while the advance guard went on a further two and a half miles to Adwabin, where stronger resistance was expected. M'Leod was there by five o'clock and by that time the Ashanti had gone, so he sent half a company back for his baggage and camped for the night. The General fetched his own baggage train up from Amoaful, escorted by detachments from each regiment with the Naval Brigade as rearguard. As this rearguard passed by, so each picquet came in to join it and the whole convoy was in Aggemmamu soon after dark.

Colley had gone back to Ahkankuassie on 1 February, as soon as he knew of the General's plans to advance and as the General left Amoaful, so he departed for Fommanah. When he got there he had to find a way through an Ashanti force which had the base surrounded and was attacking it from all sides. The town was far too big to be held by its small garrison of forty West Indians and a hundred of Russell's Mumford company, so the sick from the hospital were removed to a stockade at the north end of the town and the neighbouring houses were pulled down to give a field of fire. The attacks stopped at one'clock in the afternoon, but the carriers had been so frightened by the ferocity of the assault that they were in shock, and it proved impossible to move them for some days, a most unfortunate thing to happen at this crucial stage of the war. In fact, the first proper convoy to go up the line was of Royal Navy Kroomen who reached Aggemmamu on 6 February.

Sir Garnet was now within fifteen miles of Kumasi, and in view of this new supply situation he had to be there in two days. He asked the men if they were prepared to make four days rations last for six and they agreed willingly. So he decided to operate as a self-contained flying column. All 'weakly' men were to be left at Aggemmamu under command of Captain Cope with the additional garrison of one of Russell's companies brought back from Adwabin. Most vigorously did Cope set about preparing his defences, helped by the whole force during that afternoon. There was a greatly distressed civilian officer whose baggage had been incorporated in the perimeter wall, but on no account would Cope dismantle the wall to let him have it back!

M'Leod and the advance guard stayed in Adwabin until the main body came up on the morning of 3 February, and then marched on. After three-quarters of an hour Gifford met the enemy occupying a position in dense bush on rising ground on the far side of a little stream. He had been careless and got too far ahead of the rest of the advance guard, became too heavily involved and lost a quarter of his men killed or wounded before Russell came to his assistance. M'Leod made the engineer labourers cut a path around to the left, sent two companies of the Rifle Brigade up it to outflank the enemy, used his pistol gun to good effect and launched Russell in a successful frontal assault. Slowly the advance guard moved ahead, fighting all the way, losing men at every enemy ambuscade.

We last heard of Colley at half-past two on 2 February at Fommanah. Now at eleven o'clock on the 3rd he appeared on the scene of action after a twenty-five mile march with a hundred and fifty loads of provisions carried by picked men. His exceptional mobility and dedication had brought the force's ration state up from four to five and a half days' supply.

Half an hour later messengers arrived under a flag of truce from King Kofi Karikari in Kumasi. The King wrote that things were going far too fast for him; in any case, he could not possibly send his mother and brother as hostages as they were his most important helpers and advisers. Mr Dawson also wrote a personal plea to the General, begging him to stop lest he, Dawson, should be killed. 'I humbly beg your Excellency on my knees, to let the forces stop, and everything will be settled.' The messengers said that a ten-thousand-strong Ashanti force comprising the defeated Amoaful army and reinforcements from Kumasi were in the first village after the Ordah River, two hours march ahead, and that there they would fight.

Sir Garnet replied within a few minutes of receiving the King's letter, 'You have deceived me so before, that I cannot halt until the hostages are in my possession. If you send them to me this evening, I shall halt my army this side of the River Ordah.' As the messengers departed, they were heard shouting instructions to the Ashanti in the bush all around the advance guard to cease operations, which was just as well. The scouts had come up against one of the worst ambushes of the day! A prisoner claimed later that there were still ten thousand Ashanti south of the Ordah and the only reason they did not attack was because they had been forbidden to do so.

The advance guard reached the Ordah River at two and the main body at three o'clock. It was fifty feet wide, but only waist-deep, so Russell's regiment waded across to establish a bridgehead. This time M'Leod had reported that 'they had been in front all day and behaved with remarkable steadiness under trying circumstances, reserving their fire with remarkable self-control.' They dug in, made a clearing and then the whole of the advance guard crossed over. Major Home and his men had already started to build a bridge.

On the south bank some attempts were made to clear ground for a camp and construct rough shelter huts of palm-stems and plantain leaves. The troops bivouacked in a square, but there was no likelihood of a night attack, it was not in accordance with Ashanti rules. Besides, a tropical storm which had been banking up all afternoon now burst upon them with all its fury—thunder, lightning and torrential rain all through the night. The improvised shelters were utterly useless and everybody was drenched, passing a nearly sleepless night. Throughout it all, Home and the engineers toiled on the bridge. At one in the morning the major gave them two hours rest, then started again; by dawn, despite the appalling weather conditions, there stood a good strong bridge, complete with hand-rails.

No hostages were brought in and prisoners captured by advance-guard patrols during the night said that the enemy were in great numbers in the town of Ordahsu, three-quarters of a mile north of the river.

Back in hospital at Quarman, Evelyn Wood had received a pathetic note from Arthur Eyre, lamenting his absence and com-plaining that the General had forgotten his promise that Wood's regiment should be represented when they entered Kumasi. 'Our last compay has now been left to garrison a post, and we shall never see Kumasi until it falls.' Within half an hour Wood had discharged himself from hospital and was marching forward through the dark. He picked up Eyre on the way and reached Headquarters at four o'clock in the morning, to be met by Baker saying, 'The Chief is asleep, but he told me to give you his love, and say that he is delighted that you have come up, and wishes you to take the advanced section of the advance guard when we move at daylight.'

He assumed the duty from Baker Russell, who grumbled good-humouredly at being superseded, and led on with his Opobo company; but they came under heavy fire and started to shoot wildly into the bush. Chief Essevie, who was close by with the Elmina company, 'showed the courage that he had always displayed, kicking and buffeting all black men, including his own sons, with the greatest impartiality, to drive them on; but we made little progress.'

While Wood was teaching a Bonny man to fire an Ashanti crept so close in the dense bush that when he fired the slugs from his musket did not even spread and the force of the impact threw the Bonny's body right across the path.

A few minutes later Baker Russell came up to chat, standing upright with his habitual complete indifference to danger. Noticing Eyre also on his feet, Wood peremptorily ordered him to kneel down, like the other Europeans; but Eyre had scarcely done so when he was shot through the body at short range. He died two hours later in great pain, despite morphia administered by the medical officer.

As there had been no progress, M'Leod, as before, passed a company of the Rifle Brigade through them and brought forward Lieutenant Saunders's 7-pounder field gun. At the same time he implemented his now standard practice of cutting a path to the left. He had two more companies of the Rifle Brigade under his immediate command and Alison sent him up an additional three, so he was able to move slowly ahead. But the enemy seemed less interested in him than in an attack on Alison's main guard in the right rear, while, from Alison's point of view, cheering and drum-beating still further back indicated that an attack on Sir Garnet's main force was probable.

However, the advance guard moved on, bound by bound. The gun would fire a few rounds, the companies would come up and halt; then the gun would come up again and repeat the performance, until Ordahsu village was captured and consolidated. Seven of Saunders's eleven Hausa gunners had been hit and still they worked their gun—it was better than slavery any day! But the enemy were not fighting with anything like the conviction that they had shown at Amoaful.

The Brigadier-General had deployed troops on both sides of the road and had cleared the bush in front of them. Soon his right and rear were heavily engaged, though not with the former savagery. There fell also quite a considerable enemy effort on his left. However, as far as Sir Garnet was concerned, the expected attack on *his* main body did not materialize and he was able to send forward the 42nd to take over Alison's position while the Brigadier-General moved on into Ordahsu. By ten o'clock Alison was ready to advance again, but was subjected suddenly to a series of violent counter-attacks. After an hour of this the Rifle Brigade were becoming weary from continual action and Alison asked for the 42nd Highlanders for use as shock troops for a break-out. But the General decided against any further move forward until the baggage and ammunition reserve had been brought into Ordahsu and all picquets and the Naval Brigade rearguard were within the defensive perimeter. As this was being done 'the whole circle around the village, cut only where the main road passed to the rear and was guarded by our troops, was for the next hour one sheet of flame, and one roar of fire. The enemy at times pressed boldly up to the attack, especially on the left and left rear of the village, cheering and shouting before they advanced.' They even formed line as well as they could in the bush and fired volleys, but these excellent targets were always mown down with Snider fire. The Chief of Staff, Colonel Greaves, was firing into the thick of the enemy with his revolver; the General's escort was hotly engaged; the General was hard hit on the helmet, but the bullet luckily did not penetrate.

Eventually the last man of the rearguard was safely inside the defences and the Ashanti were allowed to close in between the village and the river. This meant nothing to the General, whose force was self-contained, but it was of great portent to the enemy. By all indigenous protocol the British had now lost the battle and should abide by the rules and admit defeat. The Ashanti gave a great sustained shout of triumph as they closed the gap and numbers rushed off to destroy the remains of last night's dilapidated bivouacks.

At noon the General ordered the 42nd Highlanders, with artillery support, to break right through the enemy ring and drive straight for Kumasi only five miles ahead, disregarding all flank attacks. Colonel M'Leod, back again at last in command of his own regiment, placed himself at the head of his men. Brigadier-General Alison takes up the story: 'I accompanied him with my staff. On first debouching from the village, a tremendous fire was opened on the head of the column from a well-placed and strong ambuscade, six men being knocked over in an instant. But the flank companies worked steadily through the bush; the leading company on the path sprang forward with a cheer; all the pipes struck up, and the ambuscade was at once carried. Then followed one of the finest spectacles I have ever seen in war. Without stop or stay the 42nd rushed on cheering, their pipers playing, their officers to the front; ambuscade after ambuscade was successfully carried, village after village won in succession, until the whole Ashanti army broke and fled in the wildest disorder down the pathway to Kumasi. The ground was covered with traces of their flight. Umbrellas and warchairs of their chiefs, drums, muskets, killed and wounded, covered the whole way, and the bush on each side was trampled as if a torrent had flowed through it.' On they drove, the gunners could not keep up, nor were they missed, until from sheer exhaustion the infantry came to a halt in Karsi, with three miles to go before Kumasi, the Ashanti capital city. At just after one o'clock Briga- dier-General Alison sent back the message: 'We have won every village except Karsi, which I hope to take soon. Their army is flying in panic.'

A staff officer would have taken the message back over the six miles to Ordahsu, made his way through the enemy, who had just delivered another vigorous attack, and presented it to the General. Sir Garnet passed the news on to the troops and the native regi- ments raised such a ringing cheer, and shouted the tidings in Ashanti to their foes, that the crest-fallen enemy warriors took them at their word and lost heart. Not another shot was fired; they melted away into the forest.

Sir Garnet now advanced with his whole force to join Alison. The Brigadier-General had been held up for half an hour by a messenger with a letter which he thought to be from Kofi Karikari, but it turned out to be only another desperate plea to stop from Dawson, terrified for his life. He took his men on, over the Soubang swamp, and entered Kumasi without further opposition at half-past five in the evening.

The town was full of armed men assembled to watch the long column of white troops march into their city. Not a single shot was fired and the Ashanti carried on about their business of getting arms and ammunition away into the bush, while Alison started getting his men on to parade in the market square in readiness for the General.

2.   Sir Garnet Wolseley entering Kumasi.

Sir Garnet and his two senior officers arrived on mule-back as it was getting dark, took over the parade and ordered three cheers to be given for Her Majesty the Queen. Then the men were dismissed and made camp, with strong outlying picquets at all entrances to the town. The surviving enslaved Fanti were freed and immediately began looting and burning, so the General had to issue a proclamation that he would impose the death penalty on any man caught plundering. Police were made to keep up an all-night patrol, but despite this a lot of damage was done. Several natives were caught and flogged, while one Fanti policeman was hanged for looting. The General hoped to use the lure of an intact city to bring King Kofi Karikari to terms.

The King had taken up a battle position at a sensible distance in rear of his armies and had now disappeared. Nobody would say where he had gone. As Lord Kimberley had feared, there was no one left with whom to conclude a peace treaty! Dawson was found free and wandering the streets in a dazed condition; he denied knowing everything, including the way to the royal palace, but he consented to find some officials who agreed to take a letter to Kofi Karikari. Sir Garnet wrote that evening, waiving his demand for the Heir and Queen Mother as hostages and inviting the King to come in and make peace.

Casualties since Amoaful had been significantly less than in that crucial encounter. Only Eyre and one native had been killed, but six officers and sixty men had been wounded, a third of the Amoaful list. Next day all wounded unable to walk were sent back down the line, staging at Ordahsu. They crossed the River Ordah without too much trouble, although the level of the water had risen to eighteen inches above the footway of the bridge; but it held.

In Kumasi messages kept on coming in to the effect that the King was on his way, but he never arrived. There was no question of going to look for him; it might have meant another battle. The Becquah, Kokofoo and Juabin contingents had gone to meet Sir Garnet's other three thrusts and had not taken part in the battles of Amoaful or Ordahsu, but they were still intact. The General could not take the risk of incurring more casualties; the organization for evacuating wounded was stretched to its limit. He decided to stay one more night, which he could do without making his men go hungry, and then march for home. To disconcert any possible Ashanti plans for pursuit he had circulated a rumour that he intended a sweep to the north to capture their King.

During the day Sir Garnet wrote his despatch on the battles and the campaign, recommending Captain Kidston and three other ranks of the 42nd Highlanders for the Victoria Cross, and giving due credit to all ranks where it was deserved. His staff went to have a good look around. They investigated the Palace, a great rambling building with a main hall capable of holding at least two hundred people. They saw the King's pet cats, of which he was very fond, a beautiful sacred bird, and a lot of carefully packaged fetish material, the basic ingredient of which turned out to be rotten eggs. They visited the execution chamber where they saw 'the great death-drum surrounded by human skulls and thigh-bones—stools covered with clotted blood standing out from them in huge thick lumps, the blood of hundreds of human victims, in which they had been bathed as an offering to the king's ancestors, to whom they had belonged. Loathsome they were to see as the flies rose in dense clouds from them at our approach.'

During the night Redvers Buller and officers representing units were appointed 'prize-agents', and by the light of the only four candles to be found in Kumasi set about officially looting the Palace Treasury. They were told that they might have only thirty carriers to transport their spoil, so they chose as carefully as they could in the time available. They found and packed masses of pure gold, neck-laces and bracelets of the same material, and silver plate, bags of gold dust and nuggets, knives set in gold and silver, swords, even a ceremonial one presented to Kofi Karikari by Her Majesty Queen Victoria.

Major Home and his engineers prepared the Royal Palace for demolition and made arrangements for the whole town to be set on fire. At six o'clock in the morning of 6 February the column, led by the Naval Brigade, wended its way slowly back along the track over which it had advanced so speedily and so successfully only two days before. The Palace was blown up and the fires burnt furiously. Colonel M'Leod and his regiment waited until all the demolition parties had passed through their lines, then came away as rearguard to the force. Kumasi was left a heap of smoking ruins.

[4]

Captain Sartorius was in Kumasi five days later and found it completely deserted. He was the fore-runner of Glover's force, which arrived there next day. Glover had managed to cross the Prah on 15 January as ordered, with seven hundred and fifty semi-disciplined Hausas and Yorubas. He had advanced over a continuous series of mountain ranges, and on the day of Amoaful he was keeping the King of Juabin's army fully occupied thirty miles eastward of Kumasi. After the capital was captured all opposition ceased and the King of Juabin made his submission to Glover. When he entered Kumasi Glover heard that King Kofi Karikari had accepted Sir Garnet's peace terms, so made his way by easy stages to Quarman.

Butler and his friends had neared the Prah, toiling on over narrow forest paths, despite attacks of fever and dysentery. 'Some of them were worn to skeletons, all had drawn, haggard features; down with fever one day, staggering on the next; eating wretched food, fighting, urging, wrestling with recalcitrant carriers; streaming with perspiration at all times. They worked their way through great, gloomy forest, endless arches of colossal cotton trees under which flourished two other growths of forest. The lower a mass of tangled and twisted evergreens, the middle one hung with spiral creepers like huge serpents hundreds of feet in length. Below all there was the hot, wet earth emitting foul odours from its black mudholes, and many pools of slime-covered water'.

All four white officers were down with fever on 14 January, but somehow they reached the river bank next day, the date appointed for crossing into Ashanti territory. Fifty Akim were already there, but they refused to cross without reinforcements. So Butler and his officers, accompanied by six native policemen carrying luggage, waded into the Prah. In the centre it rose to their lips, then they just touched bottom, caught the branches of a fallen tree, and scrambled on to the far bank. With expressionless faces, the Akim stood in groups on their home shore, watching the inexplicable behaviour of the white men.

After dire threats from the General, they crossed over on the 18th, but then refused to advance to Moinsey. At the time when Sir Garnet crossed the Adansi Hills, Butler was still thirty miles away to the east, and the General wrote to tell him that it would be a great advantage if he could come in and strike the Ashanti left flank at Amoaful. He got his tribesmen moving at last, one thousand four hundred of them. They met a reconnaissance party from the army of the King of Kokofoo, who asked if white men really were with them, and who were heard to say in conversation among themselves that it was useless trying to stop Hausas led by Europeans. On the day before the battle of Amoaful Butler was only four or five miles distant on the General's right, but this was far too close to the enemy for the Akim chiefs. They prevaricated, they refused to go on. Suddenly in mid-afternoon the whole force turned about and fled helter-skelter back to the Prah. A very disgruntled and angry Captain Butler rejoined the General at Aggemmamu on his way back from Kumasi; but he had succeeded in the task given to him by Sir Garnet—he had kept the King of Kokofoo from joining Amanquatia and from opposing the column's advance to Kumasi. The General, in his despatch to the Secretary of State, described it as 'a most important diversion'.

Captain Dalrymple never got his men into Ashanti territory. They were indeed afraid of the Governor and his wrath, but that was nothing compared to their abject fear of their hereditary oppressors. Nonetheless, the news of his recruiting activities had reached Kumasi, and the King of Becquah assembled his men to repel the expected invasion of his lands. This was another army which fought at neither Amoaful nor at Ordahsu.

So none of the subsidiary efforts were wasted. They had diverted three Ashanti armies away from the point of main impact.

[5]

The storm had swollen the Ordah River to a breadth of two hundred yards and it had risen to a height two feet over the bridge roadway. It would be only a matter of time before the bridge gave way, so the white troops were allotted priority of passage, while the carriers with their loads were made to wade across as best they could. Greaves and Buller worked tirelessly to hurry the men over, but the bridge gave way before evening, leaving the rearguard still on the Kumasi side. So the 42nd Highlanders stripped and waded or swam to the other bank, their clothes taken over dry on the heads of the regimental porters. It was night before the last companies had crossed.

The General and his staff waited at Fommanah to continue negotiations with the Ashanti king. Sir Garnet must have been rather worried in case no overtures should be made! But a messenger from Kofi Karikari came in on 9 February saying that the King would agree to all the terms if only the General would stop Glover.

So here again a subsidiary expedition had paid off in an unexpected way. Sir Garnet had replied that he would do so if five thousand ounces of gold were sent to him at once, and surprisingly quickly envoys did arrive with gold. After an abortive attempt to square Buller they produced a thousand ounces, which they swore was all there was. An intimate search of their clothing produced another forty ounces, but that was all. However, Sir Garnet decided that the King was recognizing defeat, so he sent back a draft treaty, to be known as the Treaty of Fommanah. It covered all the original stipulations, but dropped the question of hostages, and agreed that the remainder of the gold could be paid by instalments. It never was. The draft treaty, duly signed, arrived at Cape Coast Castle after Sir Garnet's departure for England.

Meanwhile the regiments marched back down the road. The Royal Welch Fusiliers detachment met the rest of the battalion on its way up, amalgamated with them and arrived at Cape Coast Castle on 20 February, embarking the same day. The Rifle Brigade did likewise next day, but the 42nd Highlanders had to wait at Inquabim for a ship, sailing finally on the 27th.

Russell disbanded his regiment at Cape Coast Castle, as did Rait his gunners. Wood took his men to Elmina before dismissing them to their homes. Promises were kept, and all the men were transported back free of charge to the place where they had originally been recruited. Wood was rather upset when Sir Garnet, who was watching the money very carefully, refused compensation to a native who had lost an eye. As he was leaving Elmina, he said to his friend Chief Essevie, 'You have done very well throughout the four months that you have served with me, and I should like to send you a present from England. Have you any preference?' After a moment's reflection, Essevie opted for a tall black hat and an umbrella. Wood eventually despatched the hat, a vast £12 ceremonial umbrella and a ten-guinea walking stick for Chief Andoo. The gifts were presented at a full-dress parade of the Elmina Garrison.

The General and his staff stayed at Fommanah for a few days, trying to avoid the importunacies of Cobbina Obbin, King of Adansi, who wanted to bring over his whole tribe and settle in the security of the Protectorate. But Sir Garnet was afraid that this might annoy Kofi Karikari so much as to jeopardize the whole Peace Treaty. Then they all left by double-marches carried in hammocks, arriving at Cape Coast Castle on 19 February.

There remained the problem of handing over government of the

Gold Coast. The Governor-in-Chief of West African Settlements, Mr Berkeley, had no desire to come from Lagos to assume authority. However, Lord Kimberley had decided that a military governor would be the best solution and told Sir Garnet to appoint one. This was not so easy. The General himself had been promised that he would not be required to stay; Brigadier-General Sir Archibald Alison declined the honour; Colonel M'Leod insisted on returning to Scotland with his regiment; Greaves and Colley begged to be excused. So Colonel Maxwell of the 1st West India Regiment, which was taking over permanently from the 2nd West India Regiment, now returning to Jamaica, was detailed to accept the post.

Major-General Sir Garnet Wolseley and his entourage sailed from Cape Coast Castle for Portsmouth on 4 March.

Colonel Maxwell died five weeks later.

[6]

The expedition had been a great military success, recognized as such by the British public. The Ashanti Army had been defeated and Kumasi had been occupied, then destroyed. The casualties incurred had been so few that, so far from possible censure, the Government had earned considerable credit. Out of a force of nearly one thousand six hundred Europeans there had been only forty-three fatalities—fourteen all ranks killed in battle and twenty-nine dead from wounds or disease. Nearly everyone had been sick in one way or another, but they had all recovered. The campaign was, moreover, completed within the original financial ceiling of £800,000.

Politically, achievements were short-term only. The Treaty of Fommanah was initialled and generally considered to be operative, though it had been a close thing. If Kofi Karikari had not been afraid of Glover staying in Kumasi and that Sir Garnet Wolseley and his men would return, he might not have agreed to sign. The huge indemnity was never paid, but no further threat was made against the coastal settlements. Kofi Karikari was dethroned, or rather de-stooled, and Prince Mensa ruled in his stead. At intervals there were internal upheavals among the Ashanti which had sufficient import outside their borders to necessitate punitive action, and that went on until final annexation to the Crown in 1901. After that, confidence in British government grew apace and there was no more trouble.

An outstanding feature of the whole operation had been the trust and confidence that existed between Kimberley, Cardwell and Wolseley. The politicians were risking a lot; they might have been removed from office if things had gone wrong. They had picked the right man for command, not only an experienced soldier but also a skilled planner, able to accept operational control and adminis-trative responsibility. If things should go wrong he would not expect to lay the blame on the bureaucrats. After he had been selected and the decision made, they saw to it that he got what he wanted, when he wanted it, riding rough-shod over military protocol in nearly every case. When he was in the Gold Coast his despatches were acted upon with the most robust energy and speed. Even from that distance in time and space Sir Garnet's needs were met, whether for two more regiments or for the services of some individual officer such as Colley. As the Colonial Office and the War Office in the persons of Kimberley and Cardwell were in accord, their joint representative Wolseley had both civil and military command, without which so much unacceptable delay could have been im-posed by local officials standing on their rights. In the same way the General was able to insist on overall command of the line of communication with all its civilian commissariat elements being given to Colley, a military officer. It had been appreciated at the highest level that there would not be time to waste over offended dignity or hurt feelings.

One suspects that no one really expected that it would be possible to raise a large native army, though admittedly Wolseley had included accoutrements and weapons for seven thousand in his original indents for equipment. As it happened, the two regiments of levies commanded by Evelyn Wood, Russell and their specially employed officers did extraordinarily well under the circumstances, although to begin with they would have been lost without the Naval Brigade. During the last phase they took all the weight off the British battalions, leading the advance and doing all the military fatigues in camp, until it was time for the 42nd Highlanders to pass through and launch their major assault. Even after Amoaful Co-lonel M'Leod had to obtain the General's permission to put a company of the Rifle Brigade in the lead.

The mass defection of carriers at a crucial stage of the operation to stock-pile in Prahsu was unexpected, though Sir Garnet had passed the necessary legislation to deal with such an eventuality as a contingency measure. The only answer was ruthless compulsion, which was implemented without compunction. The porters were men of magnificent physique and deserved no sympathy. Not more than a dozen or so were killed or wounded by the enemy, and in exchange for three months of hardship and inconvenience the remainder gained a lifetime of security.

Through foresight and efficient preparation the White Man's Grave aspect of the Gold Coast was held in check, a remarkable achievement considering that medical knowledge of fevers and dysentery was in its infancy. Although Wolseley and his doctors were ignorant of the real source of the scourges, they knew that in certain circumstances their impact was less lethal than in others. So, whenever possible, they arranged that the more favourable conditions should apply. For example, every evening fires were lit in huts to counter the damp and, in effect, kept mosquitoes away. No man at that time wore short trousers, so bare knees were not exposed to bites, and anti-mosquito cream was known. Really filthy water was carefully filtered but, sadly, men were allowed to use water from native ponds that seemed clean to the eye.

Strange to say, no one contracted smallpox, although there had been an epidemic at Cape Coast as recently as July and Amanquatia's army was full of it. The fact that British regiments never stayed a night at the port, but moved straight up to Inquabim, probably helped. Another piece of good fortune—although yellow fever had been endemic in the West African Territories for fifty years, it had never taken hold on the Gold Coast. During the campaign a ship carrying the fever anchored in the Cape Coast Castle roads, but it was inspected and sent on its way; several passengers and crew died later at sea.

The battle-casualty proportion of fourteen British killed to two hundred and forty wounded was due to the low muzzle velocity of Ashanti muskets using bad gunpowder. Their slugs usually failed to penetrate at a distance of more than fifty yards, and it was only in the major battles of Amoaful, Ordahsu and the breakthrough to Kumasi that they were prepared to decrease this range. This was one of the main reasons why Sir Garnet's comparatively small force was able to defeat such great numbers. The General himself said, 'If they had had Sniders, we would have been destroyed.' There were, of course, other factors apart from the disparity of weapons between the two sides. The Ashanti had seen their basic principles of war confounded utterly and their military conventions flouted—no properly behaved army should press on despite heavy casualties, nor continue to fight, nor take the offensive after being outflanked and then surrounded. They needed time to go away and think it all over, but that time was denied to them.

King Kofi Karikari, fetish- and priest-ridden as he was, had been no help! His continuous vacillation, in the face of daily contradictory guidance from human sacrifices, had allowed the men of Amanquatia's army to disperse to their homes and permitted the Kings of Becquah, Kokofoo and Juabin to depart in their own territorial interests. His envoys had even ordered the Ashanti force south of the Ordah River to stop harrying the British column.

An outstanding feature of the expedition was the calibre of the General's staff and the specially employed officers, who certainly earned their extra guinea a day. They would let no difficulty stand in their way, no effort was too great for them. Two officers on the General's personal staff died through weakened resistance after over-straining themselves; they insisted on carrying on after they should have been hospitalized. Having no consideration for himself, Sir Garnet expected others to follow his example and he had chosen men whom he knew would carry on until they dropped if he called upon them to do so. Moreover, he did not want people who would slog on blindly without using their brains. He had a predilection for officers who could wield the pen as well as the sword —Alison, Colley, Huyshe, Brackenbury, Butler and Maurice. All these were men who thrived on hardship and active service, then went home, analysed the lessons learned, wrote them down and published them. Colonel Wolseley himself is believed to have been the anonymous author of an account of the Red River operation published in *Blackwood's Magazine*, as well as compiling his *Field Service Pocket Book*.

The Zulu War 1879

CHAPTER 4
The Northern Column

After the Ashanti Campaign Sir Garnet Wolseley was voted by Parliament a reward of £25,000 and promoted to the substantive rank of Major-General. He was appointed Inspector-General of the Auxiliary Forces, but was in the post for only a year before being sent to Natal as Governor and General Officer Commanding to deal with Kaffir unrest. He took with him Colley, now a Brevet-Colonel, also Butler, who was described as 'tall, strong and active, quick of observation and full of resource; genial yet with much force of character.' Butler's career troubles were over: he had been promoted major in the Ashanti Gazettes and had pulled off a successful land speculation in Canada, so was in a stable financial position at last. Also with the party was Brackenbury, who as usual suffered much from seasickness during the voyage, and Lord Gifford.

Colley was sent to reconnoitre the Transvaal, where he travelled the ground and met some of the personalities to be connected with the Boer uprising which was still five years in the future. Butler went on a similar fact-finding mission to the Orange Free State.

Brackenbury and Gifford had really not enough to do. As active in the drawing-rooms as on the battlefield, they were always falling in love—so far and so frequently that Sir Garnet began to regret having brought them with him! He was relieved when he and his staff moved up-country, away from all these diversions.

Nobody stayed in South Africa for long. Wolseley went back to England with the junior members of his staff, where he returned to the War Office. Colley was posted to India as Military Secretary, and later Private Secretary to the Viceroy, Lord Lytton. While on home leave during this tour he married a wife and took her back to Simla with him.

McCalmont went to see Wolseley in the War Office and was asked if he would like to visit some strategic areas of China and collect information useful in the event of future operations. He was told that he would have to go at his own expense, as the Intelligence Department had no funds for this sort of thing and did not obtain any until Brackenbury took charge of it ten years later. However, as McCalmont combined an enormous capacity for obtaining leave with comfortable financial circumstances, he jumped at the opportunity and later wrote a very good report on his assignment. Under similar arrangements he went the following year on leave to Istanbul to have a look round in case there should be trouble between Turkey and Russia, and got himself sent as an extra military attaché in the field with the Turkish Army for the Armenian Campaign of 1877. He got very bored after hostilities were over and made himself unpopular with the pro-Turkish diplomatic world by making friends with the famous Russian General Skoboleff, who had just defeated the Turks in several battles. So he went back to England.

In Turkey at the same time was Mr T. J. de Burgh, once a lieutenant in the 5th Dragoon Guards, but who had sold out in 1878 shortly before his marriage and retired to his place in Ireland. Still feeling the need for an active life, he took a holiday and did a reconnaissance of the Buyuk Chekmaji line of forts for Valentine Baker Pasha.

Alison became Deputy Adjutant-General in Ireland, then was promoted Major-General and commanded the Staff College for a few months before taking charge of the Military Intelligence Department in the War Office, a four-year tour which ended in 1882.

Buller was promoted major, but he also had inherited property and was not sure whether to pursue his military career. So he went to discuss it with Sir Garnet, took his advice and soon he too was out in South Africa.

There were still possibilities of another major war between Turkey and Russia, so in 1878 the Sultan ceded Cyprus, to be occupied and administered by the British as part of an alliance against the common enemy. Lieutenant-General Sir Garnet Wolseley was sent out as High Commissioner and with him he took Colonel Greaves, Baker Russell, Brackenbury and Maurice. Major McCalmont had returned to London in time to be selected as ADC. But it was not a happy tour for any of them as there was not enough interesting work for men of their calibre. It began to look as though at long last someone had succeeded in shunting Sir Garnet into a siding.

While Wolseley was trying to administer Cyprus, relations with the Zulus in South Africa were becoming critical. This warrior tribe had been involved in battles, skirmishes and border disputes with the Boers of the Transvaal for nearly forty years. The Boers had first tried to obtain land by treaty, but when this failed and their negotiators were murdered they had seized their initial requirement by force of arms. As their numbers increased with the years and it became necessary to expand again, they reverted to acquiring land by treaty, some from the Zulus and some from the Swazis and other native tribes. All went well until 1873 when Cetewayo, who had been the power behind the throne for seventeen years, at last became King of Zululand. He soon began to break his promises and tried to reclaim land given to the Boers. He even claimed, after the fashion of Kofi Karikari, that the Swazis were his vassals, that they had had no right to have given land to the Boers and therefore the territory concerned must revert to him!

The British annexed the Transvaal in 1887, whereafter Boer problems became *their* worry. A boundary commission was appointed, which found very much in favour of the Zulus, but did insist on compensation or protection for Boers caught on the Zululand side of the new boundary. Cetewayo, however, was feeling defiant and allowed his regiments to commit outrages in both the Transvaal and Natal, so it was decided that he must be brought under control. This was not a decision taken lightly, as Cetewayo was known to have an Army of forty thousand fighting men, all of whom were anxious for war. There was an incentive for many of them, particularly the younger soldiers. An essential feature of Zulu discipline was that no man could marry without direct permission from the king, and this was usually withheld until he had washed his spears—killed an enemy in battle. Sometimes it happened that the whole of a couple of years' intake would be banded into one or two regiments, with a suitable leavening of trained warriors, and in later years the whole regiment might be given permission en bloc to be married.

This rule had been relaxed slightly in recent years, but Cetewayo had reinstated it with the full force of his authority. He even sent to arrest a number of girls who had married men of their own age instead of men of an older regiment for whom they were designated and slaughtered the lot. This had elicited a strong remonstrance from the Government of Natal, inclined though they were to look kindly on the doings of the Zulu race.

While all this was going on, Evelyn Wood had spent four years on the staff at Aldershot and now began to feel the urge to rejoin his regiment, which was about to leave England for South Africa to fight in the current Kaffir War. But the problem was that there was no room for him. The regiment already had its full complement of a lieutenant-colonel and one major, so he would be surplus to establishment. However, the Commanding Officer had become a Glasite, a Christian sect with strong pacifist beliefs, and he had no desire to go on active service. He even took Wood to the War Office with him to plead his cause, but to no avail; he had to go. Despite this, Wood decided to follow his regiment and found himself on the same ship as Lieutenant-General Thesiger (soon to inherit the title of Lord Chelmsford) and Major Buller. They disembarked at East London on 4 March, 1878, to find that their port of arrival 'consisted of corrugated iron huts, surrounded by broken glass bottles and empty jam tins, dotted about on bleak, bare sand-hills. There were no roads. The so-called hotel provided shelter and food, but while there were bath-towels, there were no baths, and the one closet was common to whites of both sexes, and Kafir servants.'

In April Buller was offered command of the Frontier Light Horse, a motley collection of undisciplined Boers, Englishmen and foreigners of several races, but he soon got the regiment into good order. The final touch came when a drunk came on parade and abused the Colonel loudly to his face; Buller took no action but to give the order to march. Then, a few miles later, he halted the column, made the offender dismount and sent him packing on foot. There was no more trouble.

Buller shared his men's hardships; he led them in battle and was always just in his dealings. No man ever had to suffer unfair punishment. They feared him, but they admired him and came to obey him without question. While holding the command, Buller usually wore a broad-brimmed hat with a red cloth puggaree wound round it, a coloured flannel open-necked shirt, riding-breeches, brown butcher boots and spurs, and a revolver. He would be mounted on a stout pony of fourteen hands (four feet eight inches at the withers) which scarcely looked up to his weight. In action, he is described as 'leading his men at a swinging canter, with his reins in his teeth, a revolver in one hand, and a knobkerrie he had snatched from a Zulu in the other, his hat blown off in the mêlée, and a large streak of blood across his face, caused by a splinter of rock from above, this gallant horseman seemed a demon incarnate to the flying savages, who slunk out of his path as if he had been—as indeed they believed him—an evil spirit whose very look was death.'

The men of the Frontier Light Horse followed no exact rule for dress, but all adopted the distinguishing red puggaree worn by their colonel.

Evelyn Wood had also been fortunate. During the voyage he undoubtedly had opportunities to air his opinions and Thesiger found a very reasonable solution. Wood was sent to deal with the Gaika rebellion, commanding a mixed force of colonial and imperial troops, including his own 90th Light Infantry under Major Hackett, while the Colonel was left behind at base in charge of a few friendly Hottentots.

The Gaika problem was satisfactorily resolved and Thesiger then asked Wood to see what he could do to enlist the services of Transvaal Boers in the event of a war with Cetewayo. This was a tricky assignment, requiring every bit of Evelyn Wood's considerable powers of persuasion, as annexation had aroused bitter anti-British feeling. However, he arranged a meeting with Andries Pretorius, a former President of the Transvaal. On arrival at his destination only his host complied with protocol and came out to meet him, apologizing for the manners displayed by his score of surly kinsmen and explaining that they could not stand the sight of Englishmen. As can be imagined, Wood failed to win their cooperation; they had all sworn to be true to Kruger and Joubert who were in England pleading their cause for independence. If it were any consolation, they all liked him as an individual and expressed the hope that he personally would survive the war. On his departure they even condescended to come out and see him off.

He was more successful with the Uys clan. Their patriarch and leader Piet Uys was at first very doubtful because the British were so disliked, although he himself felt strongly that all white men should combine to protect their borders against native invasion, whatever their political differences might be. So, in the end, disregarding many of his countrymen who called him a traitor, he agreed on behalf of all his sons and nephews to fight the Zulus side by side with the British in the event of hostilities.

War there would be. An ultimatum was presented to Zulu representatives in December, 1878, insisting on reforms that would

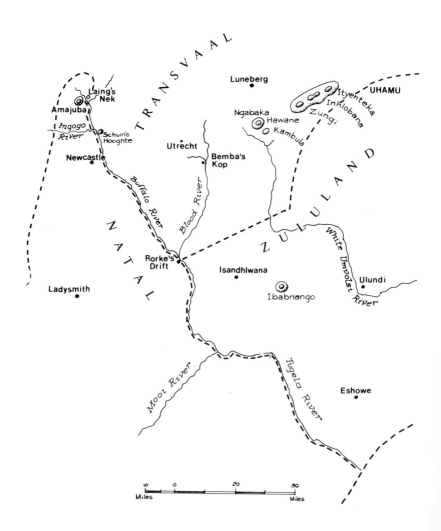

THE
ZULU AND BOER
WARS

TRANSVAL

Luneberg

Laing's
Nek

Amajuba

UHAMU

Ityenteka
InKlobana
Zungi

Ngabaka

Hawane

Ingogo
River

Schuin's
Hooghte

Kambula

Utrecht

Bemba's
Kop

Newcastle

Buffalo River

Blood River

NATAL

ZULULAND

White Umvolsi River

Rorke's
Drift

Ladysmith

Isandhlwana

Ibabnango

Ulundi

Mooi River

Tugela River

Eshowe

10   0   20   30
Miles   Miles

certainly be unacceptable to Cetewayo—one of them was a stipulation that all youths should be allowed to marry when they came to man's estate, without let or hindrance. Expiry date was 31 December, and when no reply had been received by that day three British columns were ready to cross the border into Zululand. Lord Chelmsford, who was in charge of the operation, allowed Cetewayo another ten days and then began his offensive. The northern column was to advance from Utrecht along the Blood River, the centre column would cross the Buffalo River at Rorke's Drift, the southern would move over the lower Tugela River. The crossings were made between 10 and 12 January and were unopposed.

The left-hand, northern column was commanded by Brevet-Colonel Evelyn Wood, who had concentrated his force at Bemba's Kop. Under his orders were eight companies of his own regiment, the 90th Light Infantry, now commanded by Brevet-Colonel Cherry, eight companies of the 13th Regiment of Foot (The Somerset Light Infantry) under Lieutenant-Colonel Gilbert, Brevet Lieutenant-Colonel Redvers Buller and two hundred of his Frontier Light Horse, six 7-pounder guns and two rocket-launchers under Major Tremlett, and a native contingent known as Wood's irregulars, recruited to serve under him and no one else. A very useful supplement was provided by a body of forty Boers under Piet Uys. Six hundred other Boers had been enlisted by the time that the invasion began, but at least four hundred deserted immediately, and their district field cornet made no attempt to send them back. Uys had armed, mounted and provisioned his numerous family at his own expense, refusing to accept any payment, and had brought all his sons into the field, even the thirteen-year-old Dirks.

There were no maps of Zululand, so the columns would have little to guide them except travellers' tales and the old grassed-over ruts made by pioneers' wagons. The attitude of the Zulus was still uncertain and the only way to find out their reactions was by reconnaissance. Wood received orders to make his way south down the left bank of the Blood River towards Rorke's Drift, so as to be available to give support if the centre column's crossing should be opposed. He had already taken the precaution of sending Captain Barton, an officer of the Coldstream Guards on special service with the Frontier Light Horse as second-in-command to Buller, over the proposed line of advance. Barton had done the seventy-mile round trip without incident and had reported that the natives along the route appeared to be friendly.

Having now no worries about the route, Wood moved south on 10 January, leading the way with a flying column of light horse and irregulars, bolstered by twenty-four marksmen picked from the two British infantry regiments, bumping their way uncomfortably along in mule wagons. He was already within twelve miles of Rorke's Drift when he met Lord Chelmsford who told him that the centre column had crossed the river without any trouble, and that he could return to base.

The expedition had been uneventful. Large herds of cattle had been captured and Zulus had been seen in considerable numbers, well-armed with rifles and assegais, but they had not fought to retain their property. It seems that they had not yet received instructions from Cetewayo, without which they were not prepared to take any major hostile action.

The main topographical feature in Evelyn Wood's sector was a mountain range stretching west to east for twenty miles. The Western portion was known as the Zungi Range, next came a huge central eminence called the Inhlobana Mountain, joined by a saddle, or nek, to the Ityenteka Mountain. Wood decided on a reconnaissance in force of the Zungi range for 22 January.

The force left camp at midnight, and by early morning Wood and Buller had climbed unopposed to the western summit of the Zungi Range. They swept eastwards over the plateau on which local natives had pastured their herds in safety since times immemorial, driving away the Zulu guards and rounding up their cattle. When they reached the eastern extremity of the Zungi they were interested to see some four thousand Zulus drilling and manoeuvring on the north-western slopes of the next plateau, the Inhlobana. After watching for a while, Wood took his party down the mountain to join Lieutenant-Colonel Gilbert and the 13th Foot, who had established a firm base south-east of the Zungi.

Wood stayed with Gilbert all next day, then moved out early on the 24th to have a look a the north side of Inhlobana. He met and dispersed a small band of Zulus, but while the skirmish was still in progress a messenger arrived with tidings of disaster that had overtaken the centre column.

This force had advanced from Rorke's Drift to Isandhlwana, where a camp had been made. On the morning of 22 January Lord Chelmsford had gone out on reconnaissance, and during his absence the garrison of eleven hundred British and six hundred natives had been attacked by ten thousand Zulus. The action began with the garrison deployed over a front of two thousand yards with the native contingent at the salient point closest to the advancing enemy. British rifle and artillery fire was not heavy nor concentrated enough to halt the enemy, who pressed on regardless of casualties until they were two hundred yards from the native contingent—who turned and fled. Zulus poured through the gap in the line and were in among the British with their assegais before the infantry had time to concentrate or even to fix bayonets. There was no firm base to which the troops could withdraw and make a stand, no defence had been constructed. The camp was not entrenched, nothing had been done except to start building a low stone wall along two sides. The wagons had not even been put in laager, the traditional Boer way of defence. There were a few isolated stands, where the fight was continued until the men ran out of ammunition, then they were slain. No replenishment had been possible; the Zulus had captured the ammunition wagons. Some fugitives tried to escape back to the Buffalo River, but men on foot had no hope of survival. 'The Zulus were exceptionally fleet of foot, and on rough ground were able to outstrip even horsemen.' A few got away, but British casualties in killed alone amounted to fifty-two officers and eight hundred and six men.

Morale was to some degree restored by a very gallant and successful defence of the post at Rorke's Drift by eighty men of the 24th Regiment of Foot under Lieutenants Chard and Bromhead, who had heard of the Isandhlwana debacle in time to improvise defences of a kind. They succeeded in repelling repeated attacks by four thousand Zulus, who eventually withdrew leaving three hundred and fifty of their dead lying around the small British post.

On the same day the southern column fought a victorious action at Inyezane against a large body of Zulus, inflicting three hundred casualties with little loss to themselves. Next day they reached their first objective, the Mission Station at Eshowe.

In consequence of Isandhlwana Lord Chelmsford was compelled to halt his advance pending the arrival of reinforcements. From Eshowe he withdrew most of the mounted men and the native troops to Natal, leaving a garrison of one thousand three hundred Europeans, who were soon blockaded by the Zulus.

News of Isandhlwana reached England on 11 February and that very same day ten thousand troops were put under orders for South

Africa. The leading elements arrived at Durban on 17 March and most of the remainder were in Natal by mid-April.

Meanwhile Evelyn Wood had decided to withdraw to his camp and await orders. This camp had been adequate as a temporary base, but he felt it to be unsuitable for a protracted stay, nor was it properly sited to withstand a siege or a major assault. So he moved about fifteen miles to Kambula Hill, an eminence on the south-east side of the Ngabaka Hawane mountain. Water was plentiful and firewood for cooking could be gathered from the top of the mountain, so he started to prepare a strong entrenched camp on a spur of Kambula. However, wood-gathering turned out to be a more onerous fatigue than had been anticipated, so he moved two miles further up the hill, closer to Ngabaka Hawane. The new camp, complete with a fort containing two guns, was ready on 13 February.

More expeditions were sent out. Buller went again to the Inhlobana Mountain area and captured five hundred head of cattle without serious resistance—cattle, it must be remembered, were the main currency of Zululand. On another occasion he went with some of his Frontier Light Horse and Uys's mounted burghers to intercept a Zulu column raiding into the Luneberg district. He caught up with the invaders, killed thirty-four of them and dispersed the remainder. He suffered his first casualties in this encounter, five natives killed or wounded.

Colonial reinforcements began to arrive, mostly mounted men. First were Raaf's Transvaal Rangers, a hundred whites and forty natives. Then came Schermbrucker's Corps of Kaffrarian Rifles, raised from descendants of men from the German Legion who had been granted land in British Kaffraria after the Crimean War. There rode in sixty Border Horse, a unit raised by Lieutenant-Colonel Weatherley, a retired officer living in Pretoria who owned considerable property in the Transvaal diamond fields. A veteran who had served in the Crimea in the 4th Light Dragoons, and in the Indian Mutiny, he had no intention of missing the campaign. His fifteen-year-old son, a skilled hunter, insisted on accompanying him as a Sub-Lieutenant. Finally No 1 Squadron Mounted Infantry under the command of Lieutenant-Colonel Russell of the 12th Lancers, not to be confused with Baker Russell of the 13th Hussars, came over from the centre column.

So Kambula camp was shifted yet again, partly to accommodate all these newcomers, and also for sanitary reasons. Wood's Irregulars would not practise any form of hygiene, with the result that they and the cattle so fouled the ground that frequent moves were necessary to avoid disease. Nor could Piet Uys's Boers be persuaded to use latrines, even though one was specially dug for them!

The new camp was sited on a ridge running east-west across the Kambula spur. On the eastern end a redoubt was constructed, in which two guns were incorporated. Two hundred yards further west began the main laager, roughly in the shape of a heptagon two hundred and fifty yards across. The outer defence was an entrenchment and a second line was provided by wagons lashed together when necessary. Between the two, south-west of the redoubt, was the cattle laager, defended again by entrenchments and wagons, with its eastern and southern sides on the edge of a steep rocky cliff. A plank palisade to link the redoubt with the cattle laager was put under construction.

Wood claimed that moving camp gave the men plenty to do and that it was good for morale. At the same time he made sure that he and his officers got plenty of exercise. Wherever he went he made a tennis-court and a polo-ground, attractions which induced young officers such as Lieutenants Lysons and Bright from his own regiment to come over and play with him.

He also established a form of garrison routine, including Divine Service, attendance at which was strictly voluntary. He was pleased when his tennis and polo-playing friends joined in. Moreover, the Service was held close to where two companies of infantry were digging emplacements, and the men were allowed if they wished to put down their picks and shovels and take part. They wished! The congregation was usually quite a large one.

Proud of his own regiment's prowess at the tug-of-war,—the 90th Light Infantry had been champions in England—as another diversion he challenged Piet Uys's Boers to a contest. But the burghers' team was made up of men weighing fourteen to fifteen stone, with enormous knotted arms and hands like iron. They waited until the British were exhausted and then easily pulled them over. Little things like this were good for Boer self-confidence. Wood had been rather disappointed at their reluctance to commit themselves to battle and on at least one occasion he and their patriarch had to give them a lead.

Sporting events were also arranged for the natives, including an assegai-throwing competition. Wood was surprised to find that the longest throw reached only fifty yards. It was explained to him that Zulus were not encouraged to throw, only to close and stab.

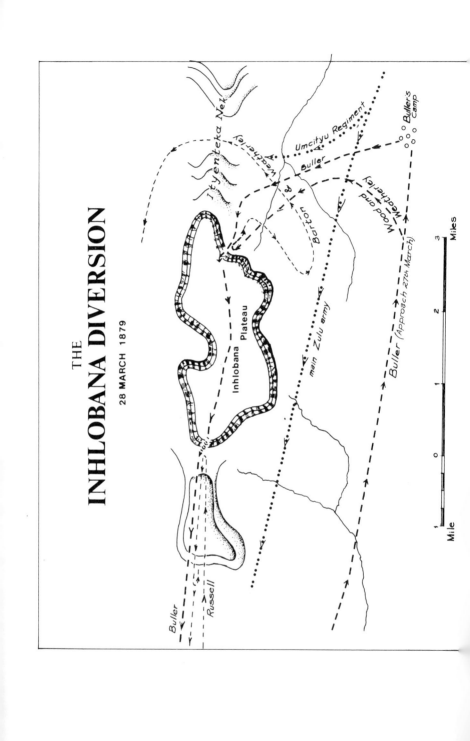

THE
INHLOBANA DIVERSION
28 MARCH 1879

In mid-March a Zulu chief named Uhamu, a brother of Cetewayo, was persuaded to renounce his allegiance to his King and work with the British. The fighting men came in to Kambula, but their families and flocks were still in the tribal area forty-five miles away beyond Inhlobana, vulnerable to any retribution that Cetewayo might take. A party had to be despatched to bring them in, so Wood led out a column consisting of Buller and three hundred and sixty mounted men, including Piet Uys and his burghers, accompanied by two hundred of Uhamu's warriors, many of whom had fought against the British at Isandhlwana.

They skirted the southern flanks of Inhlobana, which was typical of many mountains in Zululand, table-topped with precipitous sides. Rockfall lay in irregular masses at the base and on any small ledge, providing excellent cover for defenders of the summit against an assault up the slopes. The plateau could be reached only by a few difficult paths, and was used as a secure grazing-ground for their cattle by the local natives, the Makulusi, who lived in kraals built precariously on almost impossible terraces on the southern slopes. They came down to the foothills as the column passed by and engaged it with long-range rifle-fire, but stopped when the British shot back. In reprisal for their hostile activity a party, including Piet Uys's two youngest sons aged thirteen and fifteen, went to round up some cattle on the plain. Despite their age, Piet risked them in every skirmish, as he did the rest of his family, but that did not mean he was not worried about them. On this occasion he became anxious when he heard firing, but it was only his youngest son Dirks shooting a Zulu.

They reached Uhamu's territory and collected nearly a thousand men, women and children. Even five-year-olds were now faced with a thirty-mile march, but they managed it. Buller was in charge of the rearguard and swore that he would have nothing to do with the verminous little beasts, but Evelyn Wood noticed on several occasions that he was carrying up to six at a time, some in front and some behind him on his horse. One woman was in labour and had to be left behind when they were still ten miles from camp, but the Colonel detailed an officer to stay with her and bring her in. She had her baby, put it under her arm and was back with the others in two hours.

Piet Uys seems to have had some form of premonition and swore an undertaking with Evelyn Wood that, if either one of them should be killed, then the other would take steps to safeguard his children.

CHAPTER 5
Inhlobana, Kambula and Ulundi

[1]

A few days later Lord Chelmsford decided to try and relieve Eshowe and he ordered Wood to make some sort of diversion on 28 March. He had on a previous occasion told Wood that he could have a go at Inhlobana if he wanted to, and the Colonel now considered that this would be a good way of fulfilling his task, though he was 'not sanguine of success'.

There would be an element of risk, as he knew that a large Zulu army was assembling at Ulundi before marching to attack Kambula. But his informant, who was usually reliable, had said that they would not be leaving until the 27th; the witch-doctors would take that long to process them all. So there should be time to assault Inhlobana, sweep the three-mile table-land and get home again before the main Zulu impi arrived.

He would leave his British infantry and artillery at Kambula, which was, after all, the only obstacle between Zululand and the town of Utrecht, and would use a force of mounted men and his own two battalions of irregular native infantry for the operation. Uhamu's people had given good service, so he would take some of them as well to help herd cattle captured during the raid. Buller would command the assault force, Russell would create a diversion which would not be committed to action in the face of any serious resistance. Wood said specifically in his orders that scouts were to be sent to the south and south-west to watch out for any signs of the expected Zulu army.

On 27 March Buller left Kambula early in the morning with a Royal Artillery rocket-launcher detachment under Major Tremlett, Piet Uys's Dutch burghers, the Frontier Light Horse, the Transvaal Rangers under Raaf, the Border Horse under Weatherley, who had his son with him, and Baker's Horse, something like four hundred mounted men. Behind them marched Major Leet and nearly three hundred men of the 2nd Battalion of Wood's Irregulars. He covered thirty miles, then bivouacked for the night three miles south-east of Inhlobana.

Russell left at noon on the same day, as he had less far to go, and bivouacked four miles from the western extremity of the mountain. Under his command also there was a rocket-launcher detachment, with forty of Schermbrucker's men, eighty mounted infantry, seventy mounted Basutos, the 1st Battalion of Wood's Irregulars and two hundred of Uhamu's people. Wood, with his staff and a small escort, joined Russell at dusk.

Next morning Buller left his bivouac at 3.30 am with all his column except Weatherley, who had lost his way and failed to turn up on the previous evening. Although the Makulusi, from their villages on Inhlobana, must have seen the British column making camp, they had never expected an attack on the plateau and were not watching out for one. Besides, Buller's advance up the hill was screened by the morning mist, which was just as well, for the only track was rocky, steep and hardly passable for mounted men. As a result his way up was marked by a trail of dead or maimed horses which had missed their footing and come crashing down the precipices. Despite the noise that they must have made, the few Zulus on the top were taken completely by surprise, but even so came to full awareness in time to kill the leading two officers as they came up to the crest. There was only one other fatal casualty, but a number of horses were hit by rifle bullets.

The plateau turned out to be about three miles long and a mile and a half wide, and was covered with herds of cattle. There was no difficulty in collecting two thousand head and dispersing the Zulus who were guarding them. While this was going on, Buller and Piet Uys rode around looking for ways down to the plain. They found only two possible descents at the western end of the main plateau, both more difficult than their ascent, but of these the more northerly was secure from flanking fire and Buller decided to use it for at least a portion of his force. He went back to the east end of the plateau and sent Captain Barton with thirty men to bury the two officers killed, and then to find Weatherley and go back with him to Kambula by the track south of Inhlobana, the way that they had all come out on the previous day.

Wood had left Russell's bivouac, also at 3.30 am, and soon encountered the Weatherleys and their Border Horse. Moving on together, they soon heard the noise of firing from the top of the mountain and Wood ordered Weatherley to push on up after Buller. They found the ascent very difficult, as indeed had Buller, and were slow getting started. Wood therefore decided to go on ahead and see what was happening. They intended to return the same way, so his staff left their horses at the bottom of the path, but the Colonel, who hated walking, led his horse with him in case he should need it on the plateau. Accompanied by six of the better riders from the Border Horse, they all pressed on and were soon within a hundred feet of the top. But they had missed the way; they were not on Buller's track and their route had not been cleared of enemy. Only fifty yards away some Zulus were hiding in a cave and in the first volley the Political Agent, Mr Lloyd, was mortally wounded, his back broken by a bullet. Captain Campbell, the Chief Staff Officer, carried him down the hill, where he died. Wood tried to climb on and get through the enemy fire, but a Zulu shot his horse from twenty yards' range. The horse fell back on Wood, knocking him down, but he was able to struggle clear and get away to join Campbell. He told his Chief Staff Officer to order Weatherley's men to clear the rocky area of enemy, but they replied that the position was unassailable. Disgusted by this, Campbell, Lieutenant Lysons the Orderly Officer, and three men of the 90th Foot from the Colonel's escort decided to do the job themselves. Campbell was killed in the mouth of the cave, the Zulu's rifle almost touching his chest when it was fired, but Lysons and Private Fowler charged in over his body and killed the man, the remainder escaping through a back entrance.

Weatherley now came up, but found it quite impossible to get any further with horses, so back he went down the mountain to find where they had diverged from Buller's route, and then follow the correct track up to the plateau.

Wood stayed to bury his friends. It took time, as he wanted the two graves to be four feet deep, and the only implements for digging were the assegais of his native escort, Zulus from Natal. Then he retraced his steps to rejoin Russell.

Russell had occupied a smaller, subsidiary plateau west of the main Inhlobana table-land and about a hundred and fifty feet below it. He saw a track leading upwards, but judged it to be quite impractical for men on horseback, so he sent up an officer and twenty men on foot to make contact with Buller's force. They made it to the top and there they met Major Tremlett and Major Leet, after which they returned to report that the track was difficult even for men without horses, and that all was quiet on the main table-land.

Scarcely had they said so, at about nine o'clock, when Russell observed a large Zulu army advancing from the east. Wood's informant had miscalculated; the religious ceremonial had been completed earlier than he had anticipated and the impi had left Ulundi on 25 March. Lacking proper maps, Wood had expected them to appear from the south or south-west and had deployed his screen of scouts accordingly. In fact Ulundi lay south of Inhlobana, and the Zulus had marched north until they had reached Uhamu's country and then swung west for Kambula. They had covered sixty-five miles on short commons, intending to rest and eat well when within striking distance of their objective.

Russell thought that Wood must be on the main plateau, so he sent up a messenger to warn him and ask for orders. But by ten o'clock he had received no instructions—Wood was still burying Lloyd and Campbell—and, as the Zulu army was closing rather quickly, he decided to act on his own initiative. He got his men off the hills on to the plain, gave orders that the usual herd of looted cattle should be abandoned (an order ignored by Uhamu's people), sent his irregulars marching back to Kambula and positioned his mounted men on some rising ground close to the western base of the Inhlobana complex to cover Buller's retreat.

Wood, down on the flat, did not see the Zulu army until it was only two miles away. Nobody on the mountain knew where he was, so he had received no earlier notification by messenger. He sent Lysons to warn Russell and tell him to 'get into position on the Zunguin neck', while he and his remaining staff set out for that place at all speed. Russell received the order, but as there were no proper maps, so also there was no standardized nomenclature of place-names. Wood wanted Russell at the eastern end of the Zungi mountain, but Russell, in consultation with his officers, thought that he meant the place where the track from Kambula crossed the western part of the Zungi, six miles further on towards base, and there he went.

Buller had seen the Zulus at about the same time as Russell, soon after despatching Barton on his errand. Highest on the mountain, he was in the best place to see, and he estimated that there were about twenty thousand of the enemy six miles distant at the time. Obviously this posed a threat to Barton and Weatherley, so he sent off two troopers, to warn them to return to camp 'by the right of the mountain'. He was presumably facing west at the time, for he meant them to use the north side of Inhlobana as an escape route, rather than be boxed in between the mountain and the Zulu army advancing from the south. He then collected all the rest of his force at the head of the track at the north-west end of the main plateau. But now from every cave and cranny emerged the Makulusi to do battle and harass the withdrawal. More and more of them arrived on the scene, and hurrying to their support was the local regular regiment, the four thousand men seen drilling on the northern slopes during an earlier reconnaissance.

The track down was very much worse than Buller had realized. The steep downward slope resembled, if anything, a descending series of ledges, each eight to twelve feet wide, on which it was just possible for steady, docile horses to get some form of a precarious landing before making the three to four foot drop to the next ledge. This was asking a lot of any horse, but Buller's mounts were rather specially selected. 'They did not as a rule average more than fourteen hands two inches (fifty-eight inches) at the withers, but all were stout, short-backed, well-drilled animals and up to far more weight than their appearance would have given a novice to suppose'. Moreover, they were all in good condition, as Wood had inspected all horses intended for the expedition and had rejected any that he thought to be unfit.

Buller sent his native irregular battalion down first, and very slow they were, despite being on foot. He kept his mounted men on the plateau to act as rearguard and cover their retreat. Then was made a fatal error of judgement. The rearguard saw a body of natives approaching and took them to be a belated party of Wood's Irregulars. But they were Zulus, perhaps regulars advancing in some form of military formation. Buller's men held their fire and did not realize their mistake until it was too late and the Zulus had got safely into the protection of rocky formations flanking the track down. So when it came to their turn to withdraw, the mounted men in addition to the great difficulty of the descent down the terraces had to run the gauntlet of short-range rifle fire. Casualties began to mount. The Zulus infiltrated the retreat and some managed to close with the assegai. That hardened campaigner, Piet Uys, went back to help a son who was in trouble with his horse and was killed by an assegai thrust from a Zulu who had crept up to hide behind a boulder.

The last nine men at the top were Buller, Lieutenant Everitt and seven men of the Frontier Light Horse. As they turned to go, the Zulus charged, killed four troopers and stabbed Everitt's horse. Buller dragged him clear and ordered him down the hill, then took his carbine and ammunition and joined the three surviving troopers in covering the retreat. During the remainder of the action he personally saved three more lives; one he dragged from the midst of a struggling mass of Zulus, another he picked up from just in front of the enemy. He then went back and brought in Captain D'Arcy of his regiment, who had lost his horse and was panting along on foot, tired out and about to be overtaken by his pursuers. When eventually he reached the foot of the mountain he found the men thoroughly demoralized. However, he managed to restore order; wounded men and those who had lost their horses were put up behind those more fortunate and they set off back to Kambula.

Meanwhile Wood had been pursued by a regiment of the Ngoba-makosi regiment, but he had outdistanced them and they had turned back when they found that they could not catch him. But they got among Buller's battalion of Wood's Irregulars, killing two officers and eighty men. They also slew about a hundred of Uhamu's people, who had stuck stubbornly to their spoil of cattle and now paid the penalty with their lives. By then the Zulus had had enough; they were weary after their rapid approach march and they called off the pursuit. So Buller was able to make his way back to the Zungi, bothered only by long-range rifle fire from the Makulusi following him, until that too died away.

Barton had received Buller's message directing him to return to Kambula 'by the right of the mountain'. Sad to say, he was facing east at the time and thought he was meant to do as originally ordered and travel by the track running south alongside Inhlobana. Collecting Weatherley, off he went, only to find that he was becoming hemmed in between the whole Zulu army and the precipices of Inhlobana. There was no way of getting through and there was nothing for it but to retrace their steps, cross the Ityenteka Nek and make their escape along the north base of Inhlobana, as Buller had meant them to do. To begin with all went well. They were pursued by a small detachment of Zulus on foot, which caused them no concern as they were well-mounted. But on the Nek between Inhlobana and Ityenteka were Zulus of the Umcityu

Regiment blocking their way in great numbers. The British tried to fight their path through the enemy hordes and about a quarter of them succeeded in getting by. Weatherley was killed, so was his fifteen-year-old son and forty of the Border Horse; so were twenty of the Frontier Light Horse accompanying Barton. Barton himself broke through, but then took Lieutenant Poole, who had been dismounted, behind him on his horse. In pursuit came a band of mounted men from the Umcityu Regiment, led by one Chicheeli, who later told the story of Barton's death. Chicheeli had already caught and killed half a dozen whites, not including a trooper who had shot himself with his own carbine rather than risk capture. Then he came up with Barton and Poole who abandoned their exhausted horse and separated, hoping that one would get away while the attention of the Zulus was taken up with the other. It was of no avail. Chicheeli first shot Poole, who was unarmed, then galloped up to Barton. According to his story, he summoned Barton to surrender. He had already killed enough men that day to assuage his appetite and Cetewayo had ordered that one or two British officers should be brought back in triumph to Ulundi. Barton was armed only with a pistol with a faulty striker-pin—it had misfired three times—so, in reply to Chicheeli, all he did was to raise his hat in a derisive manner, at which moment he was shot by another Zulu and Chicheeli then finished him off with his assegai, thereby presumably claiming the credit.

When Buller realized what had happened he went out to find and bring in any survivors, and through his efforts twenty men of the original eighty reached the safety of Kambula.

The Inhlobana diversion had been effectively carried out, at an expense of fifteen officers and seventy-nine NCOs and men from the European element killed, and one officer and seven men wounded. Wood's Irregulars had started the day eight hundred strong and had lost eighty from the 2nd Battalion. All but fifty from both battalions deserted that night from Kambula, so casualties could not be calculated accurately. A few hundred returned later, after they had regained their confidence.

[2]

While still conducting the withdrawal from Inhlobana, Wood had sent a messenger back to Kambula with orders that the camp be put

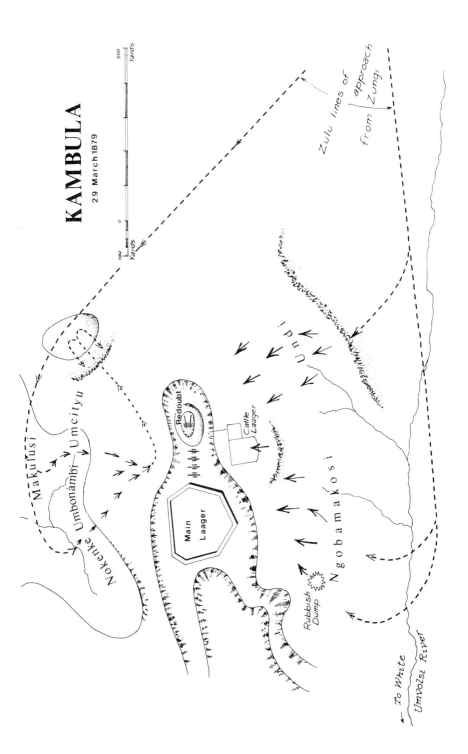

KAMBULA
29 March 1879

Yards

0

500

Yards

Zulu lines of approach from Zungi

Makulusi

Umcityu

Umbonambi

Nokenke

Redoubt

Main Laager

Cattle Laager

Undi

Ngobamakosi

Rubbish Dump

To White Umvolsi River

in readiness for defence. This meant that the wagons would be made into a chain all around the inner perimeter behind the entrenchments and their poles lashed together so that no attacker could push them aside. It was also fairly standard practice to fill the gaps between them and between the wheels with thorn branches, and this was probably done, though there is no specific mention of the fact. Apart from continuing work on the palisade between the redoubt and the cattle kraal there was nothing else that required immediate attention. Everybody knew what to do as rehearsals had been carried out. Tents could be struck (to give a clear field of fire) and every man in position within seventy seconds from the last note of the 'Alert' bugle call.

Sentries were posted after the Inhlobana column had straggled back into camp and twice during the night Evelyn Wood personally made his round, visiting all posts. Then, before first light, Raaf set out with twenty men for Zungi, where he found the Zulu army resting and cooking. He was fortunate enough to pick up one of Uhamu's people whose friends had not been aware that he had changed sides. He had managed to mingle with them unsuspected, and had heard them say that an attack on Kambula would be made that day 'at about dinner time'. Raaf sent him back to give the news to the Colonel and stayed out with his patrol to watch for any signs of Zulu activity.

So sure was Wood of the reliability of this intelligence that he forbore from recalling two companies of the 13th Foot from fuel-gathering fatigues on Ngabaka Hawane. However, he ordered two subaltern officers to keep their horses saddled, ready to gallop off and bring in the companies if necessary.

During the morning the Uys family announced that they wanted no further part in the war now that their patriarch had been killed. They inspanned and departed, leaving behind only those Boers who had hired out their wagons to the British under contract.

At eleven o'clock Raaf reported that the Zulu army was on the move. So the two lieutenants were despatched, the companies came back to camp with the fuel they had collected, and arrived in time to have a hasty meal before taking up their allotted posts in the defences.

The redoubt garrison consisted of a company each from the 90th Light Infantry and the 13th Foot, with two guns under Lieutenant Nicholson. The west, north and east flanks of the main laager were manned by the 90th, while the 13th Foot held the southern perimeter. The mounted corps assembled in the centre, except for the mounted Basutos who stayed outside and harried the Zulu rear throughout the day. The remaining four guns under Major Tremlett were brought into action in the open on the ridge joining the main laager and the redoubt, able to fire north and south. The gun-teams were sent back into the safety of the main defences and Tremlett was told to keep firing until the last possible moment before making a dash back to the laager—about a hundred and ninety yards; the distance had been paced. Range cards had been made for both infantry and artillery showing the correct distance to every feature of the ground surrounding Kambula camp, so that no ammunition would be wasted through bad judging of distance.

It was two hours before dense masses of Zulus came in sight from the direction of Zungi, marching steadily in five columns. There had been all the time needed in Kambula; dinners were over; cattle had been rounded up and driven in. Reserve ammunition boxes had been put in strategic places, opened and ready for use. At a quarter past one o'clock tents were struck, the infantry manned the perimeter, the artillery detachments took up their posts.

As the Zulus drew nearer, it appeared at first that they were going to pass south of Kambula and go on to attack Utrecht, the contingency so greatly feared by the people of that town. They had pleaded with Wood to come back and protect them, so now he must have had some nasty moments. The Zulus did indeed say later that their instructions forbade them to attack a defended camp; Cetewayo had learned his lesson from Rorke's Drift. They were supposed instead to go on past Kambula, forcing the British to come out and fight them in the open. However, if this was the order, it was not obeyed. Half the Zulu regiments inclined away to the north forming the right claw of a pincer movement to surround the camp. In this horn were the Umcityu Regiment which had destroyed Weatherley's Border Horse, and the Makulusi from Inhlobana, also the Nokenke and Umbonambi Regiments. They halted and took up position out of range of the British artillery.

The remainder marched on steadily and confidently in well-disciplined ranks, the Ngobamakosi in the lead, followed by the Undi, until they wheeled north to face the southern flank of Kambula camp. British observers noted that a number of them carried both assegais, their traditional battle-weapon, and rifles.

Wood had no intention of leaving the initiative in the hands of the

Zulus. He sent Buller and Russell with a hundred mounted men out of the main laager to engage the northern horn. They rode forward until they were within rifle range of the enemy and then halted, dismounted and opened fire. As they had hoped, this was too much for Zulu discipline. Seeing this small body of white men almost within their grasp, several thousand warriors leaped to their feet and charged. But the horsemen at once remounted and galloped out of reach, stopping after a quarter of a mile and firing again. Several times they repeated this tactic, luring the Zulus nearer and nearer to the defences, until they were within easy range. Then the mounted corps withdrew quickly into the main laager, leaving a clear field of fire. Volley after volley from the 90th Light Infantry, salvo after salvo from the guns, crashed among the Zulu ranks, dealing death and mutilation in broad and ghastly swathes through the charging host. Ox-hide shields were useless protection against Martini-Henry bullets; the bravest fell, others hesitated. The impetus was lost, the regiments hesitated and came to a standstill three hundred yards from the entrenchments. They began to draw away; some broke and ran, then they all moved back to take cover among some rocky outcrop to the north-east. Their spirit was broken and they took no further aggressive part in the battle other than some sporadic rifle fire from a safe distance.

By a quarter past two attacks by the Undi and Ngobamakosi Regiments against the south and west of Kambula camp began to develop. From the British lines the ground fell away sharply into a dip through which in the rainy season ran small tributary streams to the White Umvolosi River, rising again to a rocky slope on the opposite side where the Zulus had halted and formed their battle-line. So between the two forces lay a stretch of dead ground in which the advancing regiments would be invisible from the defences, safe cover for assembly.

The leading elements of the Undi Regiment came proudly forward, disappeared into the valley, then came surging up the rocky slopes and pouring over the crest for the assault. They were met and checked by volleys from a company of the 13th Foot manning the south entrenchments of the cattle-laager. But it was discovered immediately that this company was unable to see to its right rear, and the Ngobamakosi Regiment took advantage of this to get close enough to the main laager to form up for a charge. At the same time some forty Zulu marksmen, hunters by trade, who had acquired good Martini-Henry rifles at Isandhlwana, established themselves in a mealie patch which had grown and flourished over the rubbish-dumping area south-west of Kambula.

Wood again took the offensive and sent out Major Hackett and two companies of the 90th to cross the open ground and drive the Ngobamakosi back into the dip, clearing the rear of the cattle-laager. Steadily the British infantry drove forward with fixed bayonets, led by Hackett, except when he was passed by an enthusiastic young subaltern, sword in hand, far ahead of his company! The Zulus directly facing the attack were pushed back and Hackett took up a holding position in the open.

Wood himself was occupied. He had taken a rifle from Private Fowler and was firing at a leader of the Ngobamakosi, who, with a red flag, was urging his companions to come up out of the ravine and assault the laager. He knew the range was two hundred and fifty yards; he aimed and fired. To continue the story in the Colonel's own words: 'Hit in the pit of the stomach, he fell over backwards: another leader at once took his place, cheering his comrades on. At him I was obliged to fire unpleasantly close to the line of our officers leading the counter-attack. I saw the bullet strike some few yards over the man's shoulder, and laying the carbine next time at the Zulu's feet, the bullet struck him on the breast-bone. As he reeled lifeless backwards, another leader seized and waved the flag, but he knelt only, though he continued to cheer. The fourth shot struck the ground just over his shoulder, and then, thinking the carbine was over-sighted, I aimed on the ground two yards short, and the fifth bullet struck him in the chest in the same place as his predecessor had been hit.' (They paced the distance later, and found it to be one hundred and ninety-five yards).

Hackett's companies soon came under such accurate fire from the rubbish-dump three hundred and fifty yards to their right flank and casualties began to mount to such a degree that the Colonel decided to call them back. During their withdrawal to the main laager, Hackett, who was controlling the operation, was severely wounded, a bullet passing straight through his head behind the eyes, putting an end to his military career. Lieutenant Bright fell mortally wounded.

Bereft of infantry support to the right-rear, the cattle-laager became untenable and its garrison company had to be withdrawn. Wood had never expected to be able to hold it for long in the face of sustained attack. One soldier of the 13th failed to hear the order and, running after the others, was shot from the rubbish area and was in great danger from four Zulus from the cattle-laager, now

3. The defence of Kambula.

occupied by the enemy, who were running out to finish him off. Wood was dashing to his assistance when he was forestalled by three officers, including Lysons, saying, 'Really it isn't your place to pick up single men!'

Now the assault became general. Several brave attacks were launched against the south flank of the redoubt which were as staunchly repulsed by the defenders. When Lieutenant Nicholson was mortally wounded, Major Vaughan of the Royal Artillery, the Director of Transport, took over his guns and fought them well.

In the sector of the main laager Zulus swarmed down the slope opposite in successive waves and skirmishers poured out of the ravine to within two hundred yards of the entrenchments. But the steady fire of the infantry in the laager and the redoubt and the coolness with which the guns outside were served by Major Tremlett, Lieutenants Bigge and Slade and their men, drove them back on each occasion with enormous loss. The British soldiers were completely confident, relaxed and comfortable; some even were smoking their pipes as they took aim and fired.

At last it was brought home to the Zulus that they would never succeed in crossing the last two hundred yards between themselves and the British and reaching the entrenchments alive. By half-past five the tempo of attack had slackened so evidently that Wood went over to the offensive. He sent two companies of the 13th Foot to recapture the cattle-laager and himself led a company of the 90th Light Infantry in support on their right. Both moves were successful, the 90th forcing their way forward up to the edge of the dip, from where they did great execution among the mass of retreating Zulus. Raaf, also, took out some men to deal with the sportsmen in the rubbish-dump to the Colonel's right.

All around Kambula the Zulus were on the verge of a general retreat and at this juncture Wood ordered out Buller and his mounted men. The Zulu retreat was immediately transformed into a rout. Their morale suddenly ceased to exist; the shock of defeat had robbed them of the power even to defend themselves. The Makulusi were too exhausted to use their firearms and Buller and his men, in gory revenge, killed them at will. Many simulated death, others hid in bushes or ant-bear holes. The slaughter was very great. The pursuers first shot the fugitives, then to save ammunition skewered them with assegais taken from the dead. For seven miles the pursuit continued until the survivors were reprieved by the fall of darkness.

The Zulus had started the day with an army of about twenty-three thousand men and probably lost roughly two thousand in the battle and during the retreat. Seven hundred and eighty-five corpses were buried within three hundred yards of the Kambula perimeter, but many others lay concealed in rock hollows. The stench was soon so bad that Wood had to shift camp yet again! Three hundred rifles lay abandoned on the battle-field, their owners either killed or put to flight.

Wood lost eighteen NCOs and men killed, while three officers and seven NCOs and men died of their wounds. Eight officers and fifty-seven NCOs and men were wounded but lived.

Eshowe was relieved. The column was attacked on the way by ten thousand Zulus while in laager at Ginginhlovo, but held them at bay until, as at Kambula, they wavered, were broken by mounted infantry and fled with losses of over a thousand. The relief took place on 3 April and the station was then evacuated and abandoned.

Reinforcements began to pour into South Africa during the first two weeks of April, and in the resulting reshuffle old designations were scrapped and the force was reformed into two divisions. The 1st Division operated in the southern coastal area of Zululand, while the 2nd Division was based on Utrecht and was to provide the column for a further and final march on Ulundi.

Butler arrived in Durban to take up his duties as Assistant Adjutant-General in charge of the base, working in a stifling little office, 'the corrugated iron roof of which in the semi-tropical climate of the coast made the temperature almost insupportable during the afternoons.' He lived, worked, ate and slept in that office, coping with incessant demands for remounts, medical stores, camp equipment, clothing, ammunition—and fifty other things!

Evelyn Wood stayed at Kambula, sending out mounted reconnaissance patrols. His shift of camp not only improved the atmosphere but made it possible to accommodate reinforcements of all arms who came marching or riding in to be under his command. The news that five companies of the 80th Foot were on their way to join him precipitated a crisis, and Buller hurried in to his Commander's office asking that his Regimental Sergeant-Major be given a special dispensation without delay. The Warrant-Officer was a deserter from the 80th and would have to be given a certificate condoning his offence or he would have to be off. This was speedily arranged, for Wood was not the man to be tied by any inconvenient regulations and the RSM continued to serve with credit until the end of the war.

Evelyn Wood had now received acting promotion. His command was to be given independent status and would be known as Brigadier-General Wood's Flying Column.

Lord Chelmsford came to visit him at the beginning of May, bringing the Prince Imperial of France who had been attached to the Headquarter Staff. The General and Prince Louis had a good look at the country, riding with Wood and Buller on several reconnoitring expeditions. Towards the end of the month Buller pushed forward to within six miles of the Ibabanango mountain, where he found an old trader's track which was said to lead to Ulundi. Relying on Buller, Lord Chelmsford selected this route for the advance and on 1st June Wood's Flying Column struck camp and marched south to join the 2nd Division. Riding in front to see the ground, Wood and Buller suddenly encountered one Captain Carey in full gallop, flying for his life, and learned from him of the probable death of the Prince Imperial, deserted by his escort and slain by Zulus. Buller's reaction may be quoted: 'By God, Sir, you deserve to be shot, and I hope you will be. I could shoot you myself!'

The combined forward movement began on 18 June, with Wood's Flying Column in the lead. In front of him rode Buller with his mounted men, scouting the route and gathering what information he could about the Zulu Army. He found that Cetewayo, cautious in defeat, had forbidden any more attacks on defended camps, or even laagers, and had ruled that offensive action should be taken only against columns on the move. Wood immediately initiated a drill for forming laagers from the line of march and found after some practice that it took only thirty-five minutes to complete the manoeuvre. As he expected invariably to receive longer notice than this of an impending attack, he was satisfied.

Throughout the advance there were occasional exchanges of messages and attempts at negotiation between Cetewayo and Lord Chelmsford. Most of these were merely efforts by the Zulu King to temporize and delay the British invasion but there was one benefit in that the General promised to stop burning Zulu kraals if his advance was unopposed. This was effective and, although large numbers of Zulus were seen, there was no fighting.

On 1 July Wood reached the White Umvolosi, near Ulundi, and next day the remainder of the force came up to laager beside him. Fields of fire were cleared and a small stone fort was constructed on rising ground close by. Nobody interfered with them, but next day Zulus on the far bank of the river kept up continuous sniping at watering parties. Lord Chelmsford took this to indicate that the period of negotiations was over and at midday he sent Buller and his men across the Umvolosi to drive the enemy skirmishers away. Buller chased them for nearly three miles, when he was ambushed and nearly surrounded by five thousand Zulus, but he managed to get back with only seven casualties. Apart from clearing the river bank, he had gained valuable information about the terrain between the Umvolosi and Ulundi, and useful information about the enemy forces.

That night the noise of Zulus singing in Ulundi and the neighbouring kraals could be heard, but no attack was made on the British entrenchments.

The fourth of July was battle-morning. A small garrison was left to defend the camp, while at a quarter to seven the greater part of Wood's Flying Column and the 2nd Division forded the river. Buller led the way, pushing through the thorn scrub unopposed until he reached open country at half-past seven. Lord Chelmsford then adopted a rectangular formation, the sides formed by infantry and artillery; the native contingent and administrative elements were in the centre. The 17th Lancers acted as rearguard.

Zulu regiments began to assemble as soon as the British force emerged from the scrub. It seems that they had not attacked before because they knew that Wood had a battle-drill and assumed that he would cut thorn-branches and use them to fill the gaps between his wagons and between their wheels. At least, by waiting for him to come into the open, they were spared that. Lord Chelmsford halted only a mile and a half due west of Ulundi and soon Buller's men were compelled to retire within the rectangle. The 17th Lancers followed them in, while Zulus massed on all sides.

The forward and greater part of the perimeter was held by Wood's Flying Column, consisting of his Kambula veterans: the 90th Light Infantry, and 13th Foot and the five companies of the 80th Foot who had joined the column before the advance—twenty-one companies in all. Behind them, manning the rear part of the rectangle, were twelve companies of the 2nd Division, including a wing of the 58th Foot, the Northamptonshire Regiment, whom we shall meet again in another battle. Interspersed among the infantry, and in the line with them, were twelve guns and two Gatlings.

The Zulus began to close in rather a loose, haphazard way,

a remarkable contrast to their steady, confident approach at Kambula. The British artillery opened fire, inflicting heavy loss, but the black warriors came on regardless and Lord Chelmsford's force was soon surrounded by a huge contracting circle. When this came within musketry range the engagement became general. The British were concentrated in a dense mass and would have suffered serious casualties if the enemy rifle-fire had been accurate; but the Zulus fired wildly as they tried to reach the column and use their assegais. However, the steady and well-sustained fire of the infantry, supported by the Gatlings and the artillery rendered this impossible, and at no time did Cetewayo's men succeed in approaching nearer than thirty yards. Finding themselves held on all sides, they began to falter and lose heart, exactly as they had at Kambula. Lord Chelmsford was watching carefully for this very thing and he now ordered out Colonel Drury-Lowe and his 17th Lancers. They rode out through an opening made for them in the rear face of the rectangle, formed line and charged the Zulu regiments confronting them. The enemy in their path turned and fled for safety towards the hills, pursued by the cavalry who proceeded to give abundant proof of the efficacy of the lance as a cavalry weapon! Following after them came Buller and his horsemen, chasing scattered parties of the broken regiments, whose flight had now became general.

It was half-past nine, the battle and the war were as good as over. By four o'clock Lord Chelmsford's force was back in camp behind the Umvolosi and the Zulus had dispersed to their kraals. Ulundi was in flames.

The Zulu army had been twenty thousand strong, and had lost one thousand five hundred men. British losses were twelve killed and seventy wounded.

[3]

Sir Garnet Wolseley met Lord Chelmsford on 15 July and took over command. His officers were also beginning to arrive; Brigadier-General Colley, his Chief of Staff, and Lieutenant-Colonel Baker Russell were already on their way up country. The General announced his terms to the Zulus, stressing that the war had been against Cetewayo personally, not against the Zulu people, and that there would be no question of annexation. However, the Zulu homeland would be partitioned into a number of independent chieftainships and the military system would be totally abolished.

It now remained to capture Cetewayo, who, unlike Kofi Karikari, had seen fit to attend his Army's last battle. It was also time to deal with Sekukuni, who had openly flaunted his support for the Zulu king. Evelyn Wood might be the man for both jobs; Sir Garnet intended to pay him a visit.

From the time that he had received news of Isandhlwana until after Ulundi Wood had taken his clothes off only to wash. Every night he had slept in uniform in case of a surprise attack, and every night he had twice visited his outposts. Pushing his way through the long grass, which was nearly always wet from rain or dew, he was invariably soaked to the waist, a condition which had a bad effect on his health. Sometimes he contracted neuralgia and went about with his face bound with a cloth. He had two attacks of fever. Despite all this, he did everything that he could to maintain morale among officers and men, though he would not allow any form of laziness or inefficiency. Mr Streatfield, an author in Wood's entourage, wrote: 'I feel grateful to him for many an arduous duty and weary march made light by the kindly tone in which the order was given that they should be done. . . . Let not the reader imagine that a duty slurred over, or ineffectually carried out would meet with but a gentle rebuke from Colonel Wood. Far from it. On duty he is to others as to himself, hard as adamant; and woe betide the careless, slovenly soldier who happens to serve under him.'

Wood and Buller had both been knighted for their exploits at Inhlobana and Kambula, and Buller had been awarded the Victoria Cross, recommended by Evelyn Wood. Wolseley wrote to say that the two of them had been the bright spots 'of this miserable war', with a warning that he was on his way to inspect. Wood then made the men wash out the coffee colour with which they had stained their white belts since January and apply pipe-clay once again. Next day they marched past the General with spotless equipment and rifles, wearing clean, if ragged, clothing.

Wood also took the precaution of disbanding his remaining five hundred irregulars, who had only contracted to serve under him personally. He still resented the fact that after the Ashanti campaign Sir Garnet had refused to authorize compensation to one of his irregulars who had lost an eye, on grounds of economy, and Wood had no intention of permitting any exploitation of his present followers. The General arrived to see the last of them disappearing into the distance, and was not best pleased.

Sir Garnet offered Wood command of the Sekukuni expedition, but Sir Evelyn pleaded ill-health and said that, if ordered to take the appointment, he would need at least two weeks' sea-voyage. The General then asked whether Buller could take on the task and Wood told him that Buller was in even worse condition, his legs covered with suppurating Natal sores and his hands so crippled with them as to affect his handwriting permanently.

So both officers were permitted to take ship for England. On arrival Wood took up the question of a grant of thirty-six thousand acres of government land for Piet Uys's sons. There were many difficulties, there was procrastination, but the grant was made after a direct approach by Sir Evelyn to Her Majesty Queen Victoria and her personal intervention.

[4]

The characteristics of the Zulu War differed in some respects from those of the Ashanti campaign. For one thing both sides could usually see each other. The British elements involved were very similar in equipment and training to those sent out to the Gold Coast. The Zulus were different from the Ashanti mainly in that they had better rifles and ammunition and could use them to better effect, though the great majority were still far from being marksmen. They preferred to close and use their assegais, unlike the Ashanti who relied almost entirely on their firearms.

Lord Chelmsford started the war with eighteen thousand officers and men and received a further ten thousand from England. The Zulu Army mustered forty thousand at the outset, so there was no great disparity in numbers.

The only major disaster of the war was at Isandhlwana, where nearly a thousand British were killed after slaying the same number of Zulus in a battle where they were outnumbered by a ratio of ten to one. Apart from this factor, the battle was lost because no defences had been prepared, because the infantry were deployed in line over far too broad a front and because the native contingent was placed at the point of greatest stress.

Things were quite different a few miles away at Rorke's Drift on the same day, when Lieutenants Bromhead and Chard, with a garrison of ninety effective infantrymen, and without artillery of any kind, repulsed continuous attacks by three thousand six hundred Zulus, killing at least four hundred of them for a loss of fifteen killed and ten wounded. They survived where other companies of the same regiment failed at Isandhlwana because they had prepared good defences. Then, when their native contingent deserted (except for Corporal Schiess who fought well) and the perimeter became too long to hold, they improvised an inner retrenchment from anything to hand, such as biscuit boxes. There were no natives in the line; there was no weak link; so they won.

Inhlobana is easy to summarize. The big Zulu army appeared earlier than anticipated from an unexpected direction. Buller's men were lucky to get away at all, but more of them would have been saved if it had not been for very sloppy passage of orders.

Evelyn Wood had made meticulous preparations to withstand attack at Kambula. Defences had been prepared; everything had been rehearsed; reserve ammunition had been distributed; only British infantry manned the perimeter. He had artillery and made good use of it, siting it in such a way that it did not obscure the field of fire from the main laager or the redoubt. The big step forward in this battle was that he sensed the Zulu hesitation, counter-attacked immediately and loosed the cavalry in pursuit. This was the first instance of a break in Zulu morale and the first major British victory of the war. It set the pattern for future operations.

Finally, Ulundi convinced the Zulus that the British were now undefeatable, even in the open. British infantry were massed around a small perimeter, the artillery were part of that line, every weapon could engage the enemy on its front. Ammunition was held centrally inside the rectangle, equidistant from everyone. At the crucial moment when the Zulus faltered, Lord Chelmsford broke them with his cavalry. The Zulus were sensible people; there were no more battles, no more resistance.

One wonders how it could be that Zulu morale could drop in a matter of minutes from a peak of high euphoria to rock bottom. Perhaps it was because they knew they were nearly invincible at assegai range in sufficient numbers. And the dreadful realization that they were not going to be able to cross a few hundred yards to use their spears disheartened them to such an extent that they gave up completely. Morale may not have been all that high in the beginning: Wood's Natal Zulus never had any doubt that he would win.

Seventy-six British officers and one thousand other ranks were killed in battle during the war. If the Isandhlwana losses were to be discounted, the figures would have been only twenty-four and two hundred and one respectively. The Official History lays little stress on disease, but there is a laconic statement that between 11 January and 15 October 1879 'Seventeen officers and three hundred and seventy men died of diseases consequent on the operations in Zululand.'

Thirty-seven officers and two hundred and six men were wounded in battle; ninety-nine officers and one thousand two hundred and eighty-six men were evacuated from the Command from causes incidental to the campaign.

So, including Isandhlwana, officer casualties from battle and disease were about the same; four hundred more men became casualties from illness than from operational reasons.

The irregular units had now to be disbanded and shipped back to their homes from Durban, where they caused some problems for Butler. He wrote that it would be difficult to imagine anything more irregular than the majority of the rank and file of these bodies. He picks out for special mention 'Shambuckers' Horse, Raafs' Rangers and the Buffalo Border Guards', saying that these various units of raffish swashbucklers now came to the port of embarkation to be paid their reckonings and to pay them again into innumerable public houses in Durban!

Nobody told the War Office of Evelyn Wood's little stratagem for getting command of his regiment. So he was not paid as a Commanding Officer. Whitehall also seem to have thought that there had been an omission in the recommendations for honours and awards, and the Glasite colonel sitting happily with his Hottentots five hundred miles behind the theatre of operations received suitable recognition for the achievements of his regiment.

The Boer War 1881

CHAPTER 6
Laing's Nek and Ingogo

[1]

Sir Garnet Wolseley had extracted himself from Cyprus by going on leave to England and taking most of his staff with him, leaving Greaves in charge. He had not been there long when things began to go badly in the Zulu War and it was decided that he should sail for the Cape and take over from Chelmsford. He left by special train from Paddington on 29 May, 1879, accompanied by Baker Russell, Brackenbury, Maurice and McCalmont; Colley was coming from India and would join him in South Africa.

The party arrived after the victory over the Zulus at Ulundi, when the war was virtually over. It remained to catch Cetewayo and everybody joined in the chase. McCalmont got close enough to capture the King's ceremonial war dress. Gifford, on foot in charge of the scouts again and helped by Maurice, nearly had him, but at the last moment Major Marter of the King's Dragoon Guards snatched Cetewayo from beneath their very noses. The carriage and dignity of the royal prisoner aroused the admiration of all who met him. He was escorted to the Cape by Major Poole and a great mutual liking developed between the two men.

Wolseley realized that much of the credit for the capture belonged to Gifford and, as a reward, gave him the despatches to take home, which he did, not entrusting them to the post office, and was given a grant of £300.

Zulu affairs soon ceased to present any difficulty. The chiefs realized that their numbers were of no avail against British weapons and discipline, even when in the open and not entrenched, so they decided to call it a day for the time being.

There was, however, still one more operation necessary to tidy things up. King Sekukuni, who ruled some mountainous territory a

127

hundred miles north-east of Pretoria had been a supporter of Cetewayo and was still raiding outside his own borders. He had earlier repulsed two Boer expeditions and in the previous year a British force had been unsuccessful.

Now was the opportunity to settle with him, so Sir Garnet assembled a force of British infantry, artillery, Colonial horse and Swazi fighting men. Colley was recalled almost immediately to India to help Lord Lytton with the second Afghan War, so Brackenbury took his place as Chief of Staff.

It was a one-month campaign. Wolseley was there and exercised over-all control, but he left all the tactical handling to Baker Russell and did not interfere. The final battle was to capture a rocky hill, a last stronghold where the enemy was holding out with great deter-mination. Baker Russell led the charge, Brackenbury at his side. McCalmont had been unleashed, pistol in hand, and killed his man. Maurice was in the thick of the fighting and was wounded in the shoulder, but not too seriously. It was all very successful and Sekukuni was captured and escorted by McCalmont to Pretoria.

Sir Garnet now hoped to get away, but he had to remain on as Governor until he could be relieved. At about this time he was much incensed by an article in the *Daily Telegraph* by the famous corre-spondent W. H. Russell criticizing the behaviour and discipline of the British soldiery. Russell had not been in the best of tempers during the campaign, as he had lost his false teeth when his horse dumped him in a stream; all the young officers had thought this hilariously funny. Wolseley blamed McCalmont for antagonizing the newsman, but the ADC indignantly denied the charge. He had indeed hidden an ape in the worthy gentleman's bed, thereby giving him the fright of his life, but 'not for one moment would I admit that this *beau geste* of mine could possibly be at the root of the mishap. It was not the sort of thing that any reasonable being would be disposed to take umbrage at'. However, when Brackenbury in his turn left for home, McCalmont took his place, so he must have been forgiven! And in May, 1880, they all went back to England, not waiting to hand over to Colley, who was to take Sir Garnet's place.

[2]

We must now review the history of the Transvaal, where Boer administration had been chaotic for years. Hoping to establish some form of order, and at the same time find someone who would be firm in his dealings with the British, the people had elected as their President a minister of the Dutch Reformed Church from Cape Colony. He was able, but a visionary rather than a man of affairs, and soon he was in trouble.

The Transvaal one pound note had degenerated to the value of one shilling, so the new President, the Reverend Thomas Burgers, levied taxes, which were never paid. The country was then still threatened by Zulus in the south and by Sekukuni in the north-east, so he enrolled soldiers, who would not fight. He found the Transvaal Boers' 'idea of liberty to be anarchy, their native policy to be slavery, and their Republic to be a sham'.

The British Government decided that the only hope of survival for the Transvaal would be to annex it—and did so. Needless to say this aroused great indignation among the Boers, whose fathers had trekked away from the south to avoid that very thing—British rule. They would not pay taxes to their own appointed government, certainly they would not pay them to anyone else. Rebellion smouldered. The British defeated the Zulus, then Sekukuni, so that there was no longer any threat from the natives. Sir Garnet, before his departure, called a meeting at which he announced that 'as long as the sun shone, the British flag would fly at Pretoria'.

For once Sir Garnet was wrong. The burden would be borne by Acting Major-General Sir George Colley, High Commissioner and General Officer Commanding South-East Africa, who arrived in Maritzburg to assume his post at the end of June, 1880.

The Liberal Party in opposition had championed the cause of independence for the Transvaal, leading the Boers to expect great things when they came into power, which they did in 1880. But the policies of political parties out of office can be rather different from those adopted by the same parties when they have to shoulder the responsibilities of Government. Lord Kimberley was Colonial Secretary again and his hope now was that the Boers would accept the situation. If he was going to avoid repealing the Act of Annexation, he needed to show the British public that the Transvaal was being administered with the consent of its people, not that it was being kept under subjection by force of arms. At the same time it must be seen to be paying its way, so taxes must be collected and costs reduced, particularly that of military occupation.

Colley had been briefed accordingly. As High Commissioner he was directly responsible for Natal and Zululand, and had to cope with problems regarding Griqualand, Bechuanaland and Delagoa Bay. But as far as the Transvaal was concerned he had to deal through the British Administrator in Pretoria, Colonel Sir Owen Lanyon of the 2nd West India Regiment, whom he had met during the Ashanti campaign.

After his arrival, Colley dealt first with his immediate responsibilities and then in August went north to see Lanyon. He found that the British occupation forces, consisting of a cavalry regiment, two infantry regiments and elements of a third, and a battery of artillery, were spread out over hundreds of miles, stationed in nine different places garrisoned by anything from nine hundred to eighty men. Living conditions for troops at the end of the line were primitive, leading to desertions on an alarming scale, and the cost of transporting such supplies and amenities as were made available to them was high. Something had to be done. There seemed no need for such a large body of troops, for Colley saw no evidence of serious unrest among the Boers. Besides, Lanyon assured him, even if they might be inwardly dissatisfied and rebellious, they would never dare resort to armed insurrection—they lacked the will. So Colley arranged for the King's Dragoon Guards to revert to the Home Establishment, and at the first intimation of the move a sergeant deserted to seek his fortune in the wide open spaces with £200 of troop and canteen money! In addition the General decided that four of the more remote infantry outposts were to be abandoned, enabling five companies to rejoin their parent regiments.

But Lanyon was quite wrong, for all was far from well. The Boers were determined that they were not going to pay taxes and that was that. They were no longer threatened by the Zulus or Sekukuni, so they could now afford to turn against the protecting Power that had eliminated these dangers. So when, in October, a farmer in the Potchefstroom district a hundred miles south-west of Pretoria refused to pay, and a British sheriff seized and tried to auction his wagon, a party of Boers forcibly took it back and restored it to the owner. There was so much disturbance about this that, as a temporary measure, two companies of infantry and a section of field guns were sent from Pretoria to support the local civil authority. At first Lanyon reported that he did not feel any anxiety, but by early December he was beginning to realize that, until the people had accepted that taxes must be paid, there would be trouble. Colley had to take Lanyon's advice, but his confidence was severely shaken by meeting a loyal Boer who had expressed his views with such earnest conviction that he consulted Sir Theophilus Shepstone, one of the great architects of the annexation, now retired, who laughed to scorn the idea of serious rebellion. However, within a week there were unmistakable signs of Boer mobilization, despite which Lanyon remained unperturbed and wrote to Colley to say, 'The Boers are incapable of any united action, and they are mortal cowards, so anything they may do will be but a spark in the pan'. Even when he heard that the Boers had proclaimed a Republic of the Transvaal on 13 December, he was sure that the idea could not have been premeditated, and that pressed men would not fight: 'I do not feel anxious, for I know that these people can not be united, nor can they stay in the field.' He had failed abysmally to appreciate the strength and high calibre of the Triumvirate elected to govern the new Republic: Kruger, the Vice-President; Joubert, the Commandant-General; and, in a lesser degree, Pretorius.

Colley was still in the process of concentrating the British forces in the Transvaal in pursuance of his cost-reduction plan. These moves would now give some essential tactical advantages, but they had not been completed and he was worried about some units still on the march. His forebodings were justified. On 20 December, 1880, two hundred and fifty officers and men of the Connaught Rangers were on their way from Lydenburg to Pretoria when they were accosted at Bronkhorst Spruit by a Boer carrying a white flag. He stopped Colonel Anstruther and told him that he could not proceed without authorization from the new Boer Republic. Anstruther replied he was under orders and must continue his journey, asking that the matter might be referred back to the local Boer commander, who turned out to be Joubert himself. But the Boers, very well concealed within two hundred yards of the road, opened fire almost immediately with deadly accuracy. The British were strung out along their line of march, completely unprepared for action—it was, after all, a peacetime move. The officers, on horseback, were easily distinguishable targets and were shot down in the first few minutes. After three-quarters of an hour all the officers and two-thirds of the NCOs and men were dead or wounded, and Anstruther, mortally wounded himself, signalled surrender. Total casualties were a hundred and twenty, while the Boers admitted only to one man killed and three wounded.

Colley had been forming a committee 'to give the Transvaal as free as a constitution as might be consistent with continued connection with the British Crown'. He now cancelled the project. British arms had suffered a disgrace and the Boers must be punished.

In the meantime the Boers laid siege to all British garrisons, including the small force at Potchefstroom which was not organized for a protracted defence.

Colley wrote to Kimberley: 'I think I was misled to take too sanguine a view of the Boer difficulty. The old Boer burgher organization has been most successfully applied. The men had all been regularly summoned as in the old commando days. No one can explain how so large an assemblage, drawn from every corner of the Transvaal, and from places which are nearly a month's wagon journey distant, are got together at such short notice.'

In fact Colley must have had some sort of an idea. He actually described the system in his account of a journey undertaken for Sir Garnet Wolseley five years earlier: 'Every field cornet of a district receives orders to attend at a certain place and time with so many men, provided with wagons, and supplies for so many days. He selects the men—unmarried men between twenty and thirty being taken first—and those who have not to serve personally are called on to furnish the material; one man provides a wagon and a span of oxen, another so many slaughter-cattle, another so many pounds of sugar, coffee, flour, according to their several means. When they meet, the field cornets assemble and elect their commandant.' He said in the same report that every man was well-mounted, well-armed, trained all his life to roughing it and shooting game, and with a strong sense of superiority over his adversary.

He was sad. He rather liked the Boers and had some sympathy with their cause. He had even dined with Joubert in his house, served by his host's son, with his wife, red-faced from cooking, watching from the kitchen. However, hostilities had been forced upon him, and he left for the theatre of operations on 10 January, 1881. He was in a position similar to that of Wolseley during the Ashanti campaign, both High Commissioner and General, and he too probably wanted to show everybody that the Civil Governor was also a fighting man.

Ten days later he had collected a small force, all the men who were available. These included the 3rd Battalion of the 60th King's Royal Rifle Corps under Lieutenant-Colonel Ashburnham, who had arrived recently from India to assume command. This officer had been present during the siege of Delhi and had just ridden with

General Sir Frederick Roberts from Kabul to Kandahar. He had large grey-ginger whiskers and was known affectionately as Old Bristles. Apart from that, he was a very gallant old gentleman who loved to hear the bullets fly. The battalion had taken part in the Zulu War, but many time-expired men had reverted to the Home Establishment and their replacements were recent arrivals and mostly very young. Another infantry regiment under Colley's command was the 2nd Battalion, the Northamptonshire Regiment (58th Foot). In all, there were twelve companies of infantry, from four different battalions.

There were also an artillery battery of six guns, raised by Captain Greer, and a Royal Navy detachment of a hundred and twenty sailors with two Gatling guns and three rocket launchers. But the mounted arm was very weak—an improvised squadron of mounted infantry under Major Brownlow of the King's Dragoon Guards. The first of the two troops contained a sprinkling of cavalrymen, but the second had been recruited from infantry volunteers and the Army Service Corps. Colley was aware that this was a pathetic little force and that he needed a full regiment of regular cavalry. Concerning Brownlow's squadron, an experienced officer had already commented that Tommy Atkins could not shoot well on foot and on horseback it took all he knew to keep his seat! Reinforcements were on the way from England and from India, and would reach Newcastle in three to four weeks, but Colley did not want to wait that long. He wanted to relieve the beleaguered garrisons in the Transvaal. Most of them were in fortified positions with supplies and food for two to three months, but not so the detachment of guns and infantry at Potchefstroom, who had food for only a month and were invested by an active Boer force. They had already lost two officers and twenty men from an original strength of a hundred and twenty all ranks. Colley wrote to Sir Garnet Wolseley to say, 'Unless I can in some way reduce the pressure on Potchefstroom before the middle of February, I am afraid that the garrison and its guns must fall into the Boers' hands. This is what has determined me to move on without awaiting further reinforcements.'

On 24 January Colley marched out from Newcastle into a South African summer which was at its very worst and wettest. All the dirt roads (and there were no others) had become quagmires, all the rivers were in flood; but he had only twenty-two miles to go before he expected to meet resistance. He was on the only reasonable road into the Transvaal, and across it, five or six miles inside Natal, lay a defensive position of great natural strength. The road ran south to north over a saddle known as Laing's Nek, flanked to the west by the great mountain Amajuba and to the east by another high plateau. Colley was under no illusions. He had already told his mentor, Wolseley, that he expected a stiff fight here and he doubted whether the force he was taking forward was sufficient. He had some memories of the ground, having passed over it six years earlier on the occasion when he had visited Joubert.

As anticipated, the Boers were on the ridge, so he stopped four miles short of it and established a partially-entrenched defended camp on Mount Prospect ridge, east of the road. There he began to plan his attack. He was determined to go ahead. He told his friends that some people see the difficulty of a thing and why it can not be done, while others see the way of overcoming difficulties and doing it. He claimed to belong to the latter category.

The Boer position was sited to block the road across Laing's Nek, reaching to the west into the lower slopes of Amajuba where the ground was so broken by deep ravines as to be practically unassailable, and to the east occupying the high plateau and a conical hill adjoining it at the south-east corner. Any attack on the centre would be taken in enfilade by fire from the higher ground on both sides, but there were possibilities in the east. If he could gain a foothold on the high plateau, it was quite possible that the Boers on the Nek might lose heart and withdraw back into the Transvaal. The problem was that he was outnumbered, and both he and the Boers knew it. They had an excellent intelligence organization all along the line of his march up from Newcastle and would have known exactly what he had at Mount Prospect; while they would have plenty of time to study his approach from camp and assess the size of his assault force. Colley's men had no specially designed uniforms, as Wolseley's soldiers had had in the Gold Coast, and their red coats and white helmets rendered them conspicuous for miles in daylight. Colley appreciated, therefore, that when he launched his attack the Boers would realize that he had not enough men to assault simultaneously elsewhere and would all come rushing to the point of main threat. So he must not delay, he must get his objective before reinforcements began to arrive. The conical hill was about fifteen hundred yards away from the main eastern plateau which would become known to posterity as Deane's Hill, connected to it by a saddle with fairly easy slopes and garrisoned by anything up to about two hundred Boers. He would have liked to take this hill first, but then his intentions would have been made obvious and the enemy would inevitably reinforce the high plateau with everything they had got.

So he made up his mind to send the Northamptonshire companies to capture the high plateau by working their way up a spur on which they would be invisible to the defenders on the top until the final stages of the climb, when they would be just below the crest. Moreover, the picquet on the conical hill would not be able to fire on them until they were nearly half-way up the spur—Colley, or some of his advisers, certainly knew all about dead ground! He would send Brownlow's squadron up a fairly easy slope to the saddle between the objective and the conical hill, to arrive just as the Northamptons were emerging from ground dead to the picquet. Their task would be either to charge the Boers on the hill or to keep their heads down and prevent them from interfering with the infantry. The decision was to be Brownlow's, depending on the situation at the time. The operation would take place in daylight and the only doubt in the enemy's mind would be that in the initial few minutes they would be unsure whether he meant to attack the east-centre or east of their defences.

On 28 January Colley left camp with nearly eight hundred infantry, Brownlow's squadron and some mounted police, six guns and eighty of the Naval Brigade with their rocket launchers. He left two hundred infantry and sailors with the two Gatling guns to guard Mount Prospect. The advance was made across open grassy ridges until within two thousand yards of the Boer position, where he deployed on a ridge and brought his guns into action. He sent a company of the 60th Rifles and the Naval Brigade with their rockets forward to his left, where they found a position quite close to the road, sheltered by a wall, from where they could support the attack and harass the Nek. This move may even for a time have served the dual purpose of making the enemy consider that there was going to be an attack on their centre. In reserve were three companies of the 60th Rifles and the mounted police.

Major Hingeston commanded the five companies of the Northamptons, but his duties had been usurped by Colonel Deane, Colley's Chief of Staff, who brought with him his brigade-major and orderly officer to join in the fun. Colley even permitted his ADC, Lieutenant Elwes, to go with them. It became a sort of staff jamboree, officers with little or no experience of active service

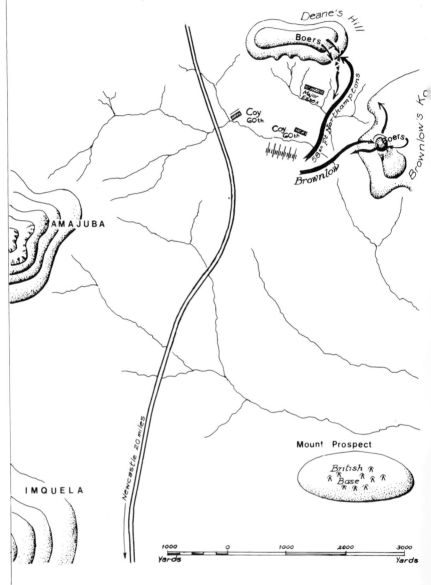

LAING'S NEK

28 January 1881

Deane's Hill

Boers

Boers

Major Essex

Coy 60th

Coy 60th

58th Ft Northamptons

Brownlow

Brownlow's Kop

AMAJUBA

Newcastle 20 miles

IMQUELA

Mount Prospect

British Base

1000   0   1000   2000   3000
Yards   Yards

thirsting for glory. They all rode their horses, so Hingeston and his officers, who probably knew better, thought that they had better do likewise. However, the artillery opened fire and off they went in great style.

At first all went well, the Northamptons moving up screened from any hostile rifle-fire. But Brownlow lost his bearings and went too far to the right until he came under fire from the conical hill. He had been given discretion and now he used it to charge at the enemy up a slope much steeper than had ever been intended. He did well; he and his leading troop, mostly true cavalrymen, reached the objective, though he lost his sergeant-major and a corporal during the charge. At the top he had his horse shot dead beneath him, but personally killed the Boer leader with his revolver, and the hill was won. The Boers had been given the order to retire and were running for their horses. But Brownlow's subaltern had also lost his horse. The squadron commander, the troop officer and the sergeant-major were dead—or so thought the follow-up troop of infantry on horseback and Army Service Corpsmen. Without a man being hit, they turned and galloped back down the hill. The reaction was immediate. Some Boer looked around and saw what was happening, shouted to his comrades and the whole picquet ran back and reoccupied the ridge, pouring fire into the remnants of the leading and once victorious troop. Brownlow made his way back down the hill with the survivors under a continuous fusillade and got back to his starting point after losing four men killed and thirteen wounded. He was disgusted with his command and would not join or talk to the men that day. They were quite useless for the rest of the battle. The spur to the right of and parallel to the Northamptons' advance which they should have occupied was now left clear and the Boers from the picquet, with their natural eye for a situation, remounted and rode forward to line its crest and fire on the infantry just as they were about to come out of dead ground and form up for the final assault.

It is not possible for everyone to keep in place while climbing a steep slope and the regiment was still in a certain amount of disorder when the Boers on the objective, far from remaining in the protection of their defences, came over the crest and took the battle to them. Colonel Deane and his three staff officers, all still on horseback, charged up the hill to try and restore the situation, but they were all shot dead. Hingeston was killed; all mounted officers were soon down; the men were still breathless after the climb and could not be rallied to charge with the bayonet. They began to fall back; there was nothing for it but to sound the retreat. As the Northamptons withdrew, more and more Boers came surging over the plateau to fire into their retreating backs. Colley switched all his artillery and rocket launchers to cover the retreat, but the fire seemed completely ineffective. The Boers' blood was up; they kept well dispersed and paid no attention to the shelling. The General also sent forward two companies of the 60th under Major Essex, one of his remaining staff officers, to occupy a line across a spur to the left of the Northamptons' retreat. Essex had his horse killed beneath him, but was unhurt and reached his lay-back position whence he succeeded in holding the Boers in check while the withdrawing infantry came away. He then in his turn brought his companies back through another company of the 60th deployed a few hundred yards in front of the guns. The Northamptonshire Regiment had fought admirably; they came back in perfect order and reformed behind the 60th Rifles. But they had lost a third of their strength, one hundred and sixty out of four hundred and eighty rank and file.

The artillery were out of rifle range and had no casualties. The Naval Brigade and the rocket-launchers, forward on the left with their comprany of the 60th, had such excellent cover behind their wall that the total casualties were but two men killed and one wounded. They got back without further loss.

Colley now withdrew his force back to Mount Prospect, where he set his men to improving the defences, as the roles had been reversed. It was now quite possible that he in his turn might be attacked by the Boers on Laing's Nek. He would have liked this to happen, hoping, he said, for a Kambula to follow his Inhlobana, but he had no such luck. There was a case for withdrawing all the way to Newcastle, there to await the imminent arrival of reinforcements, avoiding the need to keep open a line of communication which was now liable to be attacked and disrupted. But such action would have implied all the connotations of defeat. Telegraphs were humming and all England was already becoming aware of this sudden unexpected reverse suffered by British arms. A twenty-mile retreat in the face of a victorious rebel army would have had serious repercussions for the Home Government.

Colley had estimated that there were two thousand Boers astride the Nek. There were in fact only two hundred and fifty manning the defences when they saw the British force leaving camp. But there were another eight hundred six miles to the north and there was plenty of time to call them forward in support of the eastern half of the position.

Colley had taken a risk in attacking Laing's Nek. He knew that he had inferior numbers and realized that he needed at least a regiment of real cavalry. He was impelled by the need to relieve Potchefstroom before the garrison was forced to surrender. He hoped to demoralize the defenders with artillery fire, gain even a precarious foothold on his objective before Joubert could reinforce the threatened sector, and then exploit where possible, fighting a defensive battle until the Boers should lose heart and depart for home. Everything seems to have to have been based on 'hope' and Lanyon-inspired confidence in Boer low morale and even cowardice. Thinking back to the early stages of the Ashanti campaign, what a very different approach to that of Sir Garnet Wolseley, who gave complete priority to building up the morale of his own side and undermining that of Amanquatia's army. Every enterprise had to be certain of success; nothing was undertaken if there was the remotest possibility of a reverse. Colley payed no attention to this principle. He knew that the morale of his own men was high and must have been reasonably confident of winning the action or he would not have yielded to the importunities of his staff officers and his ADC, and let them get killed, instead of just having an exciting morning.

It was a close thing. The guns and rocket-launchers had nearly fulfilled their purpose. Joubert wrote to Kruger that 'the opportunity for the English artillery was too great and we suffered severely'. After a bombardment of twenty minutes the shelling was beginning to demoralize the defenders and twenty-four of the best men had been disabled; Joubert himself narrowly missed being hit by a splinter. However, they continued to hold the line.

Then came Brownlow's disaster. It did not matter that the Major got his time and route wrong; the conical hill was as good as his when the follow-up troop turned and ran. If they had not done so, letting the Boers recapture the hill, the Northamptons would surely have got on to their objective. It has been said in extenuation that the improvised troop could not be expected to control horses unused to rifle-fire. This is difficult to accept—they had got nearly all the way up, otherwise they would not have been able to see that Brownlow, his subaltern and sergeant-major had fallen. They could have ridden the rest of the way if they had had the determination. They were galloping after the leading troop and it is very unlikely that horses under such circumstances would turn away unless they had sensed the lack of confidence in their riders. However, Colley was a kindly man, he found excuses for everybody, nobody was court-martialled, nobody was shot. Buller's approach would have been of another kind! But his Frontier Light Horse troopers were now on the other side—or at best had stayed neutral.

There is a strange discrepancy between Colley's story of the action, which has been used as the basis for this account, and those of others who ought to have known the truth. They say nothing about Brownlow pistolling the enemy leader, but they do say that Sergeant-Major Lunny shot one man with his revolver and wounded another, jumping right over a small wall into the Boer trenches where he was killed.

If the Northamptons had got on to the high plateau, the Boers might indeed have withdrawn from the battlefield; the men in the picquet on the conical hill were in process of running to their horses when things went wrong from the British point of view. There will be more indications to consider at a later stage.

Colley paraded the troops and told them that they had all done very well. He promised the Northamptonshires that when he made his next assault on the position he would be sure to take them with him. He said that the failure was all his fault and took all the blame. The men were duly gratified and loved him dearly; it is conceivable, however, that some of the older soldiers may have begun to suspect that they had not got a very good General.

Boer morale had received a tremendous boost. It was the first time that they had met the British on anything like equal terms and they had advanced boldly down the hill to meet the attacking infantry, exposing themselves freely to artillery fire as they did so. They had established their valour; they had shown their mobility and inherent quick reaction to changing circumstances. They had been left in possession of the battlefield and Colley had to ask permission to recover his dead and wounded, another fillip to their new-found fine opinion of themselves. At the end of the day their own losses were fourteen killed and twenty wounded, of whom two died later. The source for figures of Boer casualties was the Rev Dr Merensky, Superintendent of the Berlin Mission to the Transvaal, who reluctantly acceded to Joubert's appeal to run his hospital. Merensky kept a nominal roll of those who passed through his hands, but there would have been many more with minor hurts, of a category which would have been included in British statistics, whose wounds were treated by their friends or by their wives. These hardy men would not have bothered to 'go sick'.

Colley was greatly distressed at nearly all his officers' mess companions having been killed. The only ones left were Captain Essex and his other ADC, Lieutenant Bruce Hamilton, his wife's favourite younger brother. He wrote to say that he would not next time delegate command, but would himself take the lead.

[3]

Soon came reports of Boers infiltrating into the area of the line of communication, and then on 7 February the mail party of mounted natives was attacked. Although they managed to break away and gallop back to Mount Prospect, Colley was not prepared to accept being cut off from all communication with Newcastle. As he was in any case expecting a convoy, he decided to go and meet it and escort it back to camp.

So next day he set out at eight o'clock with Colonel Ashburnham and two hundred and eighty men of the 60th Rifles and thirty-eight of Brownlow's mounted infantry. He took also four guns—there seemed still to be some impression that the Boers would be over-awed by the presence of artillery and would keep away. It was expected that everybody would be back in camp in time for tea!

The mounted infantry scouting ahead, they marched south eight miles to the Ingogo River, a shallow inoffensive flow which they crossed without any trouble, and made their way up a long graded slope. Then, as Brownlow's men reached the crest of the hill they sighted a strong skirmishing line of Boers astride the road, while on the slopes to the west, across a little stream, were four enemy support groups, each of fifty to sixty mounted men. The highest feature in the area was a small flat-topped hill known as Schuin's Hooghte on the east of the road. It had not yet been occupied by the Boers, so Colley deployed his infantry to hold it, company by company, as they came marching up from the Ingogo. He left two mountain guns and half a company of the 60th, including Lieutenant Marling, on the Mount Prospect side of the river to hold the ford, and sent a messenger back to call forward three companies of the Northamptonshires, first to assist the 60th secure the crossing, and then come forward to join him on the plateau.

The guns were in action almost immediately, one of the 9-pounders engaging a group of mounted Boers on the far side of the road only a thousand yards distant. An excellent target, but the first shell burst harmlessly too high in the air beyond them. The Boers, instead of galloping back out of range, charged forward down into the valley of the stream and up the other side, where they left their horses and began to work their way on foot up through the rocks and long grass towards the British position. Contemporary accounts conjecture that if only that first 9-pounder shell had struck home the whole reputation of artillery would have been re-established in Boer minds and the whole course of the battle, and even the campaign, might have been altered. But it did not. Nor was this very unusual—first rounds don't!

By a little before midday the action had become general and the Boers had surrounded all Schuin's Hooghte except for a small sector containing the road back to the river. They made expert use of rocks on the lower slopes of the hill to provide themselves with cover. The British were less fortunate; the four-acre plateau was mostly grassy, giving some concealment for men in the prone position but no protection. The Boers had their priorities clear and picked out the guns as special targets. Greer was killed early on, and the gun detachments suffered such heavy losses that they had to be reinforced by infantry volunteers, and then withdrawn to less vulnerable positions in the centre of the plateau. Horses received particular attention, and whole gun-teams lay dead in their traces. The mounted infantry, too, came in for their share of trouble. They were committed to one charge against Boers only a hundred and fifty yards away, but half of the horses were down after the first enemy volley. If nothing else, every Boer knew all about how to kill a charging animal. The survivors retreated as best they could and were too weak in numbers to charge again.

Nor did the enemy neglect the infantry; any one exposing himself was almost certainly hit. When they crawled close to the east edge of the plateau, the British left, Colley sent a staff officer, Captain MacGregor, to bring up the reserve company and plug the gap. Colonel Ashburnham had not been allowed to command his regiment, Colley having elected to do that, so he had stationed himself with the only one of his companies not yet committed to action on the perimeter. An old and experienced campaigner, he was becoming impatient with the performance of others less battle-wary than himself. Mr Carter, the press correspondent, quite bewildered by the turn of events and still mounted on his horse, was told in no uncertain terms to make himself scarce—he was attracting enemy bullets. When MacGregor arrived on horseback, Ashburnham expostulated that his company was the sole remaining reserve, and surely half a company would do? But MacGregor was adamant, quoting his General's authority, and led the whole company away to their new position on the left of the plateau. But he took them too far forward, to where the long grass gave very little concealment. An obvious target, the only mounted officer in the sector, he was killed. The company of the 6oth, despite the advantage bestowed by their black uniforms, wore the standard white helmets—wonderful marks for the Boer sharpshooters. Three hours later, of the sixty men who had come forward with MacGregor, only sixteen remained unwounded.

It was a pity about the white helmets. Marling wrote that while still in Newcastle he and his friends had realized the danger and had smeared their headgear with cow-dung, ant-bear heap mud and coffee-grounds to sully their pristine freshness. Presumably some scandalized senior officer had made them clean it all off again—Marling admitted that they had all come to smell rather oddly!

By three o'clock the firing began to die down as the Boers realized that they would not be able to take the hill that day. They started to collect their wounded and take them to an improvised dressing-station a mile away. Gradually they withdrew their riflemen from the east and south faces of the British position. But now Boer reinforcements who had made their way by a detour from Laing's Nek began to stream in, and the attack on Colley's west flank was renewed vigorously for a time. Then the newcomers too pulled back to the far side of the road to bivouac for the night. A party set off to close the river crossing, where Boers had already stopped ambulance wagons from Mount Prospect, threatening to fire on them if they advanced to the British position while the action was still in progress. But now at last the Northamptonshire companies arrived to reinforce Marling and the Boers went back to have their dinners. At five o'clock rain began to fall in torrents with the sudden rage of tropical storm, a great and merciful relief for the wounded who were short of water; but by seven it had stopped for a brief interlude. Darkness fell and all firing ceased. The officer commanding the Northamptons found that he was not going to reach the plateau in daylight, so withdrew to north of the

Ingogo, now turning into a deep, fast-rushing spate of muddy storm-water.

The Boers decided on no further action that night. Their Field-Commandant Smit tried to persuade them to attack, but the younger members of his force refused. They contended that all the horses had been killed, so the guns could not be got away; nor could the British cross the flooded Ingogo River in darkness. Colley and his men would still be on Schuin's Hooghte next day, so they would have a good night's rest and finish the business in the morning.

When it became dark enough to move without being shot, Colley counted his losses. He found that he had enough horses to pull both guns and one of the artillery wagons, so he decided to slip quietly away back to Mount Prospect. The wounded were collected together and made as comfortable as possible with such blankets and water-proof sheets as could be found. Then they were left in the care of the Church of England padre, the Rev Mr Ritchie, and Surgeon McGann. All ammunition was removed from the pouches of the dead and wounded to prevent it falling into the hands of the enemy, all rifles which could not be carried away were rendered unserviceable. Then, with the guns in the middle of a hollow square, Colley and the survivors of his force stealthily made their way down to the river. No lights showed, all orders were given in whispers, all officers were on foot. They expected at any minute to be attacked.

They reached the Ingogo. It was no longer one simple crossing: there were two channels a hundred yards apart, both raging torrents of shoulder-high swirling storm-water. Sections of men linked arms and struggled across, some even hanging on to the tail of Colley's horse. 'The passage of the flooded river in a wild night, alternately pelting rain with dazzling flashes and gleams of moonlight through rugged clouds was something to remain in one's memory,' he wrote. Eight men were swept away and drowned; it was past midnight when the last soldier was over. Of the force that had waded so cheerfully through the low water that carefree morning, only three in five came back, and only one out of every four horses. In the end the teams became too exhausted to drag the guns up the long upward gradient to Mount Prospect and the infantry, weary as they were, manned the wheels. Colley went ahead, reached camp at three in the morning and sent back relief horses. The rear of the column did not arrive until after day had broken.

A badly wounded officer of the 60th, Lieutenant Pixley, had managed to make his way over the river during daylight, shamming dead whenever he saw Boers, then taking refuge in a house on the far side. The column had been unable to pick him up and carry him back to camp. Captain Wilkinson, once ADC to Colley, and now Adjutant of the 60th Rifles, got his General's permission to take Pixley some brandy. Having done this, he decided to exceed his orders and ride across the river to help the wounded abandoned on Schuin's Hooghte. He succeeded in his self-imposed mission, but by the time that he started back the river had risen to a very dangerous height indeed. He was seized by the rushing maelstrom and drowned, though his pony scrambled ashore and made its way back to Newcastle. His body was not found until two weeks later.

In the morning Padre Ritchie went over to the Boer camp and saw both Joubert and Smit. They were quite ready to renew the attack with overwhelming forces, but agreed that first the wounded could be evacuated, insisting, however, that nothing else might go; the guns and 'Mr Colley' in particular must stay. Their astonishment and disappointment when they heard that 'Mr Colley' and all his fighting men had escaped and were probably already back in camp were almost amusing! For days after, they searched the Ingogo for the two guns, which they did not believe could have been got away over the flood. Smit had a lot to say to the young Boers who had refused to stay up and guard the river-crossing; and the Laing's Nek contingent went hurrying back to man their defences again. Seven hundred of them had come south to be in at the kill.

All the conventions of civilized war were observed. Colley offered Joubert medical assistance, which was refused with due gratitude. However, the Boers had ten wounded and asked for permission for their wagon-train to pass through the British lines on its way to the Transvaal, and this request was granted. Two of the wounded died on the way, bringing their total fatal casualties for the battle up to only ten. Colley wrote that Smit was an intelligent and fine man, courageous, humane in everything connected with the wounded, and gallant in action. Ritchie considered that Colley himself was brave as a lion, and as strong, too, while Lieutenant Bruce Hamilton, the General's ADC and brother-in-law, told him 'that he certainly would be killed if he did not sit down'. Hamilton also wrote to his sister to say that the 'admirable conduct of the troops was almost certainly due to their perfect confidence in him, and to his coolness and self-possession throughout the day'.

Boer morale was high. They feared nothing. They knew that they had only to get within rifle-range and their straight shooting would do the rest. They were never foolhardy and knew instinctively what to do as a body. Their speed of movement and loose, seemingly haphazard grouping made them very difficult targets for artillery, a fact which they had now realized. The Schuin's Hooghte action had been quite different from that at Laing's Nek. In the earlier encounter, Boer reactions might have been attributed to contingency planning; before the later action they had no more than an hour or so of warning about Colley's column having left camp, and they had reacted swiftly and with offensive dash.

The British had not been defeated; in fact the young recruits had done well. But they were beginning to realize that Boer precision in shooting, together with aptitude in manoeuvre and taking cover, gave the burghers a great advantage in battle. Colley made a morale-boosting speech to his troops, and gave full credit to everybody in his despatches, but he was becoming slightly despondent himself. He was deeply grieved that all his personal staff except for Hamilton had been killed. He felt that he was in some way a jinx, to put it in modern parlance. He was particularly worried lest his wife's favourite younger brother should be the next to fall. He had known from the beginning that he needed trained cavalry and now realized that his mounted infantry were no match for the enemy; they were worse riders and worse shots. The Ingogo engagement had shown that power in war depended not on the weapon only, but also on the man who used it. Boer skilled individual effort was opposing British collective drill and doing very well.

Some facts emerge from the battle. Though it did not actually happen, because the British force had slipped away, the Boers were undoubtedly going to assault the hill and try to take it by storm in the face of rifle and gun fire. Secondly, the deadly Boer musketry was neutralized by darkness, and the British could carry out a most hazardous move through night and tempest.

Sad to say, there were a number of officers who were under no illusions as to Colley's ability as a commander in battle. A senior officer with considerable service, probably Ashburnham, said after Ingogo that Colley ought not to be trusted with a corporal's guard on active service, and that battles were not won by making speeches and writing despatches. Marling, a young subaltern, had no doubts. He just felt it extraordinary that Colley had made such a mess of things, considering that he was one of the Wolseley group!

CHAPTER 7
Amajuba

[1]

The Whitehall Government had by this time decided that they must grant some form of redress to the burghers of the Transvaal—not going so far as to redeem their pre-election indications, but something. Besides, the Dutch population in South Africa was strongly on the side of the rebels. Some advocated a peaceful settlement without delay, others, from the Orange Free State and even from Cape Colony, were considering riding to join Joubert's Commando. President Brand, from the Orange Free State, was particularly alert to the dangers of large-scale insurrection and telegraphed to Lord Kimberley early in January urging him to waste no time in bringing about an agreement.

But Gladstone's Liberal Government had their fingers on the pulse of national feeling and they wanted to stay in office. A peace, yes—but one which would placate the British public's angry reaction to the peacetime ambush of the Connaught Rangers at Bronkerspruit. The best solution would be a cessation of hostilities after the Boers had ceased armed opposition to the forces of Her Majesty's Government, preferably when they had been chastened to some degree. Kimberley told Brand on 14 January that if the Transvaal Boers desisted he would appoint a Special Commission. Brand pleaded with him to make a clear and distinct proposal straightaway; Kimberley replied that he had nothing more to say. Pressed, he amplified this to state that, 'If armed opposition should at once cease, Her Majesty's Government would thereupon endeavour to form such a scheme as in their belief would satisfy all enlightened friends of the Transvaal community.'

Colley was told nothing about all this. Kimberley wanted to leave him 'unfettered' by political implications, so as to get on with

148

defeating the Boers, after which there could be a face-saving peace. However, on the very day that Brand had telegraphed Kimberley asking why he did not tell the Transvaal people what he meant by these vague promises, and reiterating that every moment was precious, Colley was repulsed by the Boers at Laing's Nek. Brand then appealed to Colley, who had to admit that he had not the remotest idea what was going on at the political end. When he did find out, he could only repeat Kimberley's platitudes to Brand. All he could get from Kimberley were warnings that if he did succeed in re-establishing British authority in the Transvaal, all questions of amnesties and settlements were to be referred back to the Home Government for approval. How very different from Kimberley's treatment of Wolseley in the Ashanti campaign, when that General was given full cooperation and a completely free hand, undisturbed by anything more than a few querulous restatements of policy!

Brand continued to do his best, and through his good offices Colley, at Mount Prospect, received a letter from Kruger, Vice-President of the Boer Provisional Government in the Transvaal, saying that he would submit to a Royal Commission of Inquiry. If one was established, he would permit British troops in the Transvaal to depart unhindered from his country, while he in turn would withdraw from Natal. Otherwise he and his men would fight to the last for their freedom. Colley reported the contents of the letter to Whitehall and then, at last, was given some idea of Government intentions. When he found that these entailed splitting the Transvaal into small communities, some Boer and some under British rule, he disagreed so strongly that he hinted at the possibility of resignation. Eventually he received direct orders to inform Kruger that: 'If the Boers will desist from armed opposition we shall be quite ready to appoint Commissioners with extreme powers'. If the proposal was accepted, Colley was authorized to agree to a suspension of hostilities. The General passed this on to enemy headquarters on Laing's Nek for Kruger's attention, asking for a reply in forty-eight hours.

In the meantime, substantial British reinforcements were on the way. Colonel Sir Evelyn Wood, who was senior to Colley by one place in the Army List, but who had willingly consented to serve under him, had arrived in Newcastle; so had two regiments of infantry and two squadrons of the 15th Hussars. A similar force, which would be commanded in action by Sir Evelyn Wood, was on the march up-country from Durban. Two more cavalry regiments and fifteen hundred infantry were embarking from England and India to join in the fray. Colley went to Newcastle to meet Wood and explained his plan of campaign, before setting off again for Mount Prospect with a squadron of the 15th Hussars and the 92nd Regiment of Foot (The Gordon Highlanders).

Colley did not enjoy the war in which he was involved, for he had a certain liking and respect for the Boers; he wanted them to receive a fair deal. But there were other considerations in his mind. He wanted to avenge his defeats and this was made quite clear in a letter to Sir Garnet Wolseley dated 21 February, after his return to Mount Prospect: 'I am getting together a force which should command success, but the Home Government seem so anxious to terminate the conflict that I am daily expecting to find ourselves negotiating with the Triumvirate as the acknowledged rulers of a victorious people; in which case my failure at Laing's Nek will have inflicted a deep and permanent injury on the British name and power in South Africa which it is not pleasant to contemplate.'

Back in camp he saw immediately that the Boers were working hard at improving their defences. There were a great many more trenches and stone breastworks than there had been before he had gone away. The enemy were fully aware that British reinforcements were arriving and they were both strengthening and extending their line. The east end was much more strongly held and fortified than it had been when Deane and Brownlow had attacked it, and the same arguments as before were applied against assaults on the centre or against the foothills of Amajuba to the west. But the Boers had not yet any force in permanent occupation of the top of the mountain, only a picquet which withdrew to the laagers at sunset and went up again at sunrise next morning.

The General discussed this with Lieutenant-Colonel Stewart, who had joined him in Newcastle to become Chief of Staff, and they agreed that it might be possible to seize the unoccupied plateau of Amajuba by a concealed night approach. If they succeeded in doing so and the Boers found themselves overlooked by a British force on the mountain, there was a fair chance that they might withdraw from Laing's Nek; at the worst, possession of the tableland would be a great tactical advantage in the event of an attack on the Boer west or centre.

The two officers studied the ground in detail. Amajuba was two thousand five hundred feet higher than Mount Prospect, looming steeply up from a broad base, culminating in a final precipitous ascent to the edge of the plateau. Clumps of scrub and bushes grew on narrow ledges between the steeper slopes, with a few outcrops of rock interspersed. The top was four miles distant from Mount Prospect in a straight line, but an easier climb, making use of a saddle between Amajuba and Imquela, would add only two more miles to the approach march. From previous reconnaissance they already knew the nature of the slopes on the west and south-west, and the south was obvious from camp. Colley had vague recollections of the north and north-east, but that was not enough; he wanted to refresh his memory. So on 24 February he started by shelling the Boer positions on Deane's Hill and Brownlow's Kopje. Then he took a mounted reconnaissance in force across the Buffalo River as far as some high ground flanking the Boers until he could observe the far side of Amajuba. This operation was designed also to give the impression that his intention was to attack in the same sector as before, and to make doubly sure of this he sent out infantry companies next day and the day after to cover the same area. His ADC, Bruce Hamilton, accompanied the second of these patrols, although he was not in very good health at the time; his General knew this, but sent him all the same.

All this while nobody except Stewart knew what was in the General's mind until after the mounted reconnaissance on the 24th, when Colley briefed Major Fraser, his new AMG and Head of Intelligence. Surreptitiously they studied Amajuba through their field-glasses, but not so cunningly as to deceive entirely Mr Carter, who commented that 'one might have thought that they had never seen it before'. His intuition had told him that something unusual was afoot, but he did not guess what it was! A local native who knew the mountain well was brought in for questioning and had great difficulty in answering questions without pointing with his finger, which might have given the plans away, but no suspicions were aroused.

Colley had need for speed. He was quite sure that the Boers would eventually get round to occupying and fortifying Amajuba. So to make them think that there was no great urgency, he called up · his second reserve infantry battalion as far as the Ingogo and then sent it back again to Newcastle. He hoped by this to persuade the enemy that he was still worried about raids on his line of communication. Despite his sense of urgency, however, he could not really begin operations until forty-eight hours had elapsed after the Boers had acknowledged his peace offer. Their reply had been prompt, but it said that the whole matter had been referred to Kruger who had gone away. No answer would be possible for at least four days, possibly longer.

No reply had been received by the evening of 26 February, well after the stipulated time limit had expired. Colley and Stewart sat inside their tents, peering covertly through the flaps with their binoculars until at last they were rewarded by seeing the Boer day-picquet stand up and start to make their way back to their laagers for supper.

It had been a pleasant, sunny afternoon. The band had played and everybody seemed content. The infantry company had returned from reconnaissance without incident, but young Bruce Hamilton had felt so much off-colour that he had gone to bed and was soon fast asleep. At half-past six Colley and the remainder of his staff sat down to dinner. The General was cheerful; his mind was made up; he had finalized his plan. Wolseley-like, he had told no one except the essential few. He was going to secure Amajuba under cover of darkness, dropping off strong detachments along the line of approach, just as he had done between Egginassie and Amoaful, to keep open his line of supply between the mountain and Mount Prospect camp. He would defend the plateau for three days, six if necessary, until the second infantry battalion and the rest of the 15th Hussars could come up from Newcastle.

He was going to command the force himself. There would be no regimental lieutenant-colonel to question his decisions, not one would he permit to accompany him. His second-in-command would be Commander Romilly of the Royal Navy detachment. He had written earlier to his wife to tell her that he was taking the field force under his personal control—he still reproached himself because Deane had been killed and he was putting no one else in his place.

His expedition was going to be a complete dog's breakfast, a mixture of everything. There would be three companies of the 92nd Foot (The Gordon Highlanders), two companies of the 58th Foot (The Northamptonshire Regiment), two companies of the 60th King's Royal Rifles Corps and sixty-four sailors of the Naval Brigade. Another company of the 60th would follow up, bringing reserve ammunition to the base of Amajuba. Every man would carry seventy rounds of ammunition and each company would bring six picks and four shovels. The total strength was five hundred and fifty-four rifles.

Orders were issued at eight o'clock and passed quietly round the camp. The Boers on Laing's Nek would have heard 'Lights Out' sounded as usual and seen all the lanterns in tents extinguished; they slept in peace, sure of another peaceful night.

At half-past eight the Amajuba Force formed up west of the camp outside the perimeter. There was no moon, but clear starlight. Morale was high. Before they marched off, Colley bade farewell to the Rev. Ritchie and asked him to see that Bruce Hamilton was not awakened. He had never intended taking his ADC, lest he too, like everybody else connected with himself, should be killed.

They moved off at ten o'clock, Fraser and some Kaffir guides in the lead, followed by the 58th, the 60th, the 92nd Highlanders and lastly the Naval Brigade. They were on known ground over which mounted scouts had patrolled daily towards the lower slopes of Imquela, the big mountain south-west of Amajuba. After an hour they came to a point where a Kaffir track turned off at right-angles towards the north and here were left the two 60th Rifles companies to make a secure base. The ground was fairly level, but the path was narrow and the men had to form single file, spread out in one long line through the darkness. Half a mile of this brought them to the saddle between Imquela and Amajuba, a climb of twelve hundred feet above Mount Prospect and with much the same to go before reaching the objective. Now the going was better; there was more room and the advance continued with the men marching four abreast. At midnight there was a halt. Still nobody had been told of the destination! This may have been a contributory reason why the rear of the column lost its way; an hour was lost before the Zulu scouts could find them and bring them on. Here the third company of the 92nd was left, with orders to prepare a defended locality and cover for the officers' chargers, which could go no further because of the broken terrain. At one o'clock in the morning the remaining four companies of infantry and the Naval Brigade were on their way once more. Soon they reached the foot of Amajuba and began climbing up a rough path on the mountain's steep south-west flank, pushing through clumps of thorny brushwood, stumbling over rocks and boulders until the leading files came to the last spur before the summit. Only two hundred feet to go, up a rise that was smooth, but steeper than anything yet met. Grasping at tussocks, on their hands and knees, the men struggled and scrambled up and up, until the first of them reached the top. It was twenty minutes to four, still dark. Fraser took with him some of the 58th to take over the whole plateau, while Stewart went back down to guide the men up the last bit of the ascent. Colley stayed at the top to meet them as they arrived, and as they appeared over the crest in ones and twos, regiments all intermingled after the difficulties of the climb, he gave them a few minutes' rest before despatching them to their company areas. It was an hour before everybody was on the plateau. There had been some horrific, clattering falls, but total casualties were only two sprained ankles, the men concerned being helped back to Captain Robertson's company of the 92nd Highlanders at the foot of the mountain. Quietly Colley sent the men on their way after they had recovered their breath and they went willingly. 'No bullying or driving ever came from Sir George Colley,' reported one of the newspaper men.

They were in time; it was still dark. Then, as they peered over the northern edge of Amajuba, the gloom below was illuminated by hundreds of pinpoints of light. It was the Boer reveille and in every tent and wagon lanterns had been lit.

It was Sunday morning of 27 February.

[2]

As, in the half-light of pre-dawn, it gradually became possible to see more than a few yards, Colley and his staff made a thorough examination of the plateau. The tableland of Amajuba was a saucer-like depression of about ten acres, varying in depth from ten to forty feet. It was surrounded by a ring of rocks, but this limestone rampart was not the true edge of the mountain-top, which reached out beyond it for some yards before falling sharply away towards the downward slopes. There were some small eminences on the inner perimeter and two larger isolated spurs. One was in the south; another, with a rounded top slightly lower than the edge of the plateau, reached out a hundred yards or so to the north-west. The whole of Amajuba was a splendid natural fortress, there being only two or three paths whereby it was possible to clamber to the summit.

Colley deployed his troops along the outer crest of the mountain, with particular attention to the north and east, the direction of the Boer camps. Lieutenant Ian Hamilton's company of the 92nd Highlanders was allotted this part of the perimeter, a stretch of about four to five hundred yards, which meant that the men were usually deployed twelve paces apart. The Northamptons had the east and south faces to defend, a three hundred and fifty-yard front;

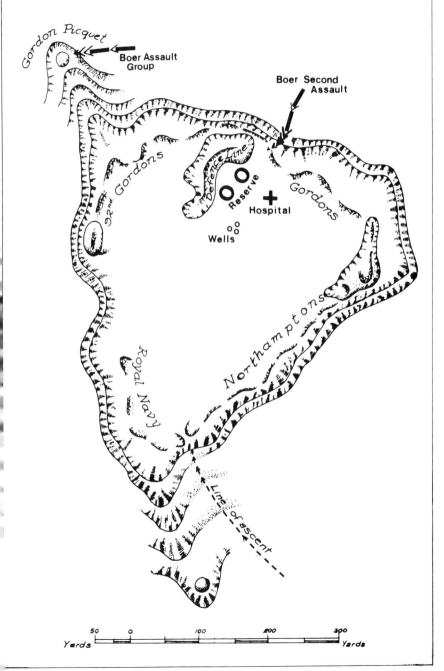

AMAJUBA

27 February 1881

Gordon Picquet

Boer Assault Group

Boer Second Assault

Defence Line

92nd Gordons

Reserve

Hospital

Gordons

Wells

Royal Navy

Northamptons

Line of descent

Yards   50   0   100   200   300   Yards

while the Naval Brigade manned the south-west and guarded the spur up which the column had so laboriously made its way in the darkness. The General established his headquarters and his reserve of about two-company strength behind a ridge in the north centre of the saucer.

Colley knew that his presence would be discovered as soon as the Boer daily patrol came up at sunrise, but he intended to stay hidden as long as possible and gave orders that there was to be no firing without orders. But the men felt so secure that they began to consider themselves immune to all the normal customs and disciplines of the Service. It was all becoming a sort of picnic; the dreaded regimental colonels were back at Mount Prospect; the General was a nice chap and so they did as they liked. Some showed themselves quite openly on the skyline, gazing at the Boer camps and defences, as every detail became clearly defined by the black shadows cast by the rising sun. It was not until about a quarter to six, when Lieutenant Lucy of the Northamptons saw fit to borrow a rifle and take a pot-shot at the Boer patrol, now on its way, that the enemy became aware of what had happened.

The result was immediate; there was frantic activity in the laagers. Oxen were yoked, wagons started to stream away to the north, while in an incredibly short space of time the plain was dotted with horsemen forming themselves into cohesion and moving towards the lower slopes of Amajuba. Colley thought these men were making a screen behind which the main enemy force hoped to retire to the Transvaal. In fact the Boers had held a quick council of war, during which it became apparent that some wanted to abandon the position but others, men who had already fought the British with success, and were full of confidence in themselves, volunteered to assault the mountain. Joubert and Smit decided to let the assault parties start up the slopes and sent numbers of sharp-shooters to give them covering fire. These latter groups occupied positions among the many rocky outcrops on the lower parts of Amajuba and kept up a continuous long-range fire on the crest. Meanwhile, patrols were sent at all speed to check the Newcastle road and see if British reinforcements were on their way to join in the battle. Dependent on this, a decision would be made whether or not to assail the summit.

Colley started to organize his defences, but with no degree of urgency. 'We could stay here for ever,' he said to Stewart. He set up his hospital south of his headquarters and started to dig for water close by. They found a plentiful supply three feet down, which was most satisfactory—humping water-containers from Mount Prospect to the summit would have been a great nuisance. He decided to build three stone redoubts, one for each regiment and one for the Naval Brigade, to be occupied at night in case of a surprise attack. But there was no hurry to begin their construction: no point in messing the men about until they had fully recovered from their night march and the steep climb. The same feeling pervaded the whole tableland. The soldiers were told to make themselves stone shelters where they lay and did so in the most perfunctory manner. The officers seemed to feel that it was a quite unnecessary fatigue to impose on tired men. Mr Carter had been at Schuin's Hooghte and knew that 'anything more trumpery or miserable as a protection against a bullet could not be conceived'. When he remonstrated, the invariable answer was, 'Oh, it will be all right, sir; it's good enough for what we shall want up here', or words to that effect! No orders were given to start digging. Even if anyone had wanted to entrench at that stage, authority would have to be obtained from the Force Commander; it was not yet axiomatic in the British Army.

By seven o'clock Boer riflemen had deployed sufficiently far up the mountain to harass the top. Their fire was ineffective in that nobody up there was hit during the next three hours, but it had some morale effect. The men on the twelve hundred yard outer perimeter had to keep down. They did not want to be hit, even by a spent bullet, and there was just the odd sniper who had crawled close enough to be potentially lethal. The British infantry replied at intervals, standing up to see their targets, careful to conserve ammunition. It was warm and comfortable in the reserve area, where the troops ate some of their rations for breakfast, then took their naps lying peacefully on the long grass in the friendly sunlight. Some of them probably divested themselves of their equipment to be more comfortable.

Colley had started to send messages. A signaller had made contact by flag with Mount Prospect and from there the telegraph to Newcastle was in working order. At eight o'clock he informed Mr Childers, the Secretary of State for War, and Evelyn Wood, that he was in possession of Amajuba. Three-quarters of an hour later he sent orders for the infantry and cavalry in Newcastle to march that afternoon and try to reach Mount Prospect next morning. At half past nine Stewart signalled that the only casualty so far was one man hit in the foot and that the Boers were wasting their ammunition.

But Smit's patrols had found out that there were no British reinforcements on the way from Newcastle. He had assessed that there was only a small force holding Amajuba and had decided to storm the summit. He formed two assault groups of picked men, proved in battle and deadly shots even by Boer standards. These two detachments were to make their ways up the northern slopes and assemble as close as possible below the rim of the plateau, there to await orders before launching the attack. The route up the slopes to their forming-up points was almost entirely over dead ground where their climb could not be observed by the defenders. There was only one stretch where they would be in view and it abounded in rocks and scrub which would provide plenty of cover. So much for Colley's reconnaissance from a distance of Amajuba's northern face! Whenever a group of Boers had to cross the open space, covering fire was increased in intensity to keep British heads down until the assault troops were in safety again.

At eleven o'clock Colley went to visit the Naval Brigade and talk to Commander Romilly. He wanted to discuss the redoubt that he wanted to build in that area and he also had ideas about handing over to the Commander and going back to camp, where he could start planning an attack on the Boer main position. As he and his staff stood conversing, bullets from an enemy marksman began to whistle past them. They amused themselves by guessing the range and concluded that the sniper was a good nine hundred yards away. Next moment Romilly fell, mortally wounded in the body. He was carried away to the hospital where he died in a few minutes. Careless exposure, designed to show a magnificent disregard for danger and to keep the sailors' morale high, had ended by having exactly the opposite effect. Colley had lost another officer. However, there was still no cause for alarm. He signalled to Childers: 'Boers still firing heavily on hill, but have broken up laager and have begun to move away.'

Midday came and there was little change. Colley still thought that the men were too exhausted for systematic entrenchment, although Major Hay, second-in-command of the 92nd Highlanders and senior officer of the regiment on Amajuba, and several others had asked for permission to dig. The General maintained that nothing substantial was required for protection against rifle-fire.

Lieutenant Ian Hamilton had seen the Boer assault party making its way across the open ground below him—more and more of them. His men stood up to fire on them, but without much luck.

Hamilton saw only three Boers hit throughout the day. Several times he went back to headquarters to report this, running the gauntlet of enemy fire to do so, but nobody was very interested. Eventually he was given a few men of the Northamptons to fill some of the gaps in his line.

Reference has already been made to a spur crowned by a small round bump, or kopje, lower than the rim of Amajuba and about seventy yards north-west of it. This kopje was vital to the defence in that from it any attacks up the two possible routes to the top on the northern flank could be taken in enfilade and easily repulsed. Colley was aware of this and had garrisoned it with a picquet of the 92nd Highlanders; there were possibly a few of the Northamptons left there after the initial posting of sentries before dawn; nonetheless it was to be named Gordon Picquet for posterity. It is likely that there were less than twenty men all told. A Boer assault group had gradually collected together only eighty yards below, in dead ground where they were invisible from above. Conversely, they themselves were unable to see the British on the kopje. But they had been able to do so when crossing the open ground close beneath; so, when orders came confirming that Amajuba was to be captured, they slid carefully backwards downhill into the scrub to positions from where they would be able to see; then in a concerted movement all rose to their feet and sent a crashing volley of sixty bullets into the Highlanders, now clearly visible and easy short-range targets. Nearly every man in the picquet was in that instant either killed or wounded. The few survivors, mentally shattered by the sudden shock of death and maiming all around them, deserted their post—which was now in any case quite untenable—and ran for safety back over the crest. The Boers made all speed to occupy the abandoned kopje, and quickly found themselves covered vantage points from which they could engage the rim.

Colley, who was at long last in process of finalizing arrangements for his three redoubts, decided to send some of his reserve to oppose any Boer penetration from the kopje. He had a mixed force of about a hundred and twenty men under his personal control and he ordered most of them forward. The men were half-asleep; some took time to collect their equipment; there were even some, according to reports, who were reluctant to move out from the security of the reserve area. Eventually they departed north-west towards the threatened area two hundred yards away; but the Boers had used the time to consolidate Gordon Picquet and now they opened fire at the Highlanders sparsely deployed along the perimeter opposite them. Ian Hamilton says, 'A space of ground sixty yards long and held by five or six of my men was *covered* with bullets. Two or three of the poor fellows were killed at once, one or two ran back.' As they went they met the reserve coming up, causing some momentary confusion. Then the newcomers deployed some distance short of the rim and opened a heavy fire, though Hamilton did not think they could see what they were firing at. But there was no respite. The Boers on the kopje turned their attention to the reserve with a murderous fusillade. Referring again to Ian Hamilton, the best eye-witness: 'About sixteen of the reserve were knocked over in no time; being unable to stand it any longer, they got up and retreated. . . . We very soon had to beat a retreat ourselves as in an incredibly short space of time the gap in our line, lately held by the reserve, was filled with Boers who advanced firing from the shoulder. Very few of our men got back to the second line. As I turned to run I saw the Boers swarming out of the ravine from which they had been for so long annoying us, and and coming straight up at us.' Officers with the reserve tried to rally the men, but their efforts were useless. There had begun a general rearward movement; then everybody broke and ran back down into the basin. Some headed straight on through the reserve ridge, set on going all the way to Mount Prospect, but others stopped and made some effort to make a delaying position.

But when Hamilton had to come back, the whole of the northern perimeter fell into enemy hands. Not only were the Gordon Picquet commando over the rim and advancing though the scrub and long grass, firing as they came, but another assault group was up and over in the right rear of the reserve position. All marksmen, they fired not only on to the reserve from its right rear, but also right across the basin into the unprotected backs of the infantry and sailors holding the south and west perimeter, giving the defenders to think that the enemy had gained the crest on all sides. Some of the men began to leave their posts and come back to the centre of the plateau, thinking it would be safer there, but there was no room for them in the reserve position. They stood in a disorganized clump and no one could sort the jumble of two regiments and the Naval Brigade into their component groupings.

The sixty Boers from the picquet now came forward (they had not lost a single man), demonstrating that skill in fire and movement which they had never been taught but which came quite naturally to them. There was more dead ground between the rim and the British last position on the central ridge and they made full use of it. They were out of sight until within forty yards of the British and, even then, there was plenty of cover in the grass and scrub. 'Nothing was to be seen of the enemy except the muzzles of rifles appearing and disappearing, the incessant spurting of smoke, and now and then a head showing for a moment over the grassy level.' The fire was as intense as it was accurate; men fell on all sides. More and more Boers were now behind them as well. It was too much; it was certain death. The men broke and ran. There was nothing for it, officers had to go too: even Major Hay saw there was no point in staying with no men to command. In a moment the Boers were on the central ridge pouring bullets into them as they fled, every man for himself. Those who were so fortunate as to reach the southern rim went at literally breakneck speed down the spur, now under fire from the Boer parties on the lower slopes, who made good practice until they were out of range.

Colley made no attempt to save himself. He stayed on the reserve ridge, revolver in hand, until a young Boer shot him at twenty yards range. Hit in the head, he was killed instantly. Stewart was wounded in the leg, but managed somehow to hide himself for a day and a half until he was found and made prisoner.

It is fair to say that some British soldiers on Amajuba fought very nearly until the last. Lieutenant MacDonald with twenty Highlanders stayed engaging the enemy until only he and one other man remained unwounded.

As happens so often when a military force gives way, more men were killed and wounded during the retreat than on top of the mountain. Some were shot in the back as they ran for the southern path down the slopes. Those who got over fled, falling, sliding down the steep approach. A Highlander put his knee out of joint; a friend put it back for him. A sailor claimed to have taken five hours to climb Amajuba, but to have touched ground only five times during his headlong descent! Fraser had found his retreat cut off and went straight over the southern precipice, but survived. As they slid and scrambled downhill, Boers on all sides shot at the fugitives, while the victors of the tableland crowded the southern rim of Amajuba to kill them from the rear. It was slaughter, but many got away or hid until dark and then made their way back to safety.

The Gold-Coast-style strong picquets along the line of communcation between Amajuba and Mount Prospect had been able to

4. Amajuba from above Prospect Camp. The Boers are in possession and the defenders in full retreat.

1. — Enemy coming round hill to attack retreating party.

2. — Enemy in possession of Majuba Mountain doing d⁰ d⁰

3. — Enemy in Dongas & side of hill . . . . d⁰ d⁰

4. — Our troops retreating down side of hill under heavy fire

5. — Shell fired from Mount Prospect Camp, about 3 m. distant.

6. — Ledge of rocks.

7. — Hussars Picket & some officers of 60ᵗʰ Rifles & others looking on at the Battle

8. — 15ᵗʰ Hussars retreating.

9. — Falls (small.)

10 — Laing's Neck.

Path

Path

Footpath

Roads   O'Neil's Farm   Cattle Laager

grass

Path   Path

Drift

River

do very little to help. Captain Robertson's company of the 92nd Highlanders had been left at the foot of the mountain and soon Captain Thurlow's company of the 60th Rifles had come up to join him, escorting the reserve ammunition. They exchanged dates of commission and established that Robertson was the senior officer, so he forthwith assumed command. He discovered that neither he nor Thurlow had any contingency instructions for future action.

At six o'clock in the morning Conductor Field had come up from camp with supplies for the top of the mountain loaded on a led mule. He had his orders and insisted on going on. The Boers were already alert to what was happening and Field was, inevitably, shot and wounded before being taken prisoner.

The other two companies of the 60th who had been left on the saddle between Amajuba and Imquela were joined by a troop of the 15th Hussars, but none of this group had any further orders either.

As soon as it became obvious that there was trouble on the mountain—and some of the early walking-wounded were beginning to come down—Robertson asked the two companies of the 60th and the cavalry to help him keep the Boers at bay until reinforcements came up from Mount Prospect—four companies would have had a much better chance of success than two—but the 60th group declined to move without orders from above. Robertson knew that he could not hold on his own. His outposts had been driven in and he was up against four hundred Boers who had come riding around the mountain to cut off the retreat. So, quietly and unobtrusively, one by one he sent away the ammunition mules in such a manner that the Boers failed to understand what he was doing. The scheme worked and all the reserve ammunition got safely back to camp. He also got most of the wounded away and sent Thurlow's company off to deploy on a lay-back position through which he would then withdraw his own company of Highlanders. He very nearly left it too late and had great difficulty in disengaging. He got his men away under fire, then found to his disgust that Thurlow had been unable to control his company, many of whom were young recruits, and that they had gone straight on to camp without staying to cover his retreat. The artillery produced some covering fire and some of the 15th Hussars came out to help, but Robertson's losses were severe. He had four killed and eleven wounded, while an officer and twenty-two Highlanders were taken prisoner. Robertson himself reached camp at five in the morning, very angry. His report was so vitriolic that Essex saw fit to 'lose' it until it was demanded by Evelyn Wood and, with reluctance, produced.

During the Amajuba operation eight British officers had been killed, five wounded and seven made prisoners; among the men eighty-six had been killed, one hundred and twenty-five wounded, fifty-one taken prisoner and two listed as missing. The Boers suffered one man killed and six wounded, of whom one later died of his injuries.

[3]

The Amajuba operation had been well-planned and had succeeded in its aim of taking the Boers by surprise. Secrecy was maintained in the Wolseley style and nobody had guessed exactly what was in the wind before the force left camp. After that security was kept up for too long. Robertson and Romilly should have been told where they were going, at latest by the time of the halt on the Imquela-Amajuba saddle; as it was they got off the right path and the whole plan might have been jeopardized if the Zulus had not found them. Nonetheless, a magnificent night operation was brought to a successful conclusion and Colley established his men on the tableland of the mountain.

At first light there were some minor cases of indiscipline. Highlanders stood up and shouted insults at the Boers who could neither see nor hear them. Lucy fired at the sunrise patrol, drawing everybody's attention to the British on the summit. None of this made the slightest difference, the Boers would have found out in another ten minutes. However, it is clear that some officers and men were not doing as they had been told. The same applied when the men were ordered to make themselves stone shelters; they skimped completely and no officer or NCO enforced the rule. The 92nd Highlanders were an excellent regiment with a fine record in the Second Afghan War, which had just ended. They had fought under Roberts around Kabul; they had marched with him to Kandahar where they helped inflict a crushing defeat on Ayub Khan. The men were all veterans. Rightly, they had a high opinion of themselves; wrongly, they had only scorn for the Boers, which was a great mistake. They were up to all the dodges of the old soldier. The trouble really started at the top. Colley was displaying no urgency in getting on with his redoubts and had decided against entrenching.

This is difficult to understand, as he must have appreciated the lethal effect of Boer marksmanship after Laing's Nek and Ingogo. One can only assume that he felt there was plenty of time, and there seems to have been something in his mind about the men being exhausted after the climb. This was not so; anybody who has operated under similar conditions will know that the sheer relief of ceasing to go up and to walk on level ground instead is all the rest one needs. However, if the General thought they needed to recuperate, the old soldiers were perfectly happy to oblige him and make the best of their good fortune.

Colley's need to show imperturbability under fire resulted in Romilly being killed. He cannot be blamed for that; standing about while being shot at remained an occupational disease of officers until well into the First World War. There were still sporadic outbreaks during the Second World War. Imperturbability in a commander is a very good thing, but it can be taken too far and degenerate into dangerous inaction. To such a degree was Colley determined not to 'flap' over Ian Hamilton's reports of Boers swarming up in greater and greater numbers that he had no counter-attack ready when the inevitable happened. This was not calmness in emergency, it was sheer bad generalship.

When the sixty-man Boer commando renewed the battle from the captured Gordon Picquet, they were opposed by six Highlanders spread over sixty yards. It is not surprising that the two or three survivors of the fusillade got out, outnumbered as they were by ten to one at a distance of only seventy yards. Nor can Ian Hamilton be criticized for pulling back his hopelessly extended company and reassembling in the rear position those that made it alive.

The behaviour of the reserve does not appear to have been all that it should have been. The men were unsteady, firing wildly into nothing. One feels that the soldiers knew that their enemy could kill them as he wished and that there was little that they could do to stop him. Seeing their comrades being cut down in swathes all around them in a matter of seconds—something which had never happened in the Afghan War—was too great a shock. They would not stay.

This might not have happened if Colley had sent a whole regiment up Amajuba under its own commanding officer. The men would have rallied around their Colonel after the initial disaster. No regiment would have accepted the ignominy of being driven from the mountain without a very hard struggle. Only nine months earlier the 66th Foot were in disorganized retreat from the field of

Maiwand in South Afghanistan when Colonel Galbraith gathered his men around him again on the outskirts of the battlefield. Two-thirds of the men who had been in the battle-line turned and stayed with him to fight it out, although retreat would have been easy. Instead, he and they died around the Regimental Colours. Given the opportunity, the 92nd Highlanders would have done the same.

But Colley had a hotch-potch of troops. He had brought some of the 92nd because they were a good regiment with a great battle reputation. He included some of the Northamptons because he had promised he would after the defeat at Laing's Nek. Some of the 60th Rifles were allowed to man the line of communication; otherwise, poor fellows, they might have been hurt at being left out. There was no regimental colonel to save the day; there was no regimental honour at stake. Everybody felt free to put the blame on somebody else and the survivors did that very thing as soon as they reached Mount Prospect camp.

Irrespective of all this, the battle was lost because no defences were constructed, no entrenchments made. Several officers asked permission to dig, but Colley is reported as saying that there was no hurry, nothing substantial would be required; they would be up against only rifle fire. There was no regimental colonel to get on with the job quietly without asking. It would have been easy to dig: they had no trouble getting down three feet when looking for water. With proper protection the men would have had the confidence to continue the battle and they would not have been such obvious targets for the enemy. The Boers would not have captured Amajuba. This may seem a categorical statement, but it is based on the fact that the Boers in the Transvaal, the same sort of Boers as those on Laing's Nek, did not succeed in capturing a single one of the beleaguered British posts with their small garrisons. They did not overcome even the extemporized fortifications of Potchefstroom.

[4]

The British Army was totally unprepared for fighting an enemy like the Boers. In all fairness, so was every other European Army. For a quarter of a century there had been only Asiatic or savage warfare in which small numbers of disciplined British or British-led soldiers were expected to defeat greatly superior enemy forces. British discipline and the ability to manoeuvre in formation and produce rapid volleys of rifle fire, the men standing shoulder to shoulder in line, nearly always won the day. Warfare was of the parade-ground; men were not trained to act as individuals; it was a crime to think. The company, or at lowest the half-company, was the smallest unit; Wolseley's section organization in the Gold Coast was his own expedient, an exception to the general rule. None of the rank and file shot at anything other than targets except on operations, when the volley rather than the individual marksman was the general procedure.

The Boers were individuals. Since boyhood they had stalked and killed wary game for the pot. The man too slow in reaction to shoot dead a charging lion or buffalo did not live to have a second chance. They went hunting in old farm clothes which blended with the terrain and did exactly the same in war. Not for them the white helmets and red coats worn by the British. As a result, when it came to action in South Africa the British could seldom see anything to shoot at, and when they could see they were likely to miss. The Boers, on the other hand, could scarcely miss the white helmets conspicuous in the grass or scrub, and went on firing until they were sure. Helmets of the British dead at Ingogo and Amajuba often had four or five bullets through them.

Before war broke out neither side was aware of these discrepancies. The British had no conception of any military inferiority and morale was complacently high. The Boers thought that they would prove to be superior, but were not sure. Of one thing they were certain, that their God was with them and that their cause was just; they were prepared to die for it, but not in too great numbers. Joubert bemoaned his comparatively negligible casualties at Laing's Nek. But after the turn of the tide of battle in that engagement Boer confidence increased progressively, while that of the British correspondingly began to drop. This made all the difference.

Laing's Nek was the first pitched battle of the war and it decided the issue of the whole campaign. Colley had good reasons for attacking with his small untrained force and he very nearly won. If the Northamptons had reached the crest of Deane's Hill, as they would have done if it had not been for the Brownlow debacle, there are strong grounds for thinking that the Boers *would* have withdrawn from the Nek. After all, they were on the point of doing so a month later, when dawn of 27 February revealed Colley in occupation of Amajuba. Many of Joubert's hastily convened council of war wanted to be off and scores of wagons had begun to break away to the north. But on this occasion a new factor, one which had not yet come into being at the time of the first battle, had a decisive influence. It was the voices of Boers who had driven the North-amptons back down the slopes of Deane's Hill, who had established their superiority in fire and movement at Ingogo. Even then, the attack would not have been unleashed if British reinforcements had been found to be coming up from Newcastle. Colley ordered them up after he was well established on top of the mountain. If he had only done so earlier, so that Joubert's scouts would have found them marching north, the campaign would have been saved. But he did not. He was probably afraid of jeopardizing surprise, and it is known that he suspected the telegraph was being tapped. He only finally decided that the attack was on after seeing the Boer daily picquet leaving the plateau. Sir Garnet would have done something like parading the Newcastle troops in battle order to move south on a reasonable pretext and then, after everyone was quite convinced that this was going to happen and the Boers on Laing's Nek felt even more secure, march them north by night on a telegraphed code word. But Colley was not Wolseley.

If he had dug-in on the top of Amajuba the battle and the war need not have been lost. As it was, his generalship on the mountain was unbelievably inefficient. Nor did his Ashanti-style picqueting of the route between Mount Prospect and Amajuba do anything to mitigate the subsequent disaster.

This account of the First Boer War began with the expectation, after Colley's brave and efficient performance in the Ashanti War, of vindicating any adverse criticism of this gallant officer. Sad to say, this is not to be. The facts elicited by research speak for themselves. He had some bad luck, admittedly, but he proved to be no General.

Colley was an intellectual. He was a kindly man, with a keen sense of justice, which made him much loved by the Kaffir races with whom he had had dealings as a young seconded officer. He understood their needs and could get them to do things for him that they would not willingly do for anyone else. He realized this and made good use of it to reorganize the carrier force in the Gold Coast. Within himself he may have been a rather diffident and unassuming man, but throughout his military career he went to great pains to conceal this trait.

He was a brilliant staff officer, second only to Sir Garnet

Wolseley, but there was no comparison between the two men. This is indicated clearly by the different treatment meted out to these officers by Lord Kimberley under fairly similar circumstances.

His major weakness as a commander lay in the fact that he had had hardly any experience of command of British troops. He had missed the Crimea and the Indian Mutiny. He had joined his regiment for the China War, but even then he was usually employed on the battalion staff. He had bad luck in that Wolseley was going to try to have him appointed to command of one of the special regiments to be formed especially for the Ashanti Campaign, but the project was vetoed by Whitehall. Now an acting Major-General, as far as his regiment was concerned he was only a junior and rather inexperienced major, and this may have rankled a bit. He may have felt, as staff officers sometimes do, that he was superior to the ordinary officer on regimental duty and that his ideas would produce the better results. Now at last he was in a position to show that this was so, and he had an additional incentive in the person of the forceful Lady Colley whom he had married two years ago.

He *knew* that, given the chance, any staff officer, even without battle experience, would show himself just as capable of leadership as the regimental officer. He gave Deane and his friends the opportunity to prove this at Laing's Nek; they were all killed and the battle lost. To demonstrate their insouciance under fire, he and his staff took quite unnecessary risks, with fatal results in most cases—all the more pity as nobody had ever thought to question their courage. As regards his handling of troops in the field Marling leaves no doubt of what the officers and men thought about that. They were only surprised that such a bad commander had got into Wolseley's good books.

The final disaster occurred because he emasculated his force of all the essential advantages of the regimental system—the driving force of the colonels, the loyalty of the men to their colours—before going up Amajuba. Half a thousand British were massacred or put to flight by a fifth of that number of Boers, who lost only one man in the process. Nobody can be blamed but Colley himself.

Yet twice in the campaign he had been so close to victory. Buller grieved at Colley's death. 'Poor Colley,' he wrote, 'it is very sad; such a career before him, such charming personal qualities, and such a talent, and all to be lost by—I don't know what to say—I suppose over-confidence will do as well as anything.' Butler says that Colley was the dearest friend that Sir Garnet had in the Army; certainly he was the one in whom he trusted most thoroughly. He felt his loss deeply.

That was Butler speaking. However, Sir Garnet was also very attached to *him*. When Butler was in Netley Hospital recovering from fever contracted during the Ashanti campaign, an illness from which he nearly died, Queen Victoria came to visit him. She said to him, 'When Sir Garnet Wolseley rode up to my carriage at the Windsor Review, the Duke of Cambridge whispered to me that if I wished to please the General, the best question should be an inquiry for Captain Butler.'

[5]

There is very little more to say about the First Boer War. Sir Evelyn Wood assumed command after Colley's death and tried to concentrate the greatly superior British forces now at his command at Mount Prospect for another attack on Laing's Nek. But the weather became so bad, with ten days of tropical storm, that no formed bodies could move forward from Newcastle. Kruger's acceptance of the British Government's bases for negotiation arrived and Gladstone saw no reason for continuing the war purely in revenge for British defeats, so he ordered Evelyn Wood to arrange an armistice with the Boers. This was concluded on 6 March and discussion of peace terms took place between Evelyn Wood and the Boer Triumvirate. Obeying Gladstone's directive with the greatest reluctance, Wood tried hard to avoid being specific, but the Triumvirate led by Kruger were adamant in refusing to accept nebulous undertakings.

Buller arrived to join Evelyn Wood on 12 March, to the gloom of those Boers who had served with him in the Frontier Light Horse. They declared it was equivalent to a reinforcement of ten thousand men to the British! Next day they went to Mount Prospect and held a review of the Boer Army—the Guard of Honour made up from ex-troopers of Buller's regiment. Three weeks later Buller was rather taken aback by finding himself promoted Brigadier-General, acting Major-General. He was genuinely upset at passing over a friend whom he considered to be the better officer, and who depended on the Army for his livelihood, while he himself could retire to his estates at any time and live easily for the rest of his life.

5. President Brand arriving at Laing's Nek with the announcement of peace.

The War Office was bitterly opposed to peace before the Boers had been taught a sharp lesson. They had sent out General Sir Frederick Roberts and ten thousand men within forty-eight hours of receiving news of Amajuba, but on the very day that he reached the Cape, 21 March, Evelyn Wood was at last reduced to signing an unequivocal agreement with the Boers. The terms gave the Boers nearly everything they wanted, and were never regarded by them and the unfortunate loyalists in South Africa as anything other than surrender. Government of the Transvaal was handed back to the Boers on 8 August, 1881.

Although Evelyn Wood had only been obeying the orders of his political masters, as was his bounden duty, Sir Garnet Wolseley never really forgave him for his part in the armistice and subsequent agreement.

The Egyptian War 1882

CHAPTER 8

Occupation of Ismailia

[1]

In the mid-nineteenth century Egypt was still vassal to an insecure suzerainty exercised by the Ottoman Sultan, although in effect the local Governor, or Wali, had a considerable degree of autonomy. As in other dependencies of the Turkish Empire, maladministration was rife and the hardship of the peasants, the fellahin, was accentuated by all the traditional plagues of Egypt. A year of cattle disease would be made worse by a disastrous Nile flood, and then within twelve months an invasion of locusts could bring starvation and the depopulation of whole villages.

An even greater menace was the urge of successive Walis to express their personalities in the form of magnificent public edifices, paid for by extortionate taxes on the fellahin, who were compelled to provide, unpaid, the labour needed for their construction.

Writing in 1867, Lady Duff Gordon says, 'I cannot describe the misery here now—every day some new tax. Every beast, camel, cow, sheep, donkey and horse is made to pay. The fellahin can no longer afford to eat bread; they are living on barley-meal mixed with water, and raw green stuffs, vetches etc. The taxation makes life almost impossible; a tax on every crop, on every animal first, and then again when it is sold in the market; on every man, on charcoal, on butter, on salt. . . . The people of Upper Egypt are running away wholesale, utterly unable to pay the new taxes and to do the work exacted. Even here (Cairo) the beating for the year's taxes is awful.'

As the need for money became more pressing, so European influence began to exploit the market. M. de Lesseps acquired his concession for the Suez Canal. The British established the Eastern Telegraph Company and the Bank of Egypt. Ismail, who no longer used the title Wali, but Khedive—more akin to Viceroy, initiated a great era of modernization during which the best European contractors built railways, lighthouses and harbours. But the funds to pay for these facilities could not be got by taxes alone. So Khedive Ismail borrowed over three million pounds, creating for the first time a national debt.

This vast sum did not last long and soon more money was needed to maintain and expand the living standards of the ruling classes. But borrowing was becoming more difficult and Ismail was reduced to gaining temporary financial relief by selling his Suez Canal shares to the British Government. This was a crucial point in Egypt's history, as the transaction drew official British attention to the financial condition of the country. Anxious to protect their now substantial interests, the British Government despatched a fact-finding mission in early 1876 and the team of experts had to report that under the existing administration bankruptcy was inevitable.

The reaction among other European nations with stakes in Egypt was immediate. Holding the purse-strings, these countries compelled the Khedive to permit international control of a large portion of the revenues. When Ismail found means to render this handicap ineffective, pressure by the British and French Governments acting on behalf of their stockholders led to the inauguration of Dual Control, whereby an Englishman supervised the revenue and a Frenchman the expenditure of the country.

The Khedive wriggled; he was not being allowed to spend where and how he wished. He got rid of Dual Control by paying lip-service to the establishment of a Constitutional Government. Then, in its turn, he disposed of this Government by arranging with the Arab officers in his Army, who were mostly of fellah origin, to riot against it in Cairo. This they did most successfully, but the operation had far-reaching effects—they learned about their own great latent strength. For the time-being, however, Ismail reverted to his old system of autocratic government, until the exasperated European Powers persuaded the Sultan in Istanbul to depose him. So one day Ismail received a letter from his overlord saying that he was no longer Khedive, but was replaced as of that date by his son Tewfik. He was so disconcerted by this unexpected action that he meekly submitted and went into retirement.

Tewfik allowed Dual Control to be re-established in the persons of Major Evelyn Baring and M. de Blignières, and the system functioned after a fashion until 1879. The problem lay in finding ways to prevent the official and land-owning classes from continuing to exercise their traditional way of living by extortion. The civilian elements of this hierarchy were not prepared to resort to violence to maintain the status quo, but they fought for their rights with every subterfuge of oriental intrigue and by non-compliance with the new edicts.

Now, however, a new personality entered the political arena. Army officers had discovered their power during the Ismail-inspired riots. One of them, of fellah origin, was named Arabi, a man of courage, with a gift of peasant oratory which could make a great impression on the rank and file. Supported and prompted by other Arab officers with more organizational ability than himself, he created a political party with the avowed aim of protecting Egyptians from the 'grasping tyranny of their Turkish and European oppressors'. Kindled by resentment at preference for promotion being given to officers of Turkish origin, the new party achieved cohesion in a campaign against all Christians, foreign and native.

The Government was weak, did not like foreigners nor Dual Control anyway, and made concession after concession to Arabi and his ever-expanding adherents. Arabi was promoted, then appointed Secretary of State for War. Ultimately, as Arabi Pasha, he became a member of the Cabinet. Soon all power was in his hands, other ministers mere puppets.

This caused alarm in international circles, as there were ninety thousand Europeans engaged in commerce in Egypt, for the most part British and French. So in May, 1882, an allied fleet of British and French warships entered Alexandria harbour to watch their countries' interests. Their presence may have had the exact opposite effect to what had been intended. Certainly serious anti-Christian riots broke out in Alexandria three weeks later and two-thirds of the European community had to fly for their lives. Finally, on 24 June, Arabi Pasha openly assumed authority. He informed the two Controllers that they might no longer sit in council with the Egyptian Cabinet. He announced that if sailors from the fleet were landed in Alexandria to restore order he would oppose them with armed force, and he began to construct fortifications east of the town. Soon threatening groups of Bedouin Arabs began to appear along the banks of the Suez Canal.

The British Government had decided steps might have to be taken to ensure the safety of the Suez Canal Zone and to allow free passage of shipping between Suez and Port Said. In the War Office, contingency planning had been going on for some time and the Adjutant-General, Sir Garnet Wolseley, had made his appreciation. He considered that permanent occupation of the strip of desert running north-south beside the Canal would be quite impractical. The Egyptian railway network was so designed that Arabi could deliver a concentration of his forces at any one of several points along the Canal at short notice, long before the widely dispersed British garrisons could collect to oppose him. Moreover, conditions were harsh and the heat was intense at some times of the year, so morale would suffer during months of static defence. Besides, the only drinking-water for the Zone came from the Nile, channelled through the Sweet-Water Canal, and the Egyptians could, if they wished, cut off this supply at source, which would give any British occupying force an administrative headache, if nothing else. Arabi would be reluctant to do such a thing, as the crops of his people, fellahin like himself, would be ruined and villagers would starve; but the threat definitely existed. The political power was situated in Cairo; from there the railways and drinking-water supplies could be controlled; there the decisions would be made. The sooner that Cairo was in British hands, the quicker would the aim of securing the Suez Canal be achieved.

　Once that had been decided, it was a question of whether to advance and seize the city from Alexandria or to land at Port Said, go south down the Canal to Ismailia and attack westwards from there. This was easily decided. It was a hundred and twenty miles from Alexandria to Cairo and only seventy-five miles from Ismailia. The Ismailia—Cairo route was across firm desert for most of the way, with no obstacles. The Alexandria advance across the Nile Delta would be hindered by a vast net of irrigation channels from August to October when the river was at its highest, and on arrival the British force would find itself on the wrong side of the Nile. There were no roads for wheeled transport at that time, everything was carried by railway, boat or by animals. A further factor in favour of Ismailia, and a very important one, was that any expedition would involve troops from both England and India. The European element could capture Port Said while the Indian contingent took Suez; they could then join forces in Ismailia. It was concluded, therefore, that the Ismailia route it would be. Earlier in the year Sir Garnet had sent Major Tulloch to make an innocent but detailed reconnaissance of the projected line of advance, and

Egyptian defences across it. As it turned out, he had done a competent and accurate job.

Sir Garnet had completed his outline operational and administrative plans by the time that the Secretary of State for War had decided on 29 June, after consultation with the Commander-in-Chief, to take such preliminary steps as could be implemented without attracting undue attention or incurring exceptional financial expenditure. It was agreed that any expeditionary force sent to Egypt would be commanded by Lieutenant-General Sir Garnet Wolseley, with the acting rank of General.

He asked for two divisions of infantry and a brigade of cavalry from England and he wanted them to be made fully mobile. No animal transport would be available in Egypt until Arabi Pasha had been defeated, so all teeth-arms must embark self-contained with full-scale regimental transport. He wanted a thousand mules to be purchased in America and shipped forthwith to the United Kingdom; more were to be bought in Malta, and pack-saddles would be needed for all these animals. He demanded also five locomotives, a hundred open goods wagons and ten miles of rail, so that he could repair and use the local railways despite demolitions carried out by the enemy.

On 4 July secret instructions were sent to commanding officers of cavalry regiments, infantry battalions and artillery batteries selected for the Force, directing them to be prepared to move at the shortest notice. A lot of preparation could be made under the pretext of getting ready for autumn manoeuvres, which would in the event be cancelled.

Regiments in the Mediterranean garrisons were already on an operational basis and they were shipped immediately to Cyprus, available to seize the Suez Canal twenty-four hours after receiving the word to go. Sir Garnet asked that his old and trusted friend from Ashanti days, Major-General Sir Archibald Alison, should be in command of this force. Alison left England four days after Sir Garnet had first applied for his services and was in Cyprus with two battalions of infantry and a company of Naval Engineers on 14 July.

After the Canal Zone and Ismailia had been secured, Sir Garnet would advance to capture Cairo. He expected, however, to have to fight at Tel el-Kebir where Major Tulloch had reported entrenchments and defences under construction. It had always been a military station and had once for a time been commanded by Arabi

Pasha, who might well elect to give battle on ground already known to him. The General was determined to win a quick decisive victory, followed by a cavalry advance at all speed to the gates of Cairo while the garrison and inhabitants were still in shock from the tidings of military disaster.

All this had to be kept secret and in Whitehall the future base for operations was always referred to as Alexandria although most planners knew this to mean Ismailia.

The Egyptian forces in Alexandria acknowledged only Arabi Pasha's orders and paid no attention to any edicts from Khedive Tewfik, aware that he favoured the continuation of European control. They worked through the nights strengthening the fortifications around the harbour, emplacing guns, even dropping rocks to block the entrance. They denied any such activity, but the Navy had only to play their searchlights around the harbour to see exactly what was going on. This pseudo-clandestine building and damming began to constitute a definite threat to the allied fleet, but Admiral Sir Beauchamp Seymour waited to allow the last European fugitives opportunities to escape. When he was satisfied that they were all safe, he then informed the local Egyptian commander that unless forts commanding the anchorage were surrendered to him within twenty-four hours, he would bombard them. Nothing happened, no agreement was reached, so the fleets began firing at seven o'clock on the morning of 11 July. By nightfall the forts had ceased to reply and they were evacuated next day when Arabi Pasha withdrew his forces out of the city to Kafr ed-Duaur along the Cairo railway. His rearguard joined with the Alexandria mob to burn and pillage until the greater part of the city's European quarter had been destroyed, then withdrew under the cover of outposts to join their Pasha. The whole of Alexandria was soon being looted by the native criminal classes.

Arabi had half the Egyptian Army with him, but that was only four thousand five hundred officers and men. A similar number was spread all over the country, as was the artillery; there were plenty of good field guns, two hundred and fifty, but only seven hundred and fifty horses to pull them.

On 26 July Arabi Pasha was officially dismissed by the Khedive, but still considered himself to be Commander-in-Chief and Ruler of the country. Nominally he was subject to a Military Committee in Cairo, who now recalled all reservists, some of them over fifty years old, to the colours, raising the strength of the Army to sixty thousand men. Two thousand regulars and a few Bedouin were sent to reinforce Kafr ed-Duaur.

The combined fleets, having destroyed what force existed to preserve law and order, were now under a moral obligation to take over police duties and control the mob. So detachments of sailors and marines were landed and began to patrol the streets.

Alison in Cyprus had no idea what was going on as the telegraph was out of order. But something important was happening; it could be that full-scale hostilities had broken out, in which case his place was in Port Said. No Wolseley officer would have sat still in such circumstances, so he took ship, went first to Port Said where he learned the true situation, and thence to Alexandria, where he arrived on 17 July, a welcome reinforcement to the Royal Navy security forces. However, this was not the only problem; preparations had to be made to defend the remains of the city and the harbour against any attempt at recapture by Arabi's main army, which was only fourteen miles away.

Alison's two infantry regiments were disembarked next day. One of them was that same 3rd Battalion of the 60th King's Rifle Corps which had fought at Ingogo and it was still commanded by Colonel Ashburnham. Captain Pigott and some of the men had fought as mounted infantry in South Africa, as had others in the South Staffordshire Regiment, also now with Alison. The Khedive willingly supplied some excellent horses from his own stables and in next to no time a mounted infantry unit of two officers and thirty men had come into existence. They were operational that evening and patrolled ten miles towards the Egyptian lines. Four days later they went into action, drove back Arabi's outposts and cut the railway line on his side of Mahalla station. This lay on the only direct route by which the Egyptians could advance to attack Alexandria —a narrow strip of ground bounded on either side by Lakes Mariut and Aboukir. The lake-beds were still impassible to any wheeled traffic, but soon they would dry out, giving any force ample room to manoeuvre. By 24 July Alison had organized a defensive position based on the ridge at Ramleh north-east of the city, incorporating the Duke of Cornwall's Light Infantry and a wing of the Sussex Regiment as fresh reinforcements.

Communication and supply for the British forward elements were maintained by an armoured train, manned by two hundred bluejackets and mounting Gatling guns, a 9-pounder and eventually a

40-pounder gun on trucks, protected by railway iron plate and slung sand-bags.

[2]

On 15 July the European Powers had delivered a note to the Sultan of Turkey asking him to despatch troops to Egypt to prevent disorder. When it became obvious that he was going to do absolutely nothing the British and French Cabinets decided to send a joint expedition and deal with the situation themselves. This was all very well, but they had to go to their Parliaments to have the expenditure authorized; and while the House of Commons voted adequate money for a campaign, the French Chambers by a huge majority refused any credit at all! No other European Power showed any inclination to become involved and it was soon clear that Britain would have to 'go it alone'. The French Navy, except for one representative gun-boat, withdrew from Alexandria.

In England, men who had left the Colours during the previous two years were recalled, and open preparations were set in hand to despatch an Expeditionary Force. All British action, needless to say, would be taken in the name of the Khedive. The original Ismailia plan would be implemented, but as through fortuitous circumstances a large brigade was already at Alexandria, it would be used to persuade Arabi Pasha that the advance on Cairo would be from there. Alison was told to 'keep Arabi constantly alarmed'. This he did by daily patrols and reconnaissances of Kafr ed-Duaur, some on a small scale, others in full force supported by the armoured train. The series of operations had to be planned with great care to avoid alarming Arabi too much; they must not be pressed too hard and troops must be withdrawn before they could become heavily involved. At the same time the British soldiery must not be allowed to become exasperated by their General's apparent lack of determination and lose confidence in him. They could not be told the true story, for the news would inevitably have leaked to the horde of international press correspondents who had swarmed into Alexandria, and would soon have reached Arabi's camp. As it was, some gentlemen of the press were of the greatest assistance to British subterfuge, grossly exaggerating the importance of every little action and castigating the vaccillatory tactics and constant failures of the taciturn Sir Archibald. In Britain some national daily newspapers rumbled and grumbled, reproducing reports by foreign newsmen, which did no harm at all to security, though unfortunately some distress was caused to officers' relatives.

M. de Lesseps, too, unwittingly played his part. Hearing that Arabi Pasha was going to order the destruction of the Suez Canal, he went to Kafr ed-Duaur and told him that if he left the Canal alone neither France nor Italy would intervene, while the British would never dare invade de Lesseps territory!

Everything worked well. Pigott's small band of mounted infantry were operating so frequently, so offensively and in so many places that Arabi thought that he was faced by two regiments of cavalry. He also appreciated that Alison's force consisted of twice as many infantry and guns as were actually present.

The Khedive now issued express authority for the Canal to be occupied by England. M. de Lesseps objected, but despite this the Royal Navy made all necessary preparations. Admiral Hoskins lay off Port Said, Admiral Hewett arrived off Suez and a British warship anchored in Lake Timsah, by Ismailia. The first troopship of the Expeditionary Force left England on 30 July, followed by a steady stream until 11 August. First arrival at Alexandria was on 10 August, the same day that Sir Garnet reached Gibraltar. He and his staff had hoped to save time by going overland and taking ship from Brindisi, but the General had been ill and needed a sea-voyage to recover.

From Gibraltar he sent a secret telegram to Lieutenant-General Sir John Adye, his Chief of Staff, at that time in command in Alexandria, telling him to warn Admiral Hoskins that when the operation began it would be necessary to move five regiments of infantry, one of cavalry and a battery of artillery down the Canal from Port Said to Ismailia. He was also to tell the Khedive and his staff that rolling stock was needed in Cyprus to make a rail link between Limassol and a projected hospital in the mountains, and on that pretext to acquire and ship four engines and eighty light carriages on board a vessel that could then quietly be diverted to Ismailia; at the very least he must obtain six light carriages which could be drawn on the railway by horses if necessary.

Admiral Hewett occupied Suez on 2 August, meeting no resistance, so the Indian Contingent sailed from Bombay a week later. Arabi though that this was just a diversion to distract his attention from the British main assault from Alexandria.

Wolseley arrived in Alexandria on the night of 15 August. The first thing that he found was that nothing had been done about his trains: there was no infallible Colley there implement his orders. The matter was rectified immediately.

Three squadrons of the Household Cavalry and a battery of artillery had already arrived and disembarked to exercise their horses. The Guards Brigade were there, and it was now known that the whole of the infantry of Lieutenant-General Willis's 1st Division would arrive by the 19th. The remainder of the cavalry and artillery were still at sea, but they could easily be diverted to Ismailia. Sir Garnet, therefore, spent his first day in Alexandria working out with Sir Beauchamp Seymour the whole of his detailed plan for seizing the Suez Canal. His plan was still to inflict one decisive defeat on the Egyptian Army at Tel el-Kebir, followed by a dash for Cairo, and occupation of all strategic points through which the remainder of the enemy formations would have to pass in order to join and become once more a viable fighting entity.

After the capture and occupation of Ismailia it would be necessary to establish a forward base where sufficient stores and ammunition could be accumulated to supply the whole Expeditionary Force for its advance to take Tel el-Kebir, the battle and the pursuit to Cairo. It was the same principle as his build-up at Prahsu before going for Kumasi, but this time there would be no Fanti porters. Instead, full use would have to be made of the railway and the Sweet-Water Canal for transportation. This would probably entail repairing demolitions, broken railways and canals; also replacing boats and rolling stock which had been removed or damaged, all with the minimum of delay.

The first problem would be getting ships to Ismailia as quickly as possible, which would need careful planning and organization. The Suez Canal had not been designed for rapid transit of shipping, and no advantage would be gained by steaming faster than usual. Passage through the short straight stretches and tight bends needed pilots experienced in this type of navigation; the deep channel was very much narrower than the whole width from bank to bank, and the smallest error resulted in grounding, delaying the ship in question and holding up all traffic on the waterway. But there would be no experienced pilots available; they were all in the employ of M. de Lesseps who was unlikely to place them at Sir Garnet's disposal! So the Royal Navy would improvise, placing a naval officer in authority aboard every transport. It was accepted that inevitably some grounding would take place, but Thorneycroft torpedo-boats had very shallow draughts and could steam outside the main channel at twenty knots if need be. Some of these craft were given the role of maintaining communication between one end of the long convoy and the other, so that, as soon as a grounding occurred, assistance could be provided enabling it to back off and proceed, or to be towed to a side to let the others pass.

There was plenty of room in Lake Timsah for shipping to assemble but no transport would be able to reach closer to shore than half a mile, due to shallow water. So every man, horse and gun, with all supplies and ammunition would have to be trans-shipped into barges and small boats, tugged or rowed to shore, and there in the initial stages landed at the one and only small pier in existence at Ismailia. Tools and materials would be landed, indeed, to improve the port facilities, but not before sufficient fighting men, animals and war material had been disembarked to consolidate the capture of Ismailia and seize ground as far forward as possible along the railway and Sweet-Water Canal for the future advance of the whole Force. When that had been done, then equipment for landing the main body could be brought in. A lot would depend on careful loading before ships left the United Kingdom: it would not be helpful if engines had been loaded on top of the cranes supposed to lift them off ship on to the quay at their destination!

The War Office was already putting a third division in readiness, though they hoped that Sir Garnet would not need it. He hoped so too, but agreed that it was a sensible precaution.

The Royal Navy, working simultaneously from both Port Said and Suez, were to capture the whole Canal and clear it of shipping on the morning of Sunday, 20 August. The only preliminary measures of any significance were to reinforce the *Orion* in Lake Timsah by two gun-boats and three companies of Marines, and on the evening of the 19th, at eight o'clock, a warship started down the Canal from Port Said, taking over all barges and dredges. There was no risk to security, as there was no way whereby the news could reach the Egyptians in time to warn them that something was afoot; their own engineers in the telegraphic communications centre at Kantara had already severed all links between stations along the Canal. But on arrival at Kantara the warship was to take over the station, restore it to full working order and stop all civilian shipping steaming north from Ismailia, diverting them into bays along the side of the Canal to clear the main channel. On the same day

Admiral Hewett was to stop all shipping from entering the Canal at Suez and capture his portion of the Canal.

At Port Said Lieutenant-Colonel Tulloch and six Marines landed from an open boat and suppressed the harbour sentries without any alarm being raised. A larger force then landed, surprised the Egyptian garrison in barracks and persuaded them to lay down their arms. Ismailia was cleared of enemy by four o'clock in the morning and the telegraph office was occupied. From a quick perusal of telegrams found there, it was discovered that the Nefisha garrison, two thousand strong, was about to be reinforced by train in order to attack Ismailia and the shipping in Lake Timsah. The *Orion* and the gun-boats therefore shelled Nefisha railway station so effectively from a range of four thousand yards that they wrecked a train and so damaged the Egyptian camp that the occupants withdrew into the desert. Telegrams were still coming in from Cairo for the traffic manager at Ismailia, so one was now sent back in his name, saying that five thousand British troops had already landed at Ismailia and that any attempt to relieve the place would be too late. The War Minister in Cairo in due course acknowledged the telegram and said that he had passed the contents to all concerned.

Operating from Suez, Admiral Hewett was also successful. His first objective had been an important lock on the Sweet-Water Canal, which had been opened by the Egyptians, dissipating its water into the Suez Canal, leaving the town of Suez with a rapidly dwindling supply. It was captured by a combined force of sailors, Marines and Seaforth Highlanders, the British regiment in the Indian Infantry Brigade. The enemy showed no lack of courage, but their shooting was very erratic.

In Alexandria a deception plan had been prepared to cover the re-embarkation of troops for Port Said, not only to conceal the true destination from them and from the press correspondents, but to convince both parties that something quite different was contemplated. It was fairly well known that consideration had been given to attacking the forts still held by the Egyptians at Aboukir, so Sir Garnet now issued actual orders for a naval bombardment followed by an assault landing in the Bay. At the same time the 2nd Division under Lieutenant-General Sir Edward Hamley, which was to remain at Alexandria, would advance on Arabi Pasha's main position at Kafr ed-Duaur, ostensibly in conjunction with the supposed invasion from Aboukir Bay. Wolseley was so strict in limiting awareness of the true plan to those who absolutely had to know that

Hamley was not privy to it and thought it extremely odd that he had been left with no field artillery. Nonetheless he did what he could, briefing his two subordinates, Alison with his 1st Infantry Brigade and Major-General Sir Evelyn Wood who was in command of the 2nd Infantry Brigade. They were a good combination: Hamley and Alison were both military writers, while Wood had developed a great admiration for Hamley when the latter had been colonel in charge of his division at the staff college. Hamley, incidentally, had later been appointed Commandant of that institution and had had occasion to reprimand Buller for riotous conduct!

At noon on 18 August, plain for everyone to see, the fleet and transports sailed from Alexandria, twenty-five ships in five lines, and headed east for Aboukir Bay. They arrived at five o'clock and anchored, remaining there until nightfall. Then the small naval craft moved closed inshore and opened fire, while the rest of the fleet steamed away to Port Said where they arrived at sunrise.

Despite all the careful planning, they could not enter the Canal. A French mail-boat had claimed the right to leave Ismailia for Port Said and had been granted permission as a matter of international courtesy. One fast ship would not have caused very much difficulty, but unfortunately two British merchant-skippers—who else!—left their moorings as soon as the Royal Navy's back was turned and sneaked off after the mail-steamer. They were not spotted until they had reached a part of the Canal where it was pointless to stop them, so the whole operation was suspended while these three ships made their meandering way north to the Mediterranean. However, Major-General Graham, commanding 2nd Infantry Brigade of the 1st Division, boarded a torpedo-boat with half an infantry regiment to pass the offending three, transferred to a gun-boat on the other side, and went to take charge in Ismailia.

While the remainder were waiting at Port Said, M. de Lesseps arrived at the quay. He boarded Sir Beauchamp Seymour's ship and informed the Admiral that he had personally guaranteed the neutrality of the Canal to Arabi Pasha and therefore no troops could travel down it. Sir Beauchamp was very polite and even offered him champagne, but was quite firm that he was under government orders and would have to proceed. De Lesseps was furious and left in a rage. According to Marling, he watched the fleet depart for Ismailia dancing on the quay, foaming at the mouth, and shouting, '*Sacrés Anglais!*'

As soon as the Canal was clear the Expeditionary Force started south. There were now twenty-three transports and some gun-boats. The first six transports contained Sir Garnet Wolseley and staff, the Naval Commander-in-Chief Sir Beauchamp Seymour, Marines, engineers, lighters and working parties, coal and railway stock, and forage for horses and mules. The next six carried seven battalions of infantry, connected staffs, and half a battery of heavy guns to garrison Ismailia. Then came another group with more staff, commissariat personnel, two field hospitals and stretcher-bearers, six ships with cavalry, artillery and mounted infantry; finally two tugs towing lighters loaded with railway plant and personnel.

Sir Garnet was in Ismailia at nine o'clock in the morning of 21 August and at once sent Graham and his men forward to Nefisha with a Gatling gun, promising him a battalion of Marines as soon as they could be landed. As it happened, he had no trouble and even managed to capture a train of carriages, without, unfortunately, an engine.

The King's Royal Rifle Corps were the first infantry regiment to land at Ismailia and remain there, so they promptly booked up the only hotel for all meals. Marling writes that it was great fun to see hungry Guards officers prowling about trying in vain to get something to eat!

By the evening of the 23rd about nine thousand men were on shore, including the Household Cavalry and the first two Royal Horse Artillery guns. Every inch of space near the single landing-stage was piled with stores of all kinds awaiting removal. The 7th Dragoon Guards were still disembarking and the 4th Dragoon Guards had got as far as Lake Timsah; but it would be some days before the artillery could all be landed.

At this point Arabi Pasha had fifteen thousand men at Kafr ed-Duaur, and there were a further twenty-two thousand between Aboukir and Rosetta. Cairo had a garrison of eleven thousand and there were another twelve thousand stationed at Tel el-Kebir and on the eastern side of the Nile Delta. About six thousand Bedouin had come in to join the Army and were divided equally between Kafr ed-Duaur and Tel el-Kebir. The large force at Tel el-Kebir was only a precautionary measure as a result of Admiral Hewett's occupation of Suez. The Egyptians were still quite convinced by de Lesseps's assurance that the British would never take the whole Canal.

News of British plans to land at Aboukir Bay had leaked success-fully to Cairo, where the Military Committee went so far as to send three thousand reinforcements to the threatened sector. Sir Garnet's deception operation had been perfectly effective; the first news of the capture of Port Said and Ismailia had been from British-inspired telegrams couched in language designed to discourage any attempts to dispute possession. Arabi himself never *did* understand how so many British troops had managed to appear so suddenly all along the Canal.

Once this was accepted as fact the Egyptian Military Committee enlisted forty thousand new recruits, who had undergone no kind of military training, and drafted them into the ranks with the trained soldiers after only a few days of drill. There were sufficient rifles to arm them all, and enough old muskets for the Bedouin. Eleven thousand transport animals were obtained as 'free-will offerings' from the fellahin, which provided horses, albeit untrained, to pull the guns.

Orders were issued for damming the Sweet-Water Canal at Magfar, ten miles west of Ismailia, where the water level now began to drop at an alarming rate. They also blocked the railway at the same place.

CHAPTER 9
Advance to Kassassin

[1]

Several officers whom we have already met had by now arrived in Ismailia. Lieutenant-Colonel Butler was an Assistant Adjutant and Quartermaster-General on Sir Garnet's staff, and working under him was Major Maurice, who later wrote the military history of the campaign. Wolseley had sent for Buller, but that officer did not arrive until early September. The summons reached him while he was at the Hague enjoying the tenth day of his honeymoon and it was couched in such language that both he and his bride felt there was nothing for him to do but to go to Egypt at once!

On the base and lines of communication staff, but still awaiting his turn to land, was Colonel Sir Owen Lanyon.

The Cavalry Division was commanded by Major-General Drury-Lowe, and his 1st Cavalry Brigade by Brigadier-General Sir Baker Russell. Lieutenant-Colonel Hugh McCalmont had accidentally met Sir Garnet in the street on the day before mobilization, had gone to take tea with the General and Lady Wolseley, and as a result embarked as a special service officer. He had a peaceful voyage out, as he was so fortunate as to have as fellow-passenger His Serene Highness the Duke of Teck. On the first day at sea the Duke had been awakened at four o'clock in the morning by sailors holystoning the deck and had not been able to get to sleep again until ten! So the practice had been forbidden for the rest of the trip. McCalmont just happened to bump into Baker Russell in Ismailia, who promptly offered him employment as his Brigade-Major, which was accepted with alacrity. They had last been in action together at the capture of Sekukuni's stronghold, and both knew that theirs would be a good working relationship.

190

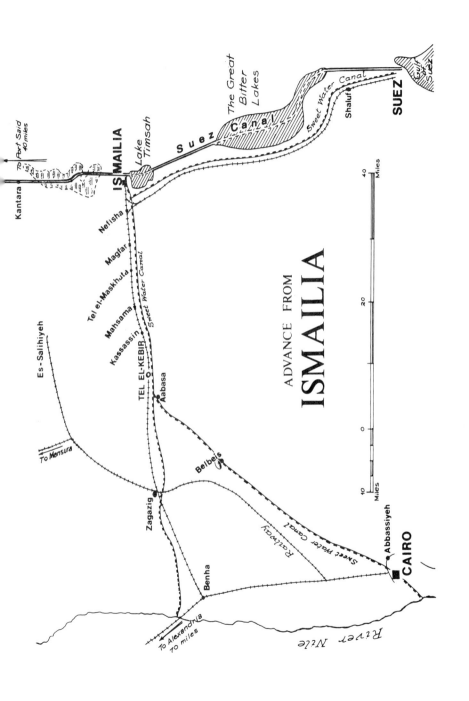

ADVANCE FROM ISMAILIA

Brackenbury had achieved a passage in an unofficial capacity, and Colonel McNeil was on the Duke of Connaught's staff.

The correspondent of the *Illustrated London News*, Mr Melton Prior, was standing by to draw graphic pictures of the fighting. Another arrival was T. J. de Burgh, who had arranged to be accredited to the Expeditionary Force as correspondent (unpaid) for the *Kildare Observer*. He had attached himself to the 7th Dragoon Guards, of which his younger brother Ulick was Adjutant.

On 23 August Sir Garnet gave orders for an advance to be made next day as far as Magfar to open the Sweet-Water Canal and restore the water supply to his base at Ismailia. Graham at Nefisha was to be reinforced by the Household Cavalry, the Mounted Infantry and a detachment of the 19th Hussars. He would then move forward with all his original force and this increment to Magfar and take up a defensive position. The Duke of Cornwall's Light Infantry would march from Ismailia at the same time as the cavalry and take over the garrison commitment at Nefisha, protecting the station, bridge and canal.

The cavalry, led by Drury-Lowe and Baker Russell, left Ismailia at four o'clock in the morning before first light, leaving McCalmont to speed disembarkation of the 4th and 7th Dragoon Guards. The mounted force moved north of the railway where the desert was fairly hard, though not sufficiently so for infantry to march or artillery teams to pull their guns with any degree of comfort. They soon found that the only practical way from Nefisha was along the railway embankment.

The Commander-in-Chief, with Butler and some of his staff, accompanied the cavalry. Lacking Buller, the General was not really happy with his intelligence, admirably though Tulloch had organized it in many ways; but he wanted to see for himself.

It was to be a morning ride of ten to twelve miles, relying on haversack rations and water from the canal; then back to tea in the Governor's house, where the Commander-in-Chief and his staff had established their headquarters. It was Butler's first sight of the desert: 'Sand, drifted into motionless waves, heaped in ridges, scooped into valleys, flattened, blown into curious cones and long yellow banks, the tops of which the wind has cut into fretted patterns as it blew over them. And all so silent, so withered, and yet so fresh; so soft, so beautiful, and yet so terrible.' The sun was soon high over the horizon and the mirage was showing distorted water-patches and inverted bushes on every side. They crossed over small hills of soft sand, skirted some brackish lakes, and eventually clashed with the Egyptian outposts who withdrew before them.

The General halted his column in the little oasis of Abu Suer, north of Magfar. From where he stood the desert rose gradually for three thousand yards to the mounds around Tel el-Maskhuta. These hillocks were now seen to be black with Egyptian infantry. 'Musket-barrels and spearheads flashed and glittered along the desert ridge, while on either side of them a long line of horsemen and camel corps stretched along the skyline far into the desert.' Prisoners captured during the outpost skirmish told their interrogator that a second dam had been constructed at Tel el-Maskhuta and that the Egyptian infantry were entrenched there in force.

Sir Garnet had come out with no purpose other than that his advance guard should seize the Magfar area while he studied the ground; but things had changed radically, so he made a new appreciation. Watching carefully through his binoculars, he saw trains arriving at Tel el-Maskhuta station; he saw the entrenchments and formed bodies of Egyptian soldiers beyond them. All indications were that that the enemy commander meant to hold his ground, if not indeed to attack. The very smallness of the British force would encourage him at least to stay where he was. Here, therefore, was an opportunity to defeat the enemy and follow up vigorously enough to secure perhaps as far as Kassassin, already chosen as the forward base for the decisive battle at Tel el-Kebir.

The urgency now was to bring up sufficient infantry, cavalry and guns from Ismailia to support Graham's small column before it was overwhelmed. Sir Garnet was fully aware that the British cavalry horses, just landed from shipboard and still unacclimatized, would be in no condition for really hard work; and that the infantry, too, would suffer considerable hardship during the ten-mile march through sand beneath an Egyptian sun beating down upon the desert at the hottest time of the year. He realized also that, even after reaching their objectives, they would be on short commons for several days until the supply organization caught up with them. It had been found that the railway engines and trucks so foresightedly brought from Alexandria could not be landed at Ismailia as there was no line from the dock to the station. They had all been shipped on to Suez, whence they would in time travel up the line to Ismailia station. For the present the forward troops would have to rely for supplies and ammunition on trucks captured by Graham at Nefisha, dragged by horses and mules. There would at least be plenty of water from the Sweet-Water Canal (water which no present-day European would dream of drinking before processing!) and the inevitable privations should not prove fatal.

Graham's half-battalion of the York and Lancaster Regiment deployed across the railway facing west, with their left flank by the dam over the canal. From their right the British force was positioned in a line roughly north-east across the higher ground west of the oasis. First the two Royal Horse Artillery guns, then the Royal Marine Artillery, the three squadrons of Household Cavalry and the 19th Hussars, and on the extreme right flank the Mounted Infantry.

At half-past eight an ADC was sent back to Ismailia to order up all cavalry and artillery that could be made ready to move and to tell the Duke of Cornwall's Light Infantry at Nefisha to drop everything and start marching west up the railway at once. Colonel Harrison, Assistant Adjutant-General for the lines of communication, returned also to get the administrative arrangements into operation. He was armed with authority to ask Admiral Sir Beauchamp Seymour to put steam launches and towing cutters on the Sweet-Water Canal. Butler calculated that it would take the ADC an hour and a half to reach Ismailia and that the troops would not be ready to move until another hour and a half after that. Then the march through heavy sand under a blazing sun would take anything up to five hours. Certainly at least eight hours must elapse before any significant assistance could reach Abu Suer. Graham would have to hold out that long.

Now that it was clear that the ensuing battle would be of great importance and have considerable bearing on the campaign as a whole, Sir Garnet ordered Lieutenant-General Willis, General Officer Commanding the 1st Infantry Division, to supersede Graham and assume command of all troops. He did not take over himself. Willis at once gave orders that the infantry were to lie down under what cover they could find among the scrub, bushes and sand-drifts, and that they were not to show themselves or to fire without special orders. There is no record of anyone disobeying *his* instructions!

The guns found a good position and came into action at about nine o'clock under the shoulder of a sandhill just north of the railway. Soon afterwards the Egyptians advanced to within two thousand yards. Their right had crossed over to the south of the canal and were shortly in contact with the York and Lancasters, whose steady disciplined fire before long brought them to a halt, then made them break off the action and withdraw. The Egyptian left tried to swing out and encircle the British position, but here the mounted infantry were responsible for flank protection. All picked marksmen (how unlike Colley's improvised troop!), they dismounted and by their effective shooting put a complete stop to any further outflanking movement on that side.

The Egyptian artillery started well with a round that passed a couple of feet over Sir Garnet's head to burst among the lead-horses of a gun-team. Soon four enemy guns were in action against the British left, so the horses were moved back to where there was some cover. Then, seeing nothing more to shoot at, as the infantry were well-concealed, they transferred their attention to the cavalry and mounted infantry, helped by two more guns. Their gun-laying was accurate, but not their fuze-setting; the shrapnel, of which they did not seem to have very much, burst so high as to be nearly harmless, while their percussion fuzes failed to explode until the shell was deep in the soft sand or irrigated ground, so that the metal fragments were buried in the desert or flew harmlessly upwards. They did little damage unless they actually hit a horse or man. Even so, Willis ordered the cavalry and mounted infantry to fall back a bit and keep moving at a walk to and fro to disconcert the Egyptian gunners.

Sir Garnet had forbidden the two British guns to reply, preferring to husband their ammunition in case the enemy should try to close. However, the cavalry were beginning to suffer casualties, so he agreed to a little counter-battery work. The first two rounds of British shrapnel, fired at half-past ten, burst directly over some newly-arrived enemy guns which were promptly withdrawn behind the crest. But the remaining six Egyptian guns then turned all their attention to the two Royal Horse Artilley 9-pounders and an artillery duel began.

At midday the ADC was back from Ismailia, reporting that the Guards Brigade under Major-General His Royal Highness the Duke of Connaught and Strathearn would march at one o'clock. But the Duke of Cornwall's Light Infantry from Nefisha were only a mile or two away and a party of sailors from the *Orion* was close at hand, manfully dragging two Gatling guns through the sand. This was as well, for more and more Egyptian reinforcements were coming in by train. Six more guns had come into action against the British right, but this time they were good, modern breech-loading

Krupp guns, not the bronze muzzle-loaders which had been firing until then. There were also so many horsemen and infantry opposite this flank that nothing the British cavalry and mounted infantry could do would drive them back.

General Willis now made fresh dispositions to strengthen his right. Where there were some low-lying sandhills he placed one of the Gatlings and had it dug in. He also found a sheltered position for one of the 9-pounders, which he moved to the same area. The other Gatling was sent to support the York and Lancaster front, where another attack was developing.

Butler was uncomfortable: 'Meanwhile, the heat had become simply outrageous, the sun stood straight overhead, the yellow sand glowed like hot coals, not a breath of air stirred over these hot hillocks.'

Shells from two directions were now passing over the heads of the Royal Horse Artillery gunners, every now and then killing a horse or breaking a leg. The greatest trial, however, was the heat. A few men succumbed, but the remainder, exhausted though they were, carried on with their task of pushing up the guns again after each recoil. Drivers came and helped with the labour, while others brought water from the canal and poured it over the heads of men who collapsed. The treatment was effective, for afterwards there were no gunner admissions to hospital from heat exhaustion. For nearly five hours the British guns engaged six times their own number, firing two hundred and eighty rounds, a fifth of the ammunition expenditure for the whole of the 1882 Egyptian campaign. Only when two lucky shells landed in succession among the battery, killing two men and several horses, did Willis send over some of the Marine Artillery to help the horse-gunners.

At one o'clock the Duke of Cornwall's Light Infantry reached the battleground and took up position in reserve. Sir Garnet then called for his horse, told Butler to come with him, and rode off towards where the Household Cavalry were manoeuvring slowly back and forth about a mile away across the desert. They came under shell-fire, but the Commander-in-Chief was not to be deterred from the real object of his journey. It transpired that one of his boots was too tight and, dressing in the semi-dark that morning, he had managed to get his riding breeches crumpled and wedged between the boot and the calf of his leg. He could not get his boot off by himself and he could not risk getting anyone else to do it for him in sight of the troops, or a rumour might have started to the effect that the General had been hit and the surgeons were cutting his leg off! Now he asked Butler to extricate him from the boot, cut a slit in the leather, straighten the breeches and help him tug the boot on again, all under artillery fire.

They reached the cavalry just as a shell hit and killed a horse. The rider was on his feet in a moment, calling three cheers for the first charger in the Life Guards killed since Waterloo!

The battle continued in a desultory manner, both sides feeling the heat, until a quarter to five, when a mass of enemy infantry and cavalry began to surge slowly down the desert slope towards the British right. Then they hesitated and stopped. Approaching from the east they had seen a cloud of dust heralding the arrival of Baker Russell and a mixed regiment of three hundred and fifty sabres from the 4th and 7th Dragoon Guards, marching straight from the quayside to the battle-line. Three quarters of an hour later the Guards Brigade arrived on the scene, bringing with them the remaining four 9-pounders of N Battery, a welcome relief for the two guns that had been in action all day.

As the sun set a cool breeze began to blow from the north, bringing comfort to men who had been exposed all day to a hot-weather sun. Better still, a steam-launch came chugging up the shallow canal towing three boats loaded with meat, biscuit and a ton of oats, all of which were unloaded without delay and made available for men and horses when the division bivouacked for the night.

Sir Garnet rode back to Ismailia, leaving Butler to see the new arrivals into their positions for the night. The Egyptians offered a slight threat to the left at half-past seven, but probably only to cover their own withdrawal. General Willis had been ordered to hold his own during the night and to attack the enemy at daybreak.

Butler rode back to Ismailia under a brilliant moon, arriving at nine o'clock. He had expected to be back in Ismailia for lunch that day, but instead had suffered sixteen hours of saddle, sun and sand, sustained by a piece of melon and occasional draughts of canal water. He got a shake-down on the office floor for a few hours until half-past three in the morning, when he rode off again with Sir Garnet through the darkness over the two miles of heavy sand between Ismailia and Nefisha, and on across the harder, more friendly desert to Magfar, where they arrived at half-past four. Beating them to it was McCalmont, who had spent the previous evening and early part of the night somehow getting every last man and horse ashore. Then, forming them up, he had marched the rear squadrons of the Dragoons to Magfar, arriving in time for the morning's advance to battle.

It was a very different story from the previous morning, the British force having swollen to an infantry division and a cavalry brigade, with gunners to match—during the night a battery of six 16-pounder guns had reached the bivouac. They moved off to attack Tel el-Maskhuta at first light, Graham's brigade north of the canal and railway, the Guards Brigade at a considerable distance to the right. On the extreme right, advancing over the ground held by the enemy during the previous afternoon, were the cavalry, mounted infantry and Royal Horse Artillery. Following behind the infantry brigades, in reserve, were Lieutenant-Colonel Ashburnham and his King's Royal Rifle Corps, who had helped push the guns through deep sand for most of the way; and the Marine Light Infantry, both of whom had arrived in the early morning. The 16-pounders moved on either side of the Guards Brigade.

As the force left, weary mules dragged a five-truck train into Magfar station. It brought a field hospital, camp equipment, more provisions and forage.

Tel el-Maskhuta and the ridge to the north of it were found clear of enemy, the Egyptians having withdrawn completely from their positions of the previous day. The sun was well up in the sky behind the British; the morning mists were dispersing; mirage had not yet established its noontime supremacy. From the ridge Sir Garnet was able to see past Mahsama towards Kassassin, ten miles away. To the immediate front clouds of dust indicated that enemy artillery was still making its laborious way back to re-deploy. More important, several trains were visible moving west along the railway in the valley to the right front. Wolseley called Butler over to him. 'Gallop to Drury-Lowe,' he said. 'Tell him to take all his cavalry and horse artillery forward and at all costs capture one of those trains. An engine could be worth a lot of money to me now.' Butler was off without waiting for written orders and soon overhauled the cavalry, who were moving at a walk over the gravelly surface, under sporadic shell-fire from Egyptian guns on lower ground to their left front. He delivered his message and Drury-Lowe went forward at the best pace he could; but the horses were already showing the strain of the last twenty-four hours in the sun. Nonetheless, the General tried to work well around the enemy left to cut off his retreat. The mounted infantry scouted ahead, their small Egyptian horses, well-bred and acclimatized, had little trouble.

No formed body of enemy was seen until they reached the heights north of Mahsama. Then Drury-Lowe judged himself to be opposed by a large force of infantry, eight to ten squadrons of cavalry and guns in position. He ordered into action his own Royal Horse Artillery guns, reinforced now by the two 16-pounders which had started the day on the right of the Guards Brigade, and very effectively they engaged the enemy, with shrapnel bursting accurately in the air over the targets. The mounted infantry were released to carry out the role for which they were designed, galloping into well-selected positions, dismounting and bringing close and aimed infantry fire to bear. Gradually the Egyptians fell back until, at last, their camp at Mahsama was captured, the mounted infantry joining in a final cavalry charge which drove all before it. Seven Krupp guns, large numbers of Remington rifles and a train were left in British hands. The engine, alas, had uncoupled and got away. Fugitives who had been unable to fight their way on to an earlier train went fleeing in all directions and the cavalry killed them by the score until the troopers became weary of slaughter. One wretched fellah soldier who had thrown away his rifle clung like grim death to McCalmont's leg, howling for mercy, and the Brigade-Major simply did not have the heart to let him be killed. He turned his attention instead to the stranded train and managed to fit himself out with a complete set of camp equipment: no more sleeping on the sand for Hugh McCalmont!

The train consisted of seventy-five wagons loaded with ammunition and, most important of all, provisions.

By eight o'clock the infantry had reached Tel el-Maskhuta and occupied the village south of the canal. As it was big enough to provide shade and shelter for the Brigade of Guards, Sir Garnet encamped them there. Graham's brigade were given time to rest while he decided whether or not to move them on to Mahsama; it would depend upon the supply situation, on whether or not he could maintain them there. He sent orders to Willis to recall the cavalry.

Before General Willis could implement this order, he received a report from Drury-Lowe about the captured provision train which altered the situation entirely. He knew that the cavalry were being brought back only because it would be too difficult to feed men and horses so far ahead, but the problem was now solved and, so far from recalling them, he told them to stay where they were and sent forward the battalion of marines and the marine artillery to help them consolidate.

When Sir Garnet received the report, he concurred with his Divisional Commander's decision and changed his own plans to be consistent with this important new factor for his administrative appreciation.

The heat became intense. By noon, when the King's Royal Rifle Corps reached the canal, it was 104 degrees Fahrenheit. Marling had been carrying the rifle belonging to a young soldier in his company for the last mile or two, but on arrival the man just lay down and died. The young subaltern had already divided the water in his bottle between his soldier-servant and two other men, so as soon as the regiment fell out he rushed straight to the canal and 'drank three great canteens full of the muddiest water I ever tasted in my life!' He mentions here that the men were still marching and fighting, as they had done in South Africa, wearing thick, black rifle serge.

It was now possible to capture and hold Kassassin Lock, so the cavalry were sent there next morning. They met with no resistance until the mounted infantry in the van were held up just short of their objective. Baker Russell was not immediately available so McCalmont took it upon himself to order off a troop of the 4th Dragoon Guards who charged home and took the lock. Baker Russell, when he heard about it, was a trifle put out.

Graham had left Tel el-Maskhuta at dawn for Mahsama, but received orders while already on the move to go on to Kassassin. He had with him the York and Lancaster Regiment, the Duke of Cornwall's Light Infantry, the Royal Marine Light Infantry and the Royal Marine Artillery. They reached Kassassin without incident and started to entrench. So, by the morning of 26 August the whole of the railway and Sweet-Water Canal from Ismailia to Kassassin were in British hands. The jumping-off place for Tel el-Kebir, only six miles further on, had been seized and defences were being prepared. It had all come about much earlier than had been anticipated as a result of Sir Garnet's flexible planning and the quick reactions by him and his officers to sudden changes in the situation. It remained now to build up depots of supplies and ammunition at Kassassin, as a preliminary to destroying the Egyptian army at Tel el-Kebir and then pressing on to Cairo.

Casualties had been light. Five men and twenty-one horses had been killed; three officers, twenty-five men and six horses had been wounded. Sixteen of the Household Cavalry and twenty-five of the York and Lancaster Regiment were admitted to hospital suffering from heat exhaustion, but all survived. Sir Garnet's calculated risk had paid off. The only death from the sun was that one unfortunate soldier in Colonel Ashburnham's regiment; none of the rest of his men even needed admission.

A very useful prisoner taken at Mahsama was Mahmoud Fehmy Pasha, Arabi's chief military adviser, who had failed to catch a train to safety. He tried to conceal his identity, which nearly led to his being shot as a spy. He then came clean and put his knowledge at the disposal of the Intelligence Department—a useful contribution, as he had designed the defences of Tel el-Kebir.

[2]

Now came the hardest part of the campaign so far. The Guards Brigade, who had been left in the fairly comfortable shade of Tel el-Maskhuta, found themselves put to work clearing dams over the Sweet-Water Canal at Magfar and Tel el-Maskhuta. Moreover, these dams had been so well constructed—the mass of earth held together by reeds, telegraph wire and other building material—that it took the men, trying to maintain their footing in a soggy, muddy canal, several days to remove the blockages. A large embankment placed over the railway had also to be dug away, but this was not so difficult. The main discomfort arose from the lack of tents and camp equipment, but these reached Tel el-Maskhuta on 28 August and the men's bedding-rolls came up on the following day. This made a great difference to the morale of the soldiers who were prepared to work hard and cheerfully from then onwards.

For troops acclimatized to Egyptian hot weather, so long as they have tents and plenty of water, there is no hardship in operating west of Ismailia in August. The same applies to horses. But that element of the Expeditionary Force which had come more or less straight from England would have found things a bit difficult to begin with. It is noticeable from contemporary accounts that the King's Royal Rifle Corps mounted infantry, coming from a nice, sunny Malta summer, and having had a month of operations around Alexandria, mounted on good local horses, had no trouble at all and were full of dash and energy.

In Ismailia Lanyon had at last been landed at the base and work was proceeding apace. As ships were emptied, so Sir Garnet used them to bring Lieutenant-General Sir Edward Hamley and some of his division from Alexandria to Ismailia. He knew from his Ashanti campaign that Alison was just the man to lead Highlanders in the storming of Tel el-Kebir; he also knew that Evelyn Wood was a genius for managing anything, somehow. So he chose Alison and his four Highland regiments to come to Ismailia, leaving a rather disgruntled Evelyn Wood to keep Arabi Pasha guessing at Kafr ed-Duaur. He gave Wood strict instructions to stay on the defensive and risk nothing—he had been left only six battalions, two batteries of garrison artillery and the Malta Fencibles. Sir Evelyn had lost every mounted man, but his protests were brushed aside by Sir Garnet with the laconic comment, 'Evelyn Wood is sure to raise more'—which he did 'somehow', though very strange they looked at first.

On 28 August Brigadier-General Wilkinson's Indian Cavalry Brigade rode into Ismailia from Suez, so a cavalry division was now constituted under the command of Major-General Drury-Lowe.

On the same morning things began to happen at Kassassin. Graham was there to hold the lock and make sure that fresh water flowed along the canal. It was overlooked from higher ground to the north-west, so was far from being an ideal defensive position. Besides, although he had two Royal Horse Artillery guns, they had left their ammunition wagons bogged down in the sand behind them. So, when his vedettes reported enemy cavalry on the hills to the north, he stood his garrison to arms and alerted Baker Russell's cavalry brigade at Mahsama. Nothing happened except for some long-range artillery fire, and at three o'clock the Egyptians seemed to be withdrawing, so everybody stood down again. At half-past four, however, the enemy sent forward a line of skirmishers, supported by heavy artillery fire, and it looked as though a serious attack was on the way after all. Graham re-occupied his position and sent a message calling up the cavalry. When his guns had expended the limited amount of ammunition they had with them, he sent them back to Mahsama, as they were useless to him.

At half-past five, when the cavalry should have been well on their way, he despatched his ADC, Lieutenant Pirie, to meet them, with a verbal message that the cavalry should come up on his right and attack the left flank of the enemy skirmishers. Poor Pirie! So much is told about ADCs galloping off to deliver vital messages that it becomes axiomatic for them to accomplish their missions. But this wretched subaltern met with a chapter of misfortunes. He missed the British cavalry in the dark and searched frantically for them all over the desert until his horse foundered from sheer fatigue. By a stroke of luck he was picked up by the Royal Horse Artillery on their way back from Kassassin and got another mount from them. At last he found General Drury-Lowe and passed on his instructions. But it seems he was so distraught after his ordeal that he got them wrong.

The cavalry were advancing over a desert lit by bright moonlight, with the 7th Dragoon Guards in the lead, steering on the evening star which happened to be directly over the Egyptian position. Behind them came artillery and the three squadrons of Household Cavalry. Drury-Lowe had meant to take his force in a wide sweep to turn the enemy's left, but suddenly made contact. The Egyptians were just as surprised to see him as he was to see them, but opened fire with rifles and artillery. The General ordered the 7th Dragoon Guards to wheel away to the left, giving the guns a clear field of fire. They came into action, fired a few rounds, then Drury-Lowe gave the order to charge. Baker Russell in the lead, the Household Cavalry—big men on big, heavy horses—charged and annihilated utterly the Egyptian infantry in their path, reforming on the enemy position.

That was all. The Egyptian cavalry made itself scarce, their artillery got away under cover of darkness and at a quarter to nine at night Graham ordered a return to camp. There had been quite a battle before the cavalry arrived, seventy of Graham's men killed or wounded. The Cavalry had twenty-five casualties, with forty horses killed or wounded, in their brief affray.

It was sad about Lieutenant Gribble, a young officer of the 3rd Dragoon Guards, attached to the 7th. He insisted on riding a horse that he could not really control and it bolted with him into the enemy lines. He never returned.

[3]

In Ismailia Indian Engineers completed a tramway from the wharf to the railway station. Trains began to run regularly along the railway; boats steamed through the Sweet-Water Canal. General Hamley arrived in Ismailia on the evening of September, but kept his men sleeping on board, providing fatigue parties for unloading during the day. Stores in excess of the daily consumption began to accumulate in Kassassin as the period of preparation drew to a

6. After the battle of Kassassin, searching for the dead and wounded.

close. The Army was deeply indebted to the Royal Navy in the persons of Admiral Sir Beauchamp Seymour and his officers for their willing cooperation, hard work and skill in organization. It is worth noting that Sir Garnet maintained good relations with his naval colleagues in every one of his campaigns requiring a Joint Service effort. We have also seen admirals in the middle of inland swamps, in the depths of tropical jungle—and Sir Beauchamp Seymour had no intention of missing the Tel el-Kebir battle.

The supply position permitted Brigadier-General Wilkinson's Indian Cavalry Brigade to move up the line to join their Divisional Commander, Drury-Lowe. Happily they rode along—spare leathery sowars, little wiry horses. It was much cooler than it had been on the plains of India and they had just had a refreshing sea-voyage. No acclimatization was necessary for *them*. With his regiment, the 6th Bengal Cavalry, was Captain Sartorius.

On 5 September Sir Garnet ordered Evelyn Wood to attract and retain the attention of the Egyptians at Kafr ed-Duaur over the vital period of his concentration of all units at Kassassin. He told him, 'Your being retained at Alexandria is a sad blow to me and I know it will be to you'. Sir Evelyn had only six battalions to cover a front of fifty-five miles, but even then believed attack to be the best form of defence. He requested permission, but the Commander-in-Chief only repeated his original orders. He had no wish to risk any form of setback to British arms and the consequent boost to enemy morale at this juncture.

On that day Colonel Sir Redvers Buller set off for Kassassin at daybreak. He had reached Ismailia with Sir Edward Hamley, to take over as Chief of Intelligence from Tulloch. Sir Garnet knew all about the importance of good intelligence and there had been no skimping over personnel. Buller found six other officers in his intelligence department.

True to form, and as Sir Garnet had expected, he was off at two o'clock in the morning next day to go and *get* his intelligence, rather than wait for it to come to him. He says that he went to reconnoitre Arabi's position, so it must have been known by then that the Pasha had shifted his attention to Tel el-Kebir. He took sixty cavalrymen with him, left fifty of them on a ridge between camp and the enemy lines, and went on with the other ten as escort. Wandering about in the dark he nearly ran into an enemy picquet, but luckily saw their camp-fire in time. However, at first light he found himself exactly where he wanted to be, directly in front of the centre of the Egyptian position and roughly a mile and a half from it. He had a good look at it in the light of the rising sun and then got safely back to his squadron on the ridge before the enemy patrols could catch him.

Next morning, 7 September, he set out again at four o'clock and this time he wanted to stay and observe for longer, so he took with him a regiment of infantry and two squadrons of cavalry to cross the canal and have a good look at the south of the defences. He stayed long enough to make a sketch and paid particular attention to a great isolated redoubt sited three-quarters of a mile forward of the main line on the Egyptian south-centre. He had two horses shot: 'One of them belonged to a correspondent who got his nag shot by going where he had no right to go.' The culprit may have been Thomas de Burgh—he certainly lost his horse at about that time. He had been present at Magfar, Tel el-Maskhuta and at Kassassin Lock for the action on 28 August, where he had been wounded, not very seriously; he had been bending over for some reason when a bullet scored his back, cutting his braces!

Up to this time garrisons at Kassassin, Mahsama and Tel el-Maskhuta had been kept to a minimum on the principle that the fewer mouths there were to feed in the forward areas, the greater amount of provisions would reach the forward depots. The Cavalry Brigade and the Guards Brigade could not have been retained so far up the line of communications if it had not been for the supplies captured in these places. But now the railway was in working order, so instructions were issued for the whole of Alison's brigade, the Indian Contingent and the remainder of the artillery to move up to Kassassin on a programme worked out to bring the last unit in on 12 September. Force Headquarters would close in Ismailia and open in Kassassin on the 9th of the month.

On that very day the Egyptians attacked. Bedouin, trying to impress, had told the Egyptian Commander in Tel el-Kebir that Kassassin was very weakly held and that they had completely severed communications between there and Ismailia. He hoped to recapture Kassassin by a combined attack from Tel el-Kebir and from Es-Salihiyeh in the north.

Buller had gone out at four o'clock in the morning with an assistant, hoping to do some surveying, and nearly got caught behind a large body of enemy cavalry. 'I need not tell you that we scuttled off towards our picquets as fast as we could, but as we were going a brute of an Arab that I was riding began to play the fool, and getting its head down bucked me clean off. I fell light, however, and never let him go, so what might have been a nasty business did not matter.' After reaching safety, he stayed to watch what was happening and thought that either the enemy was making a very strong reconnaissance in force or he was going to attack.

The 13th Bengal Lancers had been on outpost duty during the night of 8/9 September and their morning patrols soon reported the enemy to be advancing in considerable numbers. So at a quarter to seven the Indian Cavalry Brigade was sent out to delay the enemy coming east from Tel el-Kebir and Graham's infantry and artillery re-occupied their prepared defensive positions.

When it was observed that a second Egyptian force was coming south from Es-Salihiyeh to join in the fray, Baker Russell was despatched to join Wilkinson and support him in keeping the two enemy columns separated. Wilkinson was to threaten the left of the Tel el-Kebir group and Baker Russell the right of the Es-Salihiyeh enemy. The mounted infantry went first to Wilkinson, where they paid particular attention to the Egyptian artillery, harassing them with well-aimed rifle-fire and making their advance difficult until infantry came up and took over the task from them. Then the mounted infantry were transferred to Baker Russell's command.

In the early morning a troop of Bengal Lancers had charged an enemy cavalry squadron and put it to flight, but the battle proper did not begin until a quarter to eight when General Willis ordered a general advance by the whole force. The British artillery fired so effectively that the Egyptians withdrew in disorder before Graham's infantry could reach them. As the advance continued, the Royal Marines captured two guns, Colonel Ashburnham's King's Royal Rifle Corps took another, while the cavalry charged and seized a fourth with team and limber complete. Then at half-past ten the British forward elements began to come under effective fire from the guns in Tel el-Kebir, now only five thousand yards away.

General Willis knew that if he carried on in hot pursuit he could capture the fortress that day, though he would have to expect quite heavy losses in a daylight attack against a fortress manned by men armed with modern breech-loading rifles. But it would have been a stupid thing to do and in direct conflict with the Commander-in-Chief's aim. He had not the strength to annihilate the Egyptian Army at Tel el-Kebir; they would only have withdrawn to regroup somewhere further back where they would probably be reinforced. He had not the strength for a drive at Cairo, nor the administrative build-up to make one possible. So he halted.

Sir Garnet and his staff had left Ismailia at a quarter past nine, reached Kassassin at eleven, and then had some miles to ride forward before joining Willis, with whose decision to break off the action he concurred.

Buller had assessed that the Egyptian attackers at Tel el-Kebir had a strength of about thirteen thousand men and twenty guns. He then changed his horse, needless to say, and went off to join the cavalry who were coping with six thousand enemy coming from Es-Salihiyeh. They had a nice little skirmish. The correspondent of the *Kildare Observer* had been left in camp, as there was no horse to spare for him. But Captain and Adjutant Ulick de Burgh had seen fit to bring his best racehorse to Egypt to stand him in good stead in all the meetings that he expected would be held after the war was over. This fine and valuable animal was never committed to action or put to risk from enemy fire. So he was horrified, when charging the Es-Salihiyeh column, to be passed by his elder brother who had found a mount eminently suited to his taste! Mouthing dreadful imprecations, he launched himself in pursuit, shouting threats of a five-hundred pound bill if his thoroughbred was injured.

A gun was captured and then the Es-Salihiyeh Egyptians went for home as fast as they could. They withdrew so quickly that they escaped the Guards Brigade who had been ordered by telegraph to come up from Tel el-Maskhuta and cut them off. Their commander, Sultan Pasha, was a man of peace who liked his comforts. He had not acquired any great affection for the rigorous life in camp at Es-Salihiyeh and had been spending a lot of time among the flesh-pots of Ismailia, even though there was a war on and the British were in occupation. Butler had seen him there!

The Duke of Connaught and his guardsmen marched into Kassassin at four o'clock in the afternoon after a trying and wearisome march.

Losses had not been great on either side. British casualties were eighty personnel and fifteen horses.

A strong infantry and artillery outpost was now established on the high ground above Kassassin, and every morning before dawn Sir Garnet and some of his staff went there to observe the enemy fortifications at Tel el-Kebir. It was soon apparent that the Egyptians picquets and outposts were not deployed outside the entrenchments before first light, which was then at five o'clock.

CHAPTER 10
Tel el-Kebir

[1]

Sir Garnet Wolseley's aim was still to destroy the Egyptian Army at Tel el-Kebir. It must be crushed and dispersed, in no condition to offer further resistance, nor to reform and fall back on other enemy formations. The cavalry pursuit must be so speedy as to reach and capture Cairo before the authorities there had time to recover from their first shocked reaction to the news of disaster in the desert, and before they had time to implement a threat which Arabi Pasha had now made to burn Cairo as he had done Alexandria, if it looked like being taken by the British. While the cavalry were on their way to the capital city, the infantry must march to take and hold the key railway junction of Zagazig, forestalling any attempts to concentrate by the Egyptian forces in Mansura, Es-Salihiyeh, Kafr ed-Duaur or elsewhere.

A daylight attack on Tel el-Kebir would entail crossing flat ground bare of cover in the face of heavy rifle and artillery fire. Encircling movements might result in the enemy withdrawing in confusion, but more or less intact, to Zagazig and Cairo, defeating the aim. Moreover, in daylight the defeated enemy would be able to see better to escape. Another point was that the Tel el-Kebir defences were very extended, so parts of the British force would have to operate at a considerable distance from the canal and their water-supply, which would not be pleasant in the midday and afternoon sun. Lastly, Sir Garnet's essential principle of surprise would be hard to apply—the Egyptians would be able to see the advance-to-attack from three miles away and would be waiting fully prepared to meet it.

A night attack should have the advantage of complete surprise, particularly as Egyptian outposts were not deployed until daybreak.

In any case, the advance over open ground would be made under cover of darkness and, if surprise was lost, the troops would only be subjected to unaimed fire. The flatness itself would be a help, with nothing to stumble over, though special arrangements for guidance would have to be made. The troops would be moving during the cool of the night and would arrive at the start-line fresh for the assault. Lack of water would not militate against their efficiency; thirst would not be too great until the battle was over, when water-carts could be brought up. The railway and canal had been little damaged between Kassassin and Tel el-Kebir, so all the necessary supplies and baggage could be brought up without delay. The men, therefore, would not have to carry everything with them, no heavy loads to slow up the force and weary the troops.

Intelligence about the line of advance and enemy defences would have to be good. Fortunately it was; Buller had seen to that.

The final pre-dawn reconnaissance was on 12 September. All the Generals, each rationed to only one staff officer, assembled at Sir Garnet's observation post before first light. McCalmont had accompanied Baker Russell and, together, at five o'clock, with the first streak of dawn, they saw enemy vedettes emerging from Tel el-Kebir. 'Note the time,' said the Commander-in-Chief. 'Our attack must be delivered before this hour, otherwise the vedettes will detect our presence. Don't talk about it until the orders are issued!'

The troops were not told what was taking place. Sir Garnet worked on the principle that what was known in one camp would soon be known in the other, so things went on as usual during the day and in the evening, except that staff officers were hard at work preparing copies of operation orders. After darkness had fallen the three divisions moved out into the desert, leaving their fires burning in camp. Baker Russell and McCalmont were feeling on top of the world, as the Brigadier-General had previously packed his ADC off to Ismailia to procure essential supplies. Before marching out that evening, according to Hugh McCalmont, 'That enemy, my respected brigadier presented himself before my tent with a bottle of champagne in one hand and a bucket in the other, and it was then I discovered what an admirable vessel a bucket is to quaff bubbly wine out of!'

A night operation, particularly one in which it is hoped to take the enemy by surprise, has to be carried out in complete silence. There may be no loud or shouted orders, no lights. Jingling harness chains must be wrapped in cloth to stop their noise. There can be no change of plan half-way to the objective. Complete simplicity is essential in every phase of the operation, and even then things can go wrong.

In this case the starting line was about a mile and a half out in the desert, running north and south through a mound in the midst of the level, gravelly ridges north of the railway and canal. From this mound the engineers had erected a line of telegraph poles running roughly west for a thousand yards, which would indicate their direction to the divisions at the start of their advance into the night. There would be no moon. The line was not exactly parallel to the railway in order to avoid the isolated bastion to the south of the defences, which, if alerted, could give an early alarm and do great harm.

Errors could be cumulative, so Sir Garnet planned to have as many independent chances of success as possible without weakening his effort. He deployed his divisions on the starting line in the exact formation in which they would deliver their assault on the Egyptian positions, and he saw to it that they were about twelve hundred yards apart. They had tasks which were not dependent on each other, and he hoped that if one division got into trouble, then the other might still succeed, giving the laggard formation time to recover and operate in support. The field artillery would move silently in between the two infantry divisions, a body of forty-two field guns. They would therefore be immediately available at dawn to take on areas of strong resistance, to silence enemy batteries and to provide support for exploiting victory.

Buller had been made totally responsible for direction and timing: he confesses to having been horribly nervous during the advance! His survey had given a distance of three and three-quarter miles from the starting-line to the Egyptian entrenchments, and experience gained during the approach marches from Ismailia indicated that the infantry would cover about one mile in the hour. It was decided that the corps would advance at half-past one in the morning of 13 September and this should ensure them being on their objective by first light, ready to attack.

By eleven o'clock that night the whole force was in position on the starting line, lying in the desert under the stars. On the left, nearest the canal and railway, was Sir Edward Hamley's 2nd Infantry Division, led by Sir Archibald Alison's Highland Brigade of four battalions deployed in line. Sir Garnet had wanted each regiment to advance in two lines, one to assault, the other to come up in support when required; so Alison organized each of his regiments with two companies of each wing in front and a similar organization behind. In this way supporting companies coming forward would be joining their own half-battalion, retaining the normal chain of command and reducing confusion. Half a mile behind was the second brigade of only two battalions, commanded by Colonel Ashburnham. In rear of this brigade rode Sir Garnet Wolseley and his staff, and, of course, Admiral Sir Beauchamp Seymour.

In the centre was the field artillery under Brigadier-General Goodenough; on the right Lieutenant-General Willis's 1st Infantry Division led by Brigadier-General Graham's brigade with four battalions in line; behind them the Duke of Connaught's Guards Brigade of three regiments.

The Cavalry Division and the Royal Horse Artillery were at some distance to the extreme right with orders to sweep around the Egyptians' rear as soon as they were fully engaged in front, thoroughly shattering their already jittering morale, making a rally impossible, cutting off retreat and standing by for immediate pursuit.

The Indian Infantry Brigade was to move on the south side of the canal through the cultivated village area. This could be hazardous to surprise; there had been occasions in other campaigns when surprise attacks by night had failed because troops had disturbed geese or dogs, whose clamour had awakened the defenders. So Major-General Macpherson and Brigadier-General Tanner had been ordered to stay one hour's march behind the main assault force. The brigade, on arrival, would be across the enemy's line of retreat and Tanner was to be ready to move straight on to Zagazig after the battle and secure that important junction before the Egyptians could recover. Artillery support would be provided by 7 Mountain Battery and by a captured 40-pounder Krupp gun on a railway truck pushed along the railway by a two-locomotive train which also hauled wagons containing railway repair materials. Escorting the train, and keeping level with the Indian Contingent, was the Naval Brigade with its Gatlings. On the canal, ready to ferry troops across if necessary, was an engineer pontoon company.

Sir Garnet rode round the whole of the Force, checking that all units were in the correct positions. He gave Alison his own Royal Navy ADC, Lieutenant Rawson, an officer experienced in navigation by the stars, to guide him on his way.

At half-past one seventeen thousand officers and men and their guns moved west to do battle in the dawn. The desert surface undulated slightly but maintained a general uniform level varying within limits of only about twenty feet. The ground was hard enough to make movement easy, yet soft enough to render the advance almost noiseless. After an hour a short halt was ordered to ensure that all was well, but everything had worked perfectly, so the advance was resumed at three o'clock. Butler was leading the staff group, relying on the Pole Star over his shoulder to give him an alignment on another star in front, which he kept between his horse's ears. As the front star sank below the horizon, so he chose another higher up and, although there was occasional cloud, at no time were both his two stars occluded at the same time.

At half-past four Sir Garnet told Butler to go over to Alison and tell him to press on—dawn could not be far off and the enemy entrenchments must be close ahead. Maurice went with him and they found the Highland Brigade sorting out in the darkness what might have been a very dangerous piece of confusion, liable to have wrecked the whole plan. Alison had ordered another short halt to give the men a bit of a rest before the battle. He had given the order in a low tone from the middle of his forward line and the centre companies had stopped at once. But while orders were being passed from company to company, the outer elements naturally continued to move until the orders reached them, and, as at the same time they had to keep touch with the centre, the flank battalions, without realizing it, lost their sense of direction and wheeled inwards. So, when the halt was over and the brigade moved off again, the flank battalions suddenly found themselves marching straight at each other. Fortunately discipline was good and nobody started shooting. Alison halted again and set about putting things straight. Order was restored, the march was resumed, but twenty minutes had been lost. It was lucky that there was time to spare.

Butler had counted his horse's steps on the way out and worked a successful little piece of navigation to intercept the Headquarter staff, which had in the meantime been moving ahead. Suddenly at ten minutes to five a large shaft of pale light, shaped like a sheaf of corn and the colour of pale gold, became visible, rising up from the horizon into the heavens. Sir Garnet and his officers thought it must be the approaching dawn, but they were wrong; it was the Great Comet of 1882 on its way into the sun. The real dawn was not far

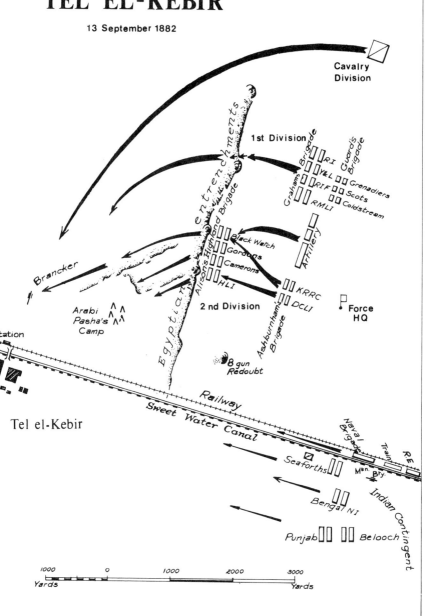

TEL EL-KEBIR

13 September 1882

Cavalry
Division

1st Division

Graham's Brigade
RI
Y&L
RIF
RMLI

Guards Brigade
Grenadiers
Scots
Coldstream

entrenchments

Alison's Highland Brigade

Black Watch
Gordons
Camerons
HLI

Artillery

KRRC
DCLI

Ashburnham's Brigade

Force
HQ

2nd Division

Brancker

Egyptian

Arabi
Pasha's
Camp

Station

8 gun
Redoubt

Railway

Sweet Water Canal

Tel el-Kebir

Naval Brigade

Seaforths

Mtn. Bty.

Train

R.E.

Bengal NI

Indian Contingent

Punjab
Belooch

1000   0   1000   2000   3000
Yards   Yards

away, but while it was still dark they heard a single shot, then two or three, followed by a thunderous roar of musketry mixed with heavy gunfire.

[2]

The Egyptian battalions detailed for defence of the outer entrenchments had been sleeping with their arms beside them and with plenty of ammunition ready for use. The whole position was held by about twenty thousand men and seventy-five guns. Some Bedouin had been ordered to stay outside on the look-out, and cavalry were posted between the outer and main defences, but neither had gone far forward. The enemy commander, Ali Rubi Pasha, had gone off to sleep in Arabi's camp, further to the rear.

It was five minutes to five o'clock when the Highland Brigade realized that they were nearing the enemy parapet. In the dim light they could just see enemy picquets a hundred and fifty yards ahead. Then a sentry saw them, a shot was fired, followed by others as Egyptian buglers sounded the alarm, and the first few shells came whizzing over their heads. The Highlanders fixed bayonets without halting and advanced another two hundred yards. Then the whole enemy entrenchment for a mile or more was lit by flashes from the rifle-muzzles of the defenders, only a hundred and fifty yards before them.

It had still been almost dark when firing broke out, but so short was the transition from darkness to light that within five minutes it was possible to distinguish objects a quarter of a mile distant, and in ten minutes everything was visible. It could be seen that Alison's brigade was the furthest forward, with the artillery in their right rear, while Graham's leading brigade of the 1st Infantry Division was still further back, about nine hundred yards from the Egyptian entrenchments. The cavalry were correspondingly further back to the right rear, nearly two thousand yards.

As soon as the enemy sounded the alarm Alison gave the prearranged signal for storming the fortifications. His bugler sounded the advance, other buglers took it up, the men responded with a roar of cheering and rushed in two long waves on the rampart before them. The gaps between battalions had closed during the night, so that there was no longer room for rear companies to come into line. General Hamley realized this and checked the advance of the

Gordon and Cameron Highlanders' rear companies, bringing them into reserve under his own hand.

In next to no time the leading companies of Highlanders were at the enemy defences, but then their fortunes varied. The two centre battalions—the Gordon Highlanders on the right, the Camerons on the left—were confronted with a ditch over nine feet wide and nearly six feet deep in places, the far side sloping steeply up to ground level. Over the top was another obstacle in the shape of a breastwork four to five feet high. The Highlanders leaped down into the ditch and started to struggle up the far side. At first it was every man for himself, slipping and sliding, seeking for some form of purchase in the soft shifting sand. Lieutenant Brooks was the first of the Gordons to mount the parapet, only to fall dead from four wounds. Private Donald Cameron led the Camerons and fell forward into the enemy trench, shot through the head. Then more individuals gained the top of the ditch, now in one place, now in another. Men began to realize the need to help each other; groups reached the summit together; little assault parties formed. They rushed the breastwork and jumped down into the enemy trenches. But in other places the defenders held so resolutely to their ground that the attackers were driven back. On the left centre Sir Archibald Alison's horse was shot as he dismounted to lead his men on foot. He crossed the ditch, but was then forced back over the parapet by sheer weight of numbers. He went back again and was more successful, but was then nearly cut off and killed by a group of Egyptians who had been driven out of another part of the line. He advanced alone, pistol in hand—he only had one hand, the other had been lost in a previous campaign. But soon an assortment of men from all regiments joined him and he led them forward.

In another sector a number of Highlanders had driven a salient into the defence line, only to find themselves under fire from the front and from both sides, for this part of the defensive position had an inner double line of works extending obliquely along it, facing north. They began to give way, but at that moment Sir Edward Hamley brought forward the reserve that he had constituted from the rear companies, rallied the broken fragments of the forward companies and from that time onward led their advance himself. It was now about twenty past five, and slowly the fight pressed on over the open ground between the outer and inner defences. Mixed groups of Camerons, Gordons and Black Watch under any officer who would lead them attacked first one party of Egyptians, then

7. Storming the trenches at Tel el-Kebir.

another, until at last the whole of the front rampart in the Highland Brigade's centre objective was won.

The Black Watch (the Ashanti battalion) on the right had been confronted by a five-gun battery protected first by a ditch similar to the one encountered by the Camerons and Gordons, and then by a second defence line behind a much worse ditch, thirteen feet wide and six feet deep. Brave and determined though they were, the defenders were equally valiant and held their ground.

The Highland Light Infantry on the left had a four-gun battery to deal with. There was only one defence line, but the ditch was also twelve feet across and nearly six feet deep. It was, moreover, held by well-disciplined Nubian regiments who counterattacked while the Highlanders were still disorganized after crossing and drove them back with the bayonet.

This was the time for committing the reserve brigade. General Hamley sent back to Colonel Ashburnham ordering him to send the King's Royal Rifle Corps to reinforce the Black Watch and the Duke of Cornwall's Light Infantry to help the Highland Light Infantry.

In the centre the Generals were right in front. Everybody had been thrown into disorder crossing the ditches. There was no cohesion and the chain of command had been broken, but the men thought of nothing but the need to get on. Wherever an officer could be found—officers *are* useful sometimes—a party formed around him.

When first light made it possible to see, Brigadier-General Graham found his brigade pointing straight at the objective but half a mile short of it. Pushing on through heavy rifle and artillery fire, they reached the defences at ten past five and found themselves in luck. On the right the Royal Irish found themselves opposed only by a shallow ditch and small rampart, so they charged home. The defenders were forced back, but remained unbroken and withdrew for only a short distance, continuing the fight. But nothing could hold the Royal Irish for long. Retaining their discipline and cohesion, they advanced by bounds from one skilfully chosen position to another, driving the enemy before them. On the brigade's left the Royal Marine Light Infantry were up against much the same as the Camerons had been and, like them, succeeded in gaining the parapet. But they had more casualties, as there had been no surprise factor in their case to get them close to the defences unseen. Here, too, the Egyptians, still unshaken, pulled back only a few yards and stubbornly held their ground. In the brigade's centre the enemy had constructed a three-gun battery with ditches and emplacements similar to the strong point met by the Black Watch. Here, in one single rush, the York and Lancaster Regiment captured the whole front of the battery and the trenches north of it; and very soon afterwards the Royal Irish Fusiliers assaulted and entered the battery from the south. By twenty past five Graham's brigade, led by their commander, had captured their objective.

The Cavalry Division, led by the Indian Brigade, found itself about two thousand yards north-east of the northern end of the Egyptian defence line when light came and began to move forward at a fast trot. Fired at from a bastion at the northern end of the Tel el-Kebir defences, General Drury-Lowe ordered his Royal Horse Artillery into action. Not only did they silence the fort, they also neutralized an enemy field battery which was shelling the cavalry from open ground behind the defences. By twenty past five, just as Graham's brigade had accomplished its first task and was reforming, and when the conglomerate mass of Highlanders in the centre was beginning to advance on the Egyptian second-line defences, Drury-Lowe was wheeling south to penetrate the enemy rear.

Also at this time Major Lugard, an officer on the headquarter staff of the 2nd Division, managed to fight his way on past the south of the strong point which had held up the Black Watch for so long. He happened to notice that the Egyptian gunners in the emplacement had left their back door open, so he collected ten Highlanders, crept in from the rear and killed the detachments as they served their guns. Almost simultaneously a joint attack by the Black Watch and King's Royal Rifle Corps carried the position.

When Marling reached the ditch it was still full of Highlanders. He jumped down into it, then got one of his men to give him a boost up to the parapet. Drawing his sword and cheering on his men, he leaped down into the enemy trench, to fall flat on his face over a dead Egyptian. 'The black Sudanese regiments fought like blazes . . . there was very little quarter given, it was most of it bayonet work when we got inside.'

This was what Brigadier-General Goodenough, Commander of the Royal Artillery, was waiting for. He straightway sent Lieutenant-Colonel Brancker's battery through a gap in the defences south of the captured bastion. Spades were brought into use, ramps were made and the guns were dragged and pushed and hauled over to the far side where they came into action. One gun was damaged and had temporarily to be left in the ditch—the battery used the honour title of Broken Wheel for the next fifty years! Of the remainder, three brought effective shrapnel fire down on the secondary defence lines which were holding up the Camerons and Gordons, while the other two faced north to engage a part of the Egyptian line that had not been in the path of the assault and was being a nuisance to the further progress of the battle. Lieutenant-Colonel Schreiber's battery was brought into action on the Kassassin side of the defences to bring additional fire on this strip. The Royal Horse Artillery with the cavalry also dropped trails and shot them up from the rear. Threatened by the cavalry sweep which they could now see moving south in their left rear, the Egyptians, who had fought so bravely and stubbornly until then, suddenly lost heart completely. When Graham's regiments, re-grouped, started to move forward again, the enemy became a mass of hopeless fugitives, just as had the Zulus at the turning-point of the battle for Kambula. The time was twenty-five minutes to six.

Five minutes later it was at last the Highland Light Infantry's turn to succeed. Backed up by some of the Duke of Cornwall's Light Infantry from Ashburnham's brigade, they launched another assault on the Nubians in their bastion, and carried it. Then they turned left and fought their way down the defence line leading away from the captured bastion, the entrenchments which had held up the Highland Brigade's centre for so long. This now permitted the Cameron/Gordon groups to push on the next and last defence line, where they met some of the most stubborn resistance of the battle. 'The Egyptians held out stiffly at each turn of the parapet, embrasure and traverse, so that it was not until six o'clock that this defence line was cleared.' The Highlanders were through and surged on towards Tel el-Kebir railway station.

Brancker now found nothing to stop him, hooked-in his guns and trotted on through the fleeing enemy to the higher ground overlooking the station and started to shell trains leaving for the west crammed with refugee soldiery. Two trains got clear, but some ammunition in a third blew up, immobilizing it. At that moment some of the Indian cavalry were seen to reach the railway line, so the guns had to cease firing.

At Brancker's battery all the commanders met together. Goodenough was with his forward gunners. General Willis was there, slightly wounded, having ridden with his staff ahead of his division which was marching steadily in his tracks. Then arrived the forward fighting groups of Highlanders, three hundred men from the Camerons, Gordons and Black Watch in an improvised battle-entity of their own, led in person by General Hamley. Alison was with his men, so were the colonels of the Gordons and Camerons.

A phase of the battle had ended and they had captured the area where regiments were supposed to reform for a final set-piece attack. But there was no need to stop and reorganize; it was obvious that all the Egyptians wanted was to get away. Hamley decided to pursue with what he had and led the Highlanders straight through the enemy abandoned camp, on to capture a hundred carriages in the railway station, on over the bridge, halting finally on the tow-path beside the canal. It was enough. His men were still shooting anything that moved; he stopped them from firing any more on the flying, defeated fellah soldiery and their wretched camels.

Sir Garnet and his staff had moved behind Hamley's division during the night and has stopped about a mile short of the main Egyptian position, by what is marked on the contemporary map as Sir Beauchamp Seymour's tree. There is no record of the use to which the Admiral had put the tree to justify the title! There they awaited the coming of first light, when the first thing they saw was the big, isolated eight-gun redoubt on their left front, firing in all directions. But as soon as the Highland Brigade became indistinguishable from the defenders, the redoubt turned its attention to Wolseley's Staff. Sir Garnet sent his telegraph troop and led horses back out of range, but, apart from that, paid little attention to the shelling, settling down to watch the progress of the battle. Once, when Butler saw a squadron of enemy cavalry moving up from behind the redoubt, he was sent to call forward the Commander-in-Chief's personal escort of 19th Hussars. They came cantering by, past the redoubt which fired four or five rounds without hitting them, but the Egyptians would not wait.

When the whole of his force was advancing from the perimeter into the depth of the Tel el-Kebir defences, Sir Garnet ordered his staff to mount and they rode forward. Irritated at still being pursued by shell from the isolated forward redoubt which had been spared any attack by the British—they had been at great pains to avoid it during the approach march—he said that it was time something was done about it. So Schreiber's battery came into action behind it, fired into its soft rear and soon exploded a magazine, which solved the problem.

The General and his staff galloped half-right across desert dotted with wounded men, mostly from the Highland Light Infantry. On their way they found the old colonel of the Duke of Cornwall's Light Infantry, down with a bullet through his jaws. They crossed the parapet through gaps made by the artillery. The sun was now well above the horizon and, by looking to their right once they were inside the defences, they could see the 1st Infantry Division in regular formation marching quickly across the sands. In front parts of the 2nd Infantry Division were still descending the slopes to the railway station. Inside the defence works the desert was strewn with dead Egyptian soldiers, dead horses and dead camels. Completely surprised through they had been, led by officers who were mostly fellahin like themselves, with little experience of war, the enemy soldiers had fought stoutly whenever ten, or twenty, or fifty of them could get together. The heaps of dead lying with their rifles, facing the up-coming sun bore eloquent testimony of the final resolve of these poor men. According to Butler, 'The wrecks of Arabi's late army were strewn in all directions. Down across the slopes, through the camps, over the railway, and across the canal, the white-clad fugitives were flying south and west in dots, in dozens, in hundreds.' At the canal bridge 'The seamy side of a battle was here painfully apparent; anything seemed to be good enough to let off a rifle at. Dead and wounded men, horses and camels were on all sides. Some of the wounded had got down to the edge of the water to quench their thirst; others were on the higher banks, unable to get down. Many of our officers dismounted and carried water to these unfortunates, but the men were not similarly disposed. I heard an officer ask a man who was filling his canteen at the canal to give a drink of water to a gasping Egyptian cavalry soldier who was lying supporting himself against the battlement of the bridge. 'I wadna wet his lips,' was the indignant reply. Many of the wounded Egyptians had managed, as they lay, to cover their heads with pieces of paper to try and keep off the flies and the scorching sun.'

The Indian Contingent south of the canal, with the Naval Brigade across the other side on their right flank, had moved off at two o'clock in the morning. They had travelled three miles when the first shots were heard from the north, and themselves came under artillery fire a quarter of an hour later. It was found that the enemy guns were protected by about four hundred infantry, so a proper attack was mounted. The Seaforth Highlanders were to assault from the front, while the 20th Punjab Native Infantry by-passed the

position and took it from a flank. The 7th Mountain Battery took on
the Egyptian guns, the six Gatlings joined in from the far bank,
while the Seaforth Highlanders advanced by short bounds, halting
to fire volleys at intervals, until Brigadier-General Tanner ordered
Lieutenant-Colonel Stockwell to fix bayonets and charge. It was
soon over, the enemy were driven from their entrenchments and the
guns were all captured. The Punjabis pushed on across the irrigated
fields and carried an enemy-held village with their bayonets. The
squadron of 6th Bengal Cavalry was sent ahead to cut off the
fugitives from Tel e-Kebir and at seven o'clock Major-General
Macpherson was able to report personally to Sir Garnet that his task
had been accomplished.

[3]

The Commander-in-Chief reached the bridge just an hour and a half
after the action had begun. There he was joined by his senior
officers and at once gave orders for the next phase. Macpherson's
Indian Contingent was to push on at all speed for Zagazig and
capture this key junction. The cavalry were to capture Cairo before
Arabi Pasha had time to burn it; he was already on his way there.
The Pasha had been awakened by the firing, but his army had been
defeated before he had finished getting dressed. He did, however,
manage to escape on horseback, whereupon General Willis and his
staff moved into his tent!

General Wilkinson, with his Indian Cavalry Brigade and the
mounted infantry, occupied Belbeis at noon, encountering little
resistance. The first thing he did was to open the lock sluices to
ensure a full supply of drinking-wayer to Tel el-Kebir. That evening
he was joined by Drury-Lowe and Baker Russell with the 4th
Dragoon Guards, but the remainder of the 'heavy' brigade and all
the guns had been delayed by deep sand and difficulty in crossing the
number of branch canals with which the area abounded.

The Indian Contingent left Tel el-Kebir at twenty minutes to
eight and was in Aabasa by ten o'clock. They were off again at noon,
marching at some speed along the railway embankment, and soon
began to overtake fugitives from Tel el-Kebir, many of them still
armed. However, these men had no intention of doing any more
fighting, and it would have taken too long to disarm them all, so the
ex-enemies went on side by side to Zagazig, one lot in regular

marching order, the other a disorderly rabble. Macpherson and his cavalry squadron pushed on through them, reaching Zagazig at just after four in the afternoon. The junction was full of trains loaded with fugitives trying to escape. There ensued a Wild-West style running cavalry action until the driver of the leading train was shot, and then in the general confusion an incoming train, presumably unaware of what was going on, collided with another that was trying to escape and blocked the line. As a result ten engines and a hundred carriages were captured and railway communications were restored with Tel el-Kebir.

Occupying the telegraph station, Macpherson immediately sent a telegram to Cairo announcing that Arabi had been utterly defeated and that Zigazig was in British hands. He forebore to mention that his force consisted of only twenty sabres! Reading from the signal traffic that three train-loads of Egyptians were about to arrive from Es-Salihiyeh, he appropriated the name of the Zagazig station-master to inform his opposite number at the next station up the line that there was an obstruction and that all troop-trains must be held up until further notice. He then sent someone to *make* the necessary obstruction, removing a couple of rails.

That evening at nine o'clock he received a telegram in reply from the Cairo Government as follows: 'The whole Egyptian Nation present their gratitude at the manner your Government have employed in supporting His Highness Tewfik Pasha, our Khedive; therefore the Nation in general acknowledge your kindness, and beg, in the name of the Nation, to stop any further action on your part until you receive orders from His Highness the Khedive. The army having laid their submission to His Gracious Highness the Khedive, we are leaving immediately by train to lay before him the submission of the army, and beg the favour of any answer to us at Kafr ed-Duaur.'

Next day, 14 September, the Indian Cavalry Brigade and 4th Dragoon Guards resumed their advance over firm desert east of the canal. They began to distribute a previously prepared Proclamation in Arabic by Sir Garnet Wolseley, informing the villagers that the war was over and that peace had come again to Egypt. Quickly as they rode, the news preceded them and the far canal bank became lined with villagers carrying white flags and crying '*Aman! Aman!*' (Peace! Peace!). The nearer they came to Cairo, the more demon-strative was the joy of the local inhabitants.

As a precautionary measure, General Drury-Lowe halted his

small force while still several miles from Abbassiyeh, the large military complex on the eastern side of the city of Cairo. He sent forward a mixed detachment of fifty 4th Dragoons and Indian cavalry under Lieutenant-Colonel Stewart, accompanied by Captain Watson as Arabic interpreter, and two Egyptian officers who had been with him throughout the march. All was well; they were met outside the barracks by a squadron of Egyptian cavalry, each trooper displaying a white flag fixed to his carbine. So Stewart sent for the officer in charge of the barracks and ordered that the citadel must be surrendered that evening. Moreover, hearing that Arabi had reached his Cairo dwelling, he said that the Pasha, too, must be given up.

Drury-Lowe still thought it advisable to hide the small numbers of his force, so that evening he sent in only Captain Watson with two squadrons of the 4th Dragoon Guards and a party of mounted infantry to take over the citadel. Watson found the whole garrison of five thousand men still in occupation, but he rode in and ordered the Governor to parade them and march out at once. There was no trouble; regiment by regiment they filed away and marched through the night to Kasr en-Nil barracks on the other side of the city where they stayed until morning. Next day, 15 September, they were quietly disarmed, together with another ten thousand cavalry, artillery and infantry who piled their arms or abandoned their guns in their barracks, were disbanded and streamed away from the city towards their homes.

Arabi Pasha had come in and surrendered his sword at a quarter to eleven the previous night.

The occupation of all points which could be used by the dispersed fragments of the Egyptian Army to concentrate proceeded apace. The Black Watch were sent by train to Zagazig on the day of the Tel el-Kebir battle and marched on to Belbeis on the 14th, relieved in Zagazig by the rest of the Highland Brigade and the artillery.

When Sir Garnet received news from Zagazig of the Egyptian Government's telegraphed surrender, he forthwith set off for Cairo by train, taking with him the Duke of Connaught and a company of the Scots Guards. Buller, trusting no one with the person of his General, travelled on the footplate of the locomotive, keeping an eye on the driver. Despite this extra precaution, the train was delayed at Zagazig, but it moved on again and reached Benha where the Commander-in-Chief received Stewart's account of the surrender of Cairo. So on he went, arriving in the capital at a quarter to ten on 15 September. Other trains followed behind him, carrying the rest of the Guards Brigade. Crowds of natives were at the station and in the streets, and all received the troops with placid submission.

Everything was so peaceful that Buller and Butler crept away and took a cab to an hotel where they had an excellent meal—so good that Butler got tight and had to be driven round the city for an hour before he dared meet his General!

There is little more to be said. Evelyn Wood took the surrender at Kafr ed-Duaur; Aboukir and Rosetta made their submission. The last armed fortress in Egypt had been given into British hands by 24 September. Next day the Khedive made a triumphant entry into Cairo, whose streets were lined with British troops.

Thanks to expert planning, the battle of Tel el-Kebir had been cheaply won. British casualties were nine officers and forty-eight men killed; twenty-seven officers and three hundred and fifty-five men wounded; missing, which is difficult to understand, were thirty men, twenty-one of them from the Royal Marine Light Infantry. Total combined casualties represented only one man in forty from the whole assaulting force. Egyptian casualties were never properly assessed, but three thousand prisoners were taken.

It was decided from England that ten thousand troops would be left in Egypt to watch British interests and re-establish a peaceful economy. Sir Archibald Alison was left in charge.

The divisions broke up, the Generals went home; the Indian contingent took ship for India and a pleasantly cool winter.

On 21 October Sir Garnet Wolseley himself sailed for England and arrived there seven days later. He received a peerage.

Delayed-action sickness soon broke out among the troops, one presumes as a result of drinking water from the Sweet-Water Canal. Butler was kept busy changing camp sites and making hospital arrangements. Cholera, in particular, was rife.

Certain interests tried to have Arabi Pasha tried in secret, thereby facilitating judicial murder. Again quoting Butler, who put things very nicely: 'All the passions were now in possession of the Egyptian vantage points: the Levantine jackal, the Khedival eunuch, the blood-thirsty Circassian, the Greek money-lender, the many representatives of Dame Quickly's old and highly endowed profession —these were now flocking into Egypt in thousands. With them were coming the former advisers of the English Foreign Office, whose persistently erroneous counsels had, as we now know, produced the crisis which had just been closed by the slaughter at Tel el-Kebir. Behind these various persons and professions this unfortunate fellah, Arabi, had ranged against him the entire tribe of the Levites and High Priests of Finance, foreign and Egyptian, from the heads of the great Jewish banking-houses in Europe to the humble 'schroff' money-changers at the street corners of Alexandria.'

However, Arabi was lucky. Mr Gladstone intervened, insisting upon a public trial, thereby undoubtedly saving his life. Instead of being shot, hanged or done to death in prison, he was sent to Ceylon and held there.

[4]

Sir Garnet Wolseley maintained his objective from start to finish of the Egyptian campaign of 1882. His task was to secure the Suez Canal for an uninterrupted flow of international shipping, and to do that he had to capture Cairo. While still in England he had chosen the Ismailia route and had decided to attack and destroy a major portion of the Egyptian Army in the field, probably at Tel el-Kebir. So he had to establish a line of communication from Ismailia to Kassassin and there built up an advanced depot of supplies and ammuniton.

This was the largest-scale operation that he had ever undertaken, so speed in all phases would be all the more essential. It had to be a quick war before heat exhaustion and sickness took their toll; besides, he was working as usual on a budget and long wars cost extra money.

He was prepared to adjust detail to exploit changes in circumstances and thereby accomplished some phases earlier than had been expected. He wasted no time, but on the other hand he never pressed on so far as to overreach himself. His subordinates understood this and supported his aims. Willis, for example, did not obey the order to withdraw the cavalry from Mahsama once he knew that they had become administratively viable. But he knew that if he went on and captured Tel el-Kebir on 9 September, the whole plan would collapse; so he withdrew until the administrative backing for the next phase was available.

Deception was masterly because security was perfect. If there was no substantial advantage to be gained by telling somebody, then he was not informed—even if he happened to be Lieutenant-General

Sir Edward Hamley! The Egyptians never knew what he was up to or what he was going to do next. He was expert at dangling the carrot of a credible plan, when in fact he was intending something quite different. Two outstanding successes were the bogus telegrams sent by Graham and Macpherson, one causing the enemy to give up any idea of re-taking Ismailia, the other eliciting a surrender telegram from the Cairo Government.

Administrative advance planning was first-class and very little went wrong; while even in the heat of battle Sir Garnet never forgot that his men and horses would have to be supplied. His ability to maintain excellent relations with the Royal Navy was a guarantee of success in this essentially Joint Service campaign. He never permitted anyone to exploit the willing help of the Senior Service: when Hamley in Alexandria signalled that he could send an additional battalion to Ismailia if Sir Garnet would make the Navy take back police duties, the answer was an unequivocal 'No'!

Sir Garnet comported himself at Tel el-Kebir as a Commander-in-Chief should do; he gave his Generals their heads and let them go. So, in the chaotic conditions amid the Egyptian forward defences, marked by the Highlanders' determination to fight on as individuals if necessary, Hamley and Alison led their improvised storming-parties like subalterns, once their reserves had been committed and Generals as such were not necessary any more.

Finally, it is only fair to pay some recognition to the Egyptians. They were up against the cream of the British and Indian Armies, many of whom had seen active service. Admittedly, they had a slight numerical superiority and were ensconced in well-constructed fixed defences. Their artillery, too, was in good condition; fifty-seven steel breech-loading rifled guns made by Krupp in Essen for the Franco-Prussian War fell into British hands at the end of the day. However, if the Tel el-Kebir garrison should be taken as homogeneous with the Egyptian Army as a whole, in each company of a hundred men, ten would have been regular soldiers; fifty were reservists of all ages who had been back with the Colours for two months, and forty were newly enrolled youngsters with three weeks' service! If this was so, and there is no reason for assuming the contrary, then they fought exceptionally bravely and well, until things suddenly became too much for them and it became a case of every man for himself.

Loose Ends

We have now followed the Ashanti Ring through six campaigns, covering their exploits sometimes in detail, at others very briefly. The wars that have been considered increase progressively in scope, as well as providing plenty of variety. Operations have been conducted along the rivers and lakes of Canada, through the primeval rain-forests and pestilential swamps of the Gold Coast, among the rolling veldt and precipitous mountains of Natal and across the desert sands of Egypt.

Resistance offered by the enemy becomes stiffer with the years. Riel and his Red River adherents faded away into the woods without a fight. The Ashanti hordes waged war with low-velocity small-arms fire and never closed with sword or spear, while the Zulus placed most reliance on their assegais in hand-to-hand combat and were lethal if they were allowed near enough to use them. This is a matter of history, though there has never been much mention of their rifles or mounted element. The deadly Boer marksmen used their rifles and their fieldcraft to win their war, while the Egyptian war was notable mainly for being a British three-divisional campaign in which the enemy employed significant strength of modern artillery.

Riel, the predominantly French half-breed with Indian and Irish ancestors, after he had fled from Fort Garry became respectable for a year or so. He was elected a member of the Dominion Parliament, but did something awful and was expelled. Re-elected, he committed further offences which resulted in his being declared outlaw, so withdrew for a quiet year as patient in the Beaufort asylum for the insane. Then he lived peacefully in Montana for five years, until called to their aid once more by his half-breed Canadian community. He instigated another rebellion, in which this time there was some hard fighting. It was suppressed after a struggle and Riel surrendered. He was tried, found guilty of treason and hanged at Regina in November, 1885.

The Red River campaign was the first experience of active service and hardship that McCalmont had experienced. He came from a wealthy Irish family with no military connection and had found that Service life provided an excellent outlet for his unbounded energy and restless spirit. He disliked the quiet life of respectability, particularly in others, and did what he could to cast stones into still waters. After a guest-night with the Blues in Regents Park barracks, he and his hosts rushed out into the night to wrench knockers off the hall-doors of houses in staid residential areas. He felt this to be a well worth-while exercise as 'Even if one could not wrench a knocker off, one could always, at the worst, give a thundering rat-tat with it and thereby cause annoyance and possibly alarm to the householder'! He was small, an expert amateur rider, and was very proud of being nick-named 'Baby'. During the voyage of the *Ambriz* to Cape Coast Castle, he talked so much about personally capturing Kofi Karikari that he was for a short time called 'King' by his friends. Unfortunately for this ambition, he was one of the first to fall ill and be evacuated home.

Butler was quite different. The seventh child of a good but not well-endowed Irish Catholic family, there was little money to spare for him. His father was initially opposed to his son entering the British Army, where in his opinion the disadvantage of an absence of hard cash could only be overcome by the surrender of one's religion. However, in due course a direct commission without purchase was obtained. With no financial resources for escapades, instead he studied military history; he visited battlefields of the past; he spent evenings with Victor Hugo; he watched the last dying efforts of the Paris Commune. He hunted buffalo over the frontier plains of Nebraska with Colonel Dodge of the United States Army. Passed over many times for promotion for the unforgivable crime of being unable to buy it, at the Red River he was junior to McCalmont, who was four years younger than himself. At last he won recognition by proving his ability on active service, though the Gold Coast nearly killed him.

Wolseley and Colley were close friends. There were only two years in age between them; they were both brought up in Ireland and they were both fascinated by administrative planning. Apart from this, they inclined to differ considerably. Wolseley as a young man was interested in every kind of sporting activity, from hunting and shooting to boxing and rowing, while Colley, although participating in the normal field sports essential to his upbringing, was perfectly content sketching old churches.

Evelyn Wood was the son of an English baronet, and the youngest son at that, so he spent most of his life arguing about money, though he could always put hands on enough of it to obtain postings and promotion when he needed them. He was a midshipman in the Naval Brigade during the siege of Sevastopol, where Wolseley also was in the trenches, and rapidly became inured to the death and mutilation of his companions. The only thing that horrified him was a mortally wounded officer who lost control and was dying noisily; greatly embarrassed by such an exhibition, the young Evelyn Wood walked away out of earshot. His best relationship in the Ring was probably with Buller, second son of an English country gentleman and only one year younger than himself. They both had strong religious beliefs, which was another point in common. Buller admitted that he actually *liked* fighting: Evelyn Wood never went so far as to say so, but certainly in his young days showed conspicuous enthusiasm in that direction.

Wolseley and Wood commanded men in battle in both the Crimea and during the Indian Mutiny and had plenty of experience of regimental duty. Buller and Butler had been too young for the big wars, but they each had ten years' service in their British regiments; Colley gained much less experience in commanding British soldiers, which was a serious deficiency.

The great Duke of Wellington made it clear to his masters in Whitehall that the first duty of his officers was to train the private soldiers under their command, rather than pay heed to the 'futile quill-driving' of War Office clerks. There is no use in producing a battalion on the battlefield beautifully dressed, equipped and having partaken of a hearty breakfast after a comfortable night's sleep if they do not know how to use their weapons, have no will to fight and can not be made to fight.

But a battleworthy regiment, even if unadministered, can at least raid the enemy for supplies and cause considerable damage to his war effort before succumbing through lack of amenities.

The whole backbone of the Army is the regimental officer and his duties are arduous and hardly learnt. He has to know his own job, teach his men, win their confidence and ensure that they will follow him in battle. If necessary, in emergency he must be able to drive them as a last resort, making them fear him more than they do the enemy. A terrible man will produce the last desperate charge which wins the battle, while the much-loved patriarchal commander may be given affectionate looks and nothing else.

An essential principle is that no officer should be allowed to command men at any level until he has shown beyond doubt that he can do so competently at the level below. Only a successful company commander should be promoted to be colonel of a regiment, and so on.

Sir Garnet Wolseley knew better than anyone who should command in a specific operation, and chose his man accordingly. For the Essaman expedition the British raiding party was of a size suited for a lieutenant-colonel, so Evelyn Wood was put in charge. Then, during the fighting in the bush it became obvious that there were insufficient officers to keep control, so the General sent his staff to help as an emergency measure only—and he lost his Chief of Staff. After that, he occasionally let some of his young staff officers go on patrol, but never let them take over from regimental officers.

When it was time to constitute an advance guard for the move north from the Prah, he chose the two levy regiments and the 2nd West India Regiment, but he did *not* put his Chief-of-Staff or Colley in charge. He sent instead for an experienced regimental commander, Colonel M'Leod of the Black Watch, taking him away from his own battalion for the purpose, and putting him at the head of it again when he was needed for the breakthrough. Nor did he, himself, decide to command the British regiments in the assault; he had a perfectly good brigadier-general for the purpose and he let him get on with it.

In Egypt Major-General Graham was in charge of the reconnaissance to Magfar, though every General in the Expeditionary Force went along too. Then, when the operation assumed battle-proportions with possible far-reaching consequences, he ordered Lieutenant-General Willis to take over. Wolseley did not even have to stay out in the desert through the night in case anything went wrong; perfectly confident in his subordinate, he rode back to Ismailia for a meal and some sleep, though one can be sure that he would have made certain that everything was functioning properly there before he retired to bed.

Before the Tel el-Kebir battle he issued clear operation instructions, made sure that every unit was in its correct position on the start-line, then left his commanders alone. He *knew* that Alison, leading Highlanders supported by Light Infantry, was a panacea for successful assault and victory, just as he *knew* that Evelyn Wood with two men and a boy would somehow contain an Egyptian army.

Colley, on the other hand, broke every principle of command and suffered for it.

During the 1870s, divisions and brigades were usually commanded by officers experienced in battle. But they needed staffs to take routine duties off their shoulders in operational detail, personnel and quartermaster administration; and some of these posts could be filled by officers who lacked that little extra something as commanders of companies, or who had little liking for the rigours of serving with troops. Some regimental offficers were apt to judge all staff officers by these criteria. Marling received a new company commander in Alexandria on 17 August and lost him eleven days later in Mahsama. 'Old Holbech,' he writes, 'has gone on the Gilded Staff. We didn't think he'd stick regimental soldiering long.'

Such is human nature that some staff officers who have escaped from regimental duty are apt soon to consider themselves as members of an elite body, reflecting the authority of their seniors. This, too, could cause friction between staff and regimental officers. The Amajuba campaign was redolent of examples of staff officers with backing from the top usurping control and over-ruling regimental officers, with the inevitable consequence of disaster and defeat.

The majority of staff officers in the field in this decade, however, were more of the calibre of Butler and Buller, good both in their regiments and on the staff.

There were always some regimental officers of the highest quality who disliked working for examinations and preferred the regimental way of life to such a degree and with such love that they wished nothing more than to stay with their men for all their lives in the Service. I will quote one fine example.

A great celebration dinner was given in Cairo towards the end of September, presided over by the Duke of Connaught and attended by the Staff and Brigade Commanders. At the close of the meal, after drinking to the health of the Queen, and the other usual toasts, the Duke stood up and said that there was one more toast that he would like to propose—the health of 'that fine old regimental officer, Colonel Sir Cromer Ashburnham, on whom everyone is delighted to see that Her Majesty has conferred a well-earned KCB.' Amidst shouts of applause, the Colonel got to his feet and returned thanks as follows: 'I'm very much obliged for the kind way His Royal Highness has proposed the toast of my health. I have been in the Rifles over thirty years, and owe everything to the Regiment. I never wore a red coat, I was never on the Staff, I hate the Staff, damn them!'

Then, gently, he subsided under the table.

[2]

Most of the officers belonging to the Ashanti Ring saw active service again in Egypt within two years; some of them even fought the Boers again in 1899. I hope to follow their fortunes once more at a later date.

For the present, suffice it to say that Wolseley and Evelyn Wood both became Field-Marshals; Buller, Baker Russell, Brackenbury, Greaves and McNeil were promoted General. Butler, who was too out-spoken, too often and at the wrong time, only made Lieutenant-General. Maurice and McCalmont both left the Service as Major-Generals.

Colonel Sir Cromer Ashburnham was appointed Aide-de-Camp to Her Majesty Queen Victoria and even attended levees. Could it be that he had become a Staff Officer—at last?

Bibliography

The Ashanti War, 1874	Captain Henry Brackenbury
The Red River Expedition	Captain G. L. Huyshe
The Story of a Soldier's Life	Field Marshal Viscount Wolseley
Life of Lord Wolseley	Sir F. Maurice
General Lord Wolseley	C. R. Low
The Wolseley Letters	Lord Wolseley
From Midshipman to Field-Marshal	Field Marshal Sir Evelyn Wood
Winnowed Memories	Field Marshal Sir Evelyn Wood
The Life of Lieutenant-General Sir Evelyn Wood	C. Williams
The Life of Sir George Pomeroy-Colley	Sir W. F. Butler
Sir William Butler	Autobiography
Sir Redvers Buller	Colonel C. H. Melville
The History of the Rifle Brigade	Sir William Cope
Narrative of the Field Operations connected with the Zulu War of 1879	War Office, 1881
In Zululand with the British throughout the War of 1879	C. L. Norris-Newman
With the Boers in the Transvaal 1880–81	C. L. Norris-Newman
A Narrative of the Boer War	T. F. Carter
Rifleman and Hussar	Colonel Sir Percival Marling
Listening for the Drums	Sir Ian Hamilton
The Life of a Regiment—the History of the Gordon Highlanders	C. G. Gardyne
The Military History of the Campaign of 1882 in Egypt	Colonel J. F. Maurice
The Memoirs of Major-General Sir Hugh McCalmont	Major-General Sir C. E. Calliwell
Illustrated London News 1873–82	
Journals of the United Services Institution 1873–82	

Index